CHIPPEWA LAKE

CHIPPEWA LAKE

A Community in Search of an Identity

Cindy L. Hull

Michigan State University Press
East Lansing

⊗ The paper used in this publication meets the minimum requirements of ANSI/NISO Z39.48-1992 (R 1997) (Permanence of Paper).

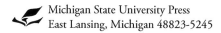 Michigan State University Press
East Lansing, Michigan 48823-5245

Printed and bound in the United States of America.

18 17 16 15 14 13 12   1 2 3 4 5 6 7 8 9 10

LIBRARY OF CONGRESS CATALOGING-IN-PUBLICATION DATA

Hull, Cindy L., 1950-
Chippewa lake : a community in search of an identity / Cindy L. Hull.
   p. cm.
   Includes bibliographical references and index.
   ISBN 978-1-61186-048-1 (pbk. : alk. paper) 1. Community life—Michigan—Mecosta County. 2. Social networks—Michigan—Mecosta County. 3. Social change—Michigan—Mecosta County. 4. Rural-urban relations—Michigan—Mecosta County. 5. Mecosta County (Mich.)—Economic conditions. 6. Mecosta County (Mich.)—Rural conditions. 7. Mecosta County (Mich.)—Social life and customs. I. Title.

   HM761.H85 2012
   977.4'91—dc23   2011050506

Book design by Scribe Inc. (www.scribenet.com)
Cover design by Erin Kirk New
Front cover image is of the Chippewa Lake Community Church and Chippewa Lake. Back cover image is of the McCormick Family c. 1906.

green press INITIATIVE Michigan State University Press is a member of the Green Press Initiative and is committed to developing and encouraging ecologically responsible publishing practices. For more information about the Green Press Initiative and the use of recycled paper in book publishing, please visit www.greenpressinitiative.org.

Visit Michigan State University Press at www.msupress.org

*To my husband, LaVail, who brought me
kicking and screaming to Chippewa Township;
to our children, Sarah, Nathan and David,
who thrived here and brought joy to our lives;
to our adorable grandchildren Adeline and Eliott;
and to the people of Chippewa and Martiny Townships
who anchored us and showed us the meaning of community.*

Contents

Acknowledgments

THIS ETHNOGRAPHIC STUDY HAS BEEN TWENTY-EIGHT YEARS IN THE making. It started when we moved to Chippewa Lake in 1982. I was arriving to live here for the first time; my husband was returning to his roots. I have been planning this ethnography for many years, but did not have the opportunity to do so until my sabbatical from Grand Valley State University in 2004. I would like to acknowledge the support I have received over the years from Grand Valley State University in both my research in Mexico and my current work in Chippewa Lake. It was exciting to bring GVSU students to my community and see it afresh through their eyes. The students who participated in the initial survey and interview sessions were all anthropology majors: Lauren Bostic, Michael Blassingame, Zachary Guy (Student Summer Scholarship recipient), Gillian Meister, Elizabeth (Libby) Michel, and Sarah Veenkamp. Lauren, Libby, and I coauthored "A Short History of Chippewa Township and Chippewa Lake," which was presented to the Township board in appreciation of the community cooperation in the project.

In preparing this monograph, I used a multitude of data sources. For information about Chippewa Township and the surrounding area, I am grateful for the cooperation and assistance from the following governmental offices: Mecosta County Registrar and Registrar of Deeds, and the Natural Resources Conservation Service, U.S. Department of Agriculture, Big Rapids, Michigan. I especially appreciate the assistance of Ms. Jennifer Taylor.

I would like to thank Dr. James McClurken and Joe Quick of James McClurken and Associates, for inviting me to use their facilities and for helping me untangle the history of the indigenous people of the area surrounding Mecosta County.

It is impossible to thank all of my friends and neighbors in Chippewa and Martiny Townships who have shared my life over the years. Many of the stories incorporated in this document are the result of personal experiences collected and nurtured over many years. I started collecting oral histories in 1983 for the Chippewa Lake Centennial celebration, and sadly, all of those whom I interviewed then have passed away. Their lives continue on through the stories that pass from generation to generation. Some of those stories are included here: Ernie (and Evelyn) Nott, Virginia Ball, Irvin and Edna Austin, and George Nott.

I am also indebted to the families who allowed my students and me into their homes and shared their life stories. You will never know the impact that your stories and your friendliness had on the students who sat nervously with you, taking notes. They talked incessantly about your lives and what it must be like to live in a small community, and what it must have been like many years ago. For those of you who did follow-up oral histories, you will also never know how much the time that I spent in your homes meant to me, listening to your stories and your concerns.

For those whom we interviewed, but whose words or stories are not included here, we apologize, and I hope that the major concerns and joys that you related to us are reflected in some way in the pages that follow.

I would like to thank Valerie Hover and Julie Austin who read earlier versions of this manuscript, and Dr. Richard Santer for sharing his expertise on the history of Big Rapids. A special thanks goes to my husband LaVail for his intrepid search across two counties for the sources of Nettie Smith's articles. And finally, I want to express my appreciation to LaVail and our children for their encouragement and patience.

I am especially grateful for my friends and neighbors in Chippewa and Martiny Townships who have accepted the city girl into their community, and have taught her how to make a sheet cake, saddle a horse, and plant a garden. I am thankful for all I have learned over the past years, and for how my children thrived in this environment. I am thankful for the lifelong friends we have made, and for the ease with which I was invited into homes to conduct interviews and learn about family history. I hope that this report reflects accurately the strength of character of rural residents today, especially those in Chippewa and Martiny Townships, as well as the challenges facing them during these precarious economic times.

Finally, I would like to remember those in my community, old and young, whom we interviewed for this project and who have passed away since I started this manuscript: Eleanor Erlenborn, Tom and Esther Hahn, Duke Metcalf, Judy Miller, Ed Nellis, Wynne Nellis, Evelyn Nott, Richard Stein, and precious Megan Miller, who brightened our lives for a little while.

Preface

I WAS FIRST INTRODUCED TO CHIPPEWA LAKE BY MY FUTURE HUS-
band, LaVail. I often accompanied him on the trek north from Grand Rapids
to visit his grandparents, who lived on a small farm about two miles from
the village of Chippewa Lake. I remember reveling in the lush greenness of
the scenery, the endless fields of corn, and the beautiful lake that gave the
community its name. LaVail's grandparents were descendants of one of the
earliest European families to settle in Chippewa Township, the township that
includes Chippewa Lake. His family came from Scotland via Canada at the
same time as other original settlers—the McCallums, Carmichaels, McLach-
lins, and Campbells. LaVail's grandfather's cousin, Mary McCormick, is
listed in the county registry as the first white child born in the township.

But, as a sociology major in college, aiming for a teaching career, I wasn't
particularly interested in that history. What struck me was the poverty of the
area, particularly the poverty in which I thought Earl and Cleva McCormick
lived. They inhabited a small two-story farmhouse with tarpaper siding, and
an open well in the front yard. Only recently had Grandma Cleva obtained
a hand pump attached to her sink that allowed her to pump water directly
from the well to the house. She heated water for dishwashing and baths on
the cooking stove or the wood stove, and the toilet and tub were also fairly
new improvements, installed by her two sons-in-law. The outhouse still sat
in the back yard, a monument to another time. The house was heated by a
wood stove, located in the kitchen that also served as the living room in the
winter. The real living room was closed off in the winter to preserve heat,
and my husband remembers icicles forming in his upstairs bedroom when
he was young. The most exciting, yet intimidating improvement was the
telephone that brought Earl and Cleva closer to their children and grandchildren, who all lived in Grand Rapids or beyond. It was a three-party
phone, and their greatest fear was having their neighbors listen in to their
phone calls. My husband's family would often receive cryptic phone calls
from up north: "You have to come up. We have to talk about something . . .
you know what we talked about . . ." This could be anything from a need to

fix the car or put up fence to discussing important family issues. We always suspected that the real reason for the call was to get their family to come up for a visit.

My memories also include the strong smell of pork cooking in lard, homemade bread, and green tea. The best time was in the fall, when the McCormick daughters and spouses, distant aunts, uncles, and cousins came up for deer hunting season. Grandpa Earl was on his best form when he had an audience. Crippled from polio as a young man, he moved slowly with a cane, his legs bowed. Surrounded with family in the warm kitchen, he sat in his favorite chair, a huge, overstuffed wooden-frame chair that smelled of cigarette smoke and the accumulated smells of the kitchen and farm. He told stories and sipped the whiskey that his sons-in-law brought for him. Cleva never sat. She was in constant motion, bustling in the small kitchen area, cooking and serving, trying to keep some order in an impossible situation, feeding and picking up after her children, grandchildren, and assorted cousins and tag-alongs like me.

This was how the elder McCormicks lived in the 1970s. I never thought that I would live in the Chippewa Lake community. Born and raised in Grand Rapids, seventy miles south, I was accustomed to urban neighborhoods, walking to school and to the local parks, having friends within walking or biking distance, as well as the mixed blessings of next-door neighbors and closely spaced houses. It was with much apprehension that I agreed to move to the rural homestead with our two young children after residing for two years in the Micronesian islands.

Returning from the semitropical island of Pohnpei to the United States was traumatic enough for us and for our children, but arriving in midwinter was insanity. The winter of 1982 was raging when we drove our Volkswagen Beetle, just out of storage, with two children in tow up to our new home, a small retirement house built by my husband's family on ten acres of the McCormick homestead. The snow was so deep that we could barely move along the gravel road, piled high with unplowed snow. Our home was newly built, but like the original homestead within our sight, had only a small wood stove to heat it, no garage for our Volkswagen, and only two small bedrooms for the four of us. Over the years, as the family grew, and as we became more established, we expanded on the house, and finally, after five or six years, we installed a propane furnace and no longer had to get up at 4:00 in the morning to stoke the wood furnace into action.

Even though LaVail and I had lived in several different cultures since our marriage—Detroit, Ann Arbor, Mexico, Micronesia, and Grand Rapids, Michigan—Chippewa Lake presented me with the same exotic awe with which I entered a Yucatecan village or adapted to life on a Pacific island.

Even though I spoke the same language as those in my new village, it was difficult for me to adapt to the rural lifestyle, the isolation in the winter, and the distances between home and anywhere else I wanted to go. My immersion in the village social life was likely easier for me than other newcomers because of my husband's ties to the community. While feeling very lonely during that first winter, I discovered that the village came to life in the spring, and it wasn't long before I was meeting people—especially the women, with whom I connected immediately despite the chasm of experience that existed between us. I joined the Young Women's Club and found playmates for our children. When the community was organizing their centennial in 1983, I became involved, and used this opportunity to learn about the history of Chippewa Lake. I utilized my anthropological skills to conduct interviews and collect oral histories of members of the community, many of whom have passed away since that time. I also assisted community members in developing a museum to display letters, photographs, and other historical items during the celebration. This participation instilled in me a desire to expand this research, which I finally was able to achieve twenty years later with the sabbatical that provided the time to fulfill that goal.

Although I have not considered my thirty years of living in Chippewa Township as research, I have been an active participant-observer. Unlike my husband and me, our children lived in the same house and attended the same schools from preschool to graduation (with the exception of study-abroad experiences for two children, and a one-year trial with a charter school for our youngest). As parents, we supported our children in sports and music programs, scouting, equestrian team, and 4-H. We attended the local church, I became involved in the Young Women's Club, LaVail was a volunteer firefighter, and thus we became enmeshed in the social fabric of this small farming community.

Over the years, I have learned a great deal about the lives of our neighbors—their joys and trials. I have made many friends, and have lost friends to accidents and cancer. I have lamented as some of them moved away. I have also seen how many lives have changed as families abandoned dairy farming for wage labor. I have seen mothers seek jobs to supplement low wages, and I have seen the impact of economic conditions on community unity and participation. I have watched as the community of Chippewa Lake has shifted from a farming township to a commuting-based community and retirement destination.

My interest in this community is not focused solely on the negative. I am also interested in the resilience of rural families. I am encouraged by the perseverance of the early settlers of this area—from Scotland, Ireland, Germany, and elsewhere—to stay here and maintain the family farm. As I visited the longtime residents and collected their oral histories, I was amazed by the wealth of information that these families have. At every interview, several members of the family came to share their stories. At each house, I was shown boxes—or in more organized families, notebooks and photo albums—filled with old photographs and mementos. I found that every family has a designated family historian, and as an anthropologist, I was amazed at the number of complex genealogies I found, in family albums or printed neatly on 8×11 sheets of paper held together with aged Scotch tape. One of these genealogists traced her ancestors from Scotland in 1870 and had the family genealogy updated to her own children. The taped sheets of paper covered an entire dining room table.

There are hundreds of fascinating stories in this township alone. I have collected a small portion of them. I hope that in the future, others will continue to collect these stories, and that families continue to share their past with their children. These histories serve as a backdrop to the present, when rural families are caught in the midst of conflicting economic and social tides. The stories describe an ideal community, defined by historic roots and an imagined community that no longer exists. I hope that I can preserve the value of the history while shedding some light on the present.

It is also my goal to link the families of the past to those of the present, for the complete story requires an examination not only of those who have left, but of those who are arriving from other worlds, bringing diverse and sometimes conflicting worldviews. I have incorporated stories, histories, and anecdotes that illustrate the dreams of the newcomers, those who are seeking an idyllic rural community or lakeside retirement. These newcomers are seeking a rural community of their own—defined by their own history and experience, and nourished by their desire to leave their urban life behind them and seek their own version of the ideal community.

Unfortunately their imagined community often contrasts with the local reality they encounter: a community with its own value system steeped in history and tradition. It is at that intersection that conflict, tension, and cultural misunderstandings occur. I hope to identify the spatial and social loci where rural agricultural values intersect with those of the newcomers, examining both the factors of conflict and those places where there may exist shared values and communal expectations.

The tension between established families and immigrants is not the only example of the disjuncture of the ideal and the real in contemporary Chippewa Township. The ideal farm community is in reality a community where, while only 10 percent of the population fall under the official guidelines for poverty, farm families struggle to pay taxes on large farms, maintain expensive equipment and buildings, and bear the increased cost of oil, gas, and their byproducts, fertilizers and pesticides. Because of these realities, Chippewa Township is a community in which today only 2.5 percent of the population are actively involved with farming, and these farmers represent the elders of the community. Further, these elders rely on supplemental income from second jobs, and the unpaid labor of children and other relatives. While their incomes might not place them within the governmental guidelines, these families are struggling, silently, but with great pride in their way of life.

While financial struggle is not unusual in farming communities, the structure of the community is no longer conducive to the mutual support and collective spirit that defined the earlier times. Commuting, the demands of dual-income strategies, and a heterogeneous population threaten the idealized rural community. In this book, I hope to outline the vast changes that are occurring in Chippewa Township, and to explore the consequences of these changes to the traditional lifestyles and established understanding of membership in community. I hope to balance a discussion of transition with an appreciation for the resilience of the community and the spirit of all residents to carve their ideal community from the rustic beauty of a struggling rural town.

A note on the ethnographic present: People's lives do not stop when the anthropologist finishes her work. Thus, there have been many changes in the lives of these families; people have passed on, divorced, and for some, family circumstances have changed since I interviewed them. The life stories I have included here reflect the situations of individuals and families during the time of the research and writing of this book. I hope that I have captured the world view of the families of Chippewa Township and that the reader will understand that the struggles and the joys of life in small communities like Chippewa Lake are ongoing and fluid, like life everywhere.

Introduction

They had a shack out here, in the opening where the garden and lawn is . . . and [Aunt Clara Nott and her dad] took off walking in the woods—of course there was no road—and they come up to the prettiest lake, it was just so green—it was Chippewa Lake.

—ERNIE NOTT, SEPTEMBER 1983

IN THE BROAD REGIONAL VIEW, THIS CURRENT RESEARCH IS A "TALE of two cities and a village." Although I propose an ethnography—that is, a study of one community—this cannot be successful without locating the research community within a larger economic and social matrix. First, the most direct impact on current trends in the village of Chippewa Lake must be viewed in relationship with both Big Rapids (population 11,000), the closest city, and Grand Rapids (200,000), located seventy miles south. Grand Rapids is a growing urban area, with both its population and manufacturing base expanding beyond its city limits to surrounding townships and small towns. Historically, the area surrounding the city was agricultural, with large family farms providing the region with fresh produce and fruit. Until quite recently, such communities were rural towns, each with its own distinctive character. Now, one can move from one town to another without being aware of where one ends and the other begins. Development has transformed rural apple orchards into bedroom communities, providing housing and apartment developments with such promising names as "Apple Ridge" and "Orchard View." The orchards themselves are only a flickering memory to those who have lived here long enough to remember them. Likewise, light manufacturing has moved outwards, further causing the newly arrived to wonder why roads in and out of these communities are named "Fruit Ridge" and "Peach Ridge."

Until the early 1990s, the only road that connected Grand Rapids to Big Rapids was "old" US 131, a poorly maintained, narrow two-lane road that meandered through numerous small rural villages, some of which offered nothing but a roadside gas station or café. It was (and still is) a dangerous road as impatient drivers take risks to pass slower traffic, including tractors and Amish horse-drawn carriages. As the US 131 expressway slowly worked its way north, many of these small communities were bypassed, but those through which the expressway passed gained new life.

Big Rapids has always been the economic hub for Mecosta County (41,000 people). Big Rapids, the county seat, has a population of 11,000 people and houses the county's only major medical center. When the expressway finally extended as far as Big Rapids in the mid-1990s, it was already a thriving town. It is the home of Ferris State University, which has been a major employer in the region for many years. Big Rapids has also been the recipient of numerous small manufacturing plants, some of which supply parts to the automotive industry in Detroit, offering tax breaks and other incentives to draw small businesses to the area which in turn have provided many nonunion jobs to county residents. With the current crisis in Michigan's automobile industry, many of these small suppliers are laying off workers, and the impact of this national and global financial crisis is affecting small towns and rural areas throughout the state.

Because of the university, its small-town atmosphere, high quality of life, and low cost of living, Big Rapids has drawn many families to the region. The expressway and improved secondary roads have also facilitated travel from the rural areas to jobs in Big Rapids, and for Big Rapids residents to find work in Grand Rapids, now only one hour away. Since the expressway arrived in Big Rapids (with two exits), the town has also earned the attention of franchises. In the past ten years, there has been a proliferation of big box stores and restaurant franchises that line the main thoroughfare into town from the west. However, as the discount stores thrive, the businesses and shops on the town's main street struggle to survive. With the arrival of Meijer and Walmart, all of the smaller, locally owned grocery stores have gone out of business.

The village of Chippewa Lake in Chippewa Township is linked to Big Rapids, and the world beyond, by a two-lane winding blacktop road. Located about fifteen miles east of Big Rapids, one can make the trip in twenty minutes in good weather. Chippewa Lake is the administrative center of the township and the only population center. It is not an incorporated entity, and has no governmental structure of its own beyond the township board, which is administered by elected officials. Big Rapids has always been the primary economic hub for the village, where farmers bought their seed, shopped for food and supplies, bought parts for their tractors and cars, and took care of their health needs. A secondary commercial hub for early farmers was the town of Evart, located fifteen miles north of Chippewa Lake in Osceola County. Most of the day-to-day lives of early settlers, however, were centered within their community.

The history of Chippewa Lake is one of boom and bust. The first European settlers displaced the small indigenous population in the mid-1800s, establishing farms and building an agricultural community. In the late 1800s, the logging industry around the lake brought new life to the area. The white pine was plentiful, and steamboats carried logs from around the township, across the lake, to the railroad that passed through the village. In those years, the village had several hotels, numerous restaurants and bars, a dance hall, livery stable, and various professionals such as a medical doctor and veterinarian. When the white pine was logged out, the railroad was pulled up and Chippewa Lake was left a skeleton of its former self. Farming continued to provide a livelihood to local residents, and ultimately, subsistence farming was replaced by dairy and crop farming.

In the 1970s, when I first started visiting the area with my husband-to-be, Chippewa Lake had three small grocery stores that served the needs of the locals as well as the summer vacationers, two gas stations, a marina, a bar, laundromat, bank, post office, bait shop, fire station (for two adjacent townships), community building, and a Methodist church. It also had a roller rink and a small restaurant. At that time, telephones were a new item, and four or five families shared a party line; some houses did not have indoor plumbing. The only major paved roads were the main thoroughfare that linked Big Rapids to Barryton, and the road that linked Chippewa Lake to Evart. This was in the 1970s in rural Michigan, seventy miles from Grand Rapids.

Today, the village looks very different. The roller rink is gone, and thus a major social gathering place for young people has disappeared with nothing to replace it. The village gas station closed as did two of the stores. The bank also closed, and the blinking light at the T-shaped intersection of town disappeared one day, never to return. There is another gas station, grocery store, and restaurant located at the marina about one mile east of the village, which serves the resort people with boat launching, ice cream, and bait.

Today, the community survives primarily because of the lake. One of the largest in the state, it is a clean lake, very deep, and good for fishing. The population of the village (1,200 according to the 2000 census) doubles in the summer as families arrive from all over Michigan, and as far away as Chicago, to rent cabins or stay in family cottages that crowd around the lake. The survival of all of the small businesses in the community depends on the summer clientele, as local dollars cannot support these businesses year round.

In this sense, the isolation of Chippewa Lake as a community is both its downfall and its salvation, depending on one's point of view. Located as it is off the main highway that links Big Rapids to cities north and south, and away from the major east-west road that links Big Rapids to the casino in Mt. Pleasant, the only way to find Chippewa Lake is to be looking for it. This adds to its appeal for those seeking the benefits of solitude, but also contributes to the lack of development that might lure tourists who are on their way to other places.

The actors in this saga include dairy and crop farmers, most of whom are descendants of the original settlers; their children and grandchildren who are being forced to leave these farms and find work elsewhere; those children who remain on the farm but work in factories in Big Rapids, Evart, or Grand Rapids; newcomers who are moving into the rural community as commuters to urban jobs; and retirees who are upgrading summer cottages into year-round homes. Over the years, I have observed this shift from farm community to commuter and retirement community, even though the process started before my arrival. I know many young men who have left their family farms to seek work elsewhere, and I have observed the changes in the rural landscape as dairy farmers sell their herds. I also know many women who found jobs in factories or restaurants in Big Rapids to supplement their family incomes. And I have watched as newcomers arrive to establish retirement homes around the lake, displacing the summer residents and seeking their own rural paradise.

My interest in this research was spurred by curiosity as to how rural families are affected by the economic and demographic changes occurring around them. I set out to investigate four questions:

- What are the strategies that rural families employ to meet their needs as the local economic structure is shifting from agricultural to wage labor?
- To what extent do commuters, retirees, and other newcomers threaten or become adapted to the local culture; to what extent do they become incorporated into the local social networks?
- To what extent do longtime residents continue to participate in community events and social organizations that reinforce social networks and reproduce the local sense of community, and to what extent do newcomers involve themselves in the daily life of the village?
- As a consequence of these issues, how do families refine or reshape their conceptualization of "community?" Will the idea of community expand to include social and familial networks beyond the village?" In other words, do local residents continue to have a sense of identity with "place," or do we need to revise our concepts of community and identity?

The answers to these questions are just the beginning, as they force us to ask more difficult questions pertaining to the future of all rural communities. Will the confluence of these processes, comprised of the disappearance of the family farm, and the emigration of farm youth to the cities, and the movement of members of the middle class and retirees to the rural communities, result in the loss of community? Does this process further ring the death knell for the rural family, which is the core of most definitions of the ideal community?

PARTICIPANT OBSERVATION

The most critical method in ethnographic research is participant observation. By both observing daily life in one's adopted community and participating in local events and rituals, anthropologists share experiences with local families and gain an appreciation for the daily struggles, concerns, and joys of life. Such observations and cross-cultural comparisons contribute to a broader understanding of both cultural difference and the ways in which cultures are similar. Anthropologists utilize the concept of cultural relativism to avoid judging other cultures whose values and worldview differ fromWestern worldviews. By recognizing that all humans view other cultures through cultural filters, anthropologists are trained to acknowledge these filters and put them aside so that we might meet our fellow human beings on their own ground, as participants within their own culture, shaped by specific forces of nature, environment, and history. Cultural relativism does not require that anthropologists accept the customs of others uncritically, but that we attempt to examine them as objectively as we can within the context of indigenous cultural experience and history. This is a very difficult task at times as anthropologists examine such traditions as female circumcision, female seclusion, or ethnic violence.

Historically, anthropologists worked and lived among non-Western societies whose cultures and customs contrast markedly with those of Western or American society. This is no longer the case. While research within the United States might seem less difficult than work in Africa or the Middle East, it has its own set of challenges. First, in contrast to our perception that our country is a melting pot, the United States is comprised of a multitude of cultures and subcultures, members of which might not speak English as a first language. Anthropologists work in indigenous communities in Alaska, Hawaii, and the continental United States, diverse cultures that predate Western conquest. Others examine the adaptation and resilience of European, Latin American, Caribbean, Asian, and other immigrant communities throughout the country, each of which has brought with it distinct histories, traditions, and languages. Research among these communities requires cultural relativism, but also a keen sense of the role of conquest, colonialism, globalization, and the other processes that have shaped the lives of indigenous populations and that have brought immigrants to our shores, including the first Europeans who stumbled upon the "New World."

Second, research among rural communities may seem simple in contrast, but the demands of research in the heartland among third- and fourth-generation farmers of European descent are no less challenging. In fact, the study of the familiar requires a critical eye, one that can see beyond the obvious and tease out the underlying patterns of behavior that have defined European American society for generations. Those of us raised as Christians, who attended public schools and participated in potluck dinners, school sports, and shopping malls will be likely to see these activities and values as "natural," but in fact, they are not. These activities and belief systems have been shaped by complex historical and social processes. Anthropologists who conduct research in the United States must take special care to recognize the patterns behind the obvious and extricate ourselves from the webs of familiarity that have shaped our own lives.

In my case, I brought a vast and varied history with me to Chippewa Lake. I spent most of my childhood in Grand Rapids, but also lived for a time in multiple settings, including the suburbs, a multiethnic neighborhood in Detroit, the middle-class academic atmosphere of Ann Arbor, followed by a rural Mexican village and a Micronesian island. When I first moved to Chippewa Lake, I felt much like I did in those first few months in Detroit, Yaxbe, and on Pohnpei—like I had just landed on the moon and found people living there! Now, having lived in Chippewa Township for so many years, I have come to see it as home, and as I began this research, I found that I had to make that step back as an anthropologist and look carefully behind the customs I have come to share and, more complicated yet, the people I have come to know.

The fact that I still live in Chippewa Township adds a challenging dimension to this research, as I respect my neighbors and have a long history of sharing with them. I have a fear that they will be unhappy with this book, and I joke that I may have to leave town when it is published. The tension between factual data collection and an ethical responsibility not to harm my "subjects" has been a constant concern during the writing of this book. Because Chippewa Lake is an identifiable location, I struggled with the dilemma of whether or not to use a pseudonym for the community and its people. As I returned to the families discussed in this book to have them review and make corrections and updates on my narrative, I found that they were appalled that I had planned to use a pseudonym for the community or for them. They wanted their family names to be in the book, flaws and all. To this end, I have acquiesced to their wishes, with several exceptions.

My experiences in Chippewa Township over the years have been positive. People have accepted me and treated me like family; they have shared experiences with me, as I have with them. Yet, I have scratched my head in confusion over some of the rituals I have observed—I still don't understand mud runs, tractor pulls, and car races on the frozen lake in winter. And I have struggled with writing about painful moments in the lives of my friends and neighbors, especially in the case of "Marijuana Mama." I do not want to benefit from their pain, yet I want to disclose their lives with honesty in an attempt to give them a voice and accurately express the reality of their struggles to raise their families with the values that shaped their own lives. As an anthropologist, it is my responsibility to portray people as accurately as possible, recognizing that I may view their lives through lenses that differ from theirs. In this case, the breadth of my experiences and the fact that I came to Chippewa Lake with a Ph.D. in Anthropology distance me considerably from the average citizen of Chippewa Lake who has a high school diploma and who is likely never to have left the state of Michigan in his/her lifetime.

However, I have lived in Chippewa Lake for nearly thirty years, and my husband and I have raised our three children here. We owned horses and watched our children participate in 4-H, the equestrian team, orchestra, marching band, and running cross-country. We planted vegetable gardens, made apple cider, and even experimented (unsuccessfully) with cattle raising. We raised chickens and traded eggs for milk with our neighbors, and my husband bartered legal services for firewood. I learned to accept deer hunting as a rural livelihood, and learned how to prepare the locally acceptable potluck dishes. These experiences have given me a strong sense of what rural life is like, what neighbors expect of one another, and what is not acceptable behavior. Many of these experiences, based on countless kitchen conversations and participation in local events, provide contextual and anecdotal depth to this analysis.

I am also an ethnographer who values quantitative data; these have been entered in SPSS and Atlas/ti databases and serve as analytical tools for the research. In pursuit of the historical and economic contexts, I have collected

TABLE I. Research Sample: Distribution of Households Interviewed

Region of Chippewa Township*	Number of households	Number of households surveyed	Percentage of all households
Rural township	224	27	12%
Lake district	196	19	10%
Village	51	9	18%
Totals	471	55	12%

* The village is defined as the area surrounding the township hall; it has its own zip code. The lake district includes those homes and cottages that surround the lake. The rural township contains the remaining areas of Chippewa Township.

plat maps, aerial photographs, and other documentation, such as census data and land-use plans that outline land-use patterns and population figures, and provide other demographic information.

As an educator, I am also committed to the idea of experiential learning, and I am grateful for the funding that I and several students received from Grand Valley State University that supported the initial data-collection phase of this project. Several additional students from Grand Valley participated in the project through a field school course that supplemented my sabbatical for the 2004–2005 academic year. These five students conducted structured interviews, collected surveys, and assisted in the recording of the data into the database. Two of the students worked with me to write a short history of the community that was presented to the township board.

THE MACRO, THE MICRO AND THE POSTMODERN

Anthropologists, in the pursuit of understanding, often take divergent roads toward this comprehension. For some, cultures can only be understood at the local or micro level, that is, an in-depth analysis of the social organization of one community. This perspective allows the anthropologist to concentrate on the daily lives and beliefs of a small community of people with the goal of "getting into the minds" of people. Customs and behaviors are shaped by worldviews. For others, knowledge of the local must be examined within the context of the global. In this view, we cannot understand the local without placing it within its larger (macro) milieu, the region, and the world. Behaviors, in this context, are shaped by events and circumstances that exist beyond the local. Still others believe that neither of these methods can culminate in a true understanding, first because the anthropologist cannot escape his or her own culture, and second, because the anthropologist is applying her/his own Western perspectives and definitions of local and worldwide institutions that may or may not apply to local groups. This perspective, known as postmodernism, represents a view that both the macro and micro perspectives are flawed in that they cannot equally reflect every voice, and that some voices, notably those of the powerful, will necessarily be privileged.

While all methods of analysis and description have potential flaws, my perspective straddles the first and second. Because I have lived in a small Mexican village and a Pacific Island culture, both caught in the vortex of devastating colonial histories and global economics, I cannot view any local community in a vacuum. On the other hand, I learned over the years that the residents of each of these communities are not passive victims of their circumstances. They use agency and multiple strategies that allow them to survive economically and maintain a viable social network, despite catastrophic events. An overview of several theoretical perspectives that have informed my research will place this monograph into a larger explanatory framework.

Dependency Theory and World Systems Theory

The impact of national- and state-level policies on local communities is a critical issue in current anthropological studies. Research in this genre often focuses on how national and state policies result in transformation of local forms of production and social organization. In developing his theory of dependency, A. Gunder Frank rejected the modernization model popular in the mid-1900s.[1] The modernization model was utilized by the United States and other powerful nations as a solution to underdevelopment in the "Third World." The premise is that development can only occur through industrialization and the extraction of valuable natural resources that replace traditional subsistence-based economic structures. Unfortunately, this type of development model did not incorporate mechanisms that would allow for viable sustenance systems at the local level. Profits from industrialization were funneled from the rural sectors through the local colonial political structure to the controlling power, such as the United States or Great Britain. Instead of development, this system resulted in a dual economic system, and a concomitant philosophy that poverty in the rural areas was the fault of the local populace, blamed for lack of skill or reluctance to abandon their backward ways. Frank argued that instead of modernization, this development model results in dependency whereby the dominant economic region or state drains labor and resources from the rural areas (satellites) to support capitalist expansion and wealth in the urban areas (metropoles).

Immanuel Wallerstein refined this theory.[2] His perspective, called World Systems Theory, was the theoretical focus for my research in Mexico. In World Systems, the metropole/satellite dichotomy is replaced by a core, periphery, and semi-periphery model that explains how natural resources and labor in the underdeveloped periphery feed the dominant core with profits, few of which flow back to the rural areas or underdeveloped nations. The semi-periphery refers to those regions intermediary to the core and periphery through which resources flow, such as large market towns, strategically located cities and nations, and seaports.

Political economists in the United States have applied this model of underdevelopment to the rural communities here. After World War II, industrialization in the United States flourished. In the 1960s, the U.S. government promoted regional clusters of industrialization as a solution to rural poverty. While manufacturing did take hold in the rural areas, it displaced people from rural communities and provided primarily unskilled and low-wage, nonunion jobs.[3] As in the modernization paradigm, the profits from these factories benefited the larger "mother" industries in the east and north.

The economic recession in the 1980s resulted in national policies that had lasting repercussions in the rural area that continue today. As farm subsidies, tax breaks, and incentives shift from family farms to corporate farms and agro-businesses, small farmers are no longer able to subsist on their earnings. Imports of inexpensive vegetables, fruits, and beef have further resulted in losses to family farms and rural communities. In addition, the loss of manufacturing jobs in both urban and rural areas starting in the 1980s, and again in the current (2009–10) economic crisis, has resulted in un- and underemployment in both areas. In the meantime, many family farms are being divided up among family members or sold due to tax structures, leaving few options for rural people who have lost jobs. Those who had jobs were earning less than their urban counterparts because rural manufacturing is largely unskilled and nonunion. Service-sector jobs in the rural area also are poor paying as a whole, because careers in health care or education, for example, that require a skilled, and thus better paid, labor force are located closer to urban areas.[4]

Social Embeddedness and Practice Theory

Within these global, national, and regional matrices, however, families live, earn a living, raise their children, and interact in social networks that are distinct yet ultimately linked to these larger matrices. To understand these networks and survival strategies, idiographic research is appropriate. I plan to employ the perspective of "practice theory" as outlined by Sherry Ortner in anthropology, and "social embeddedness" theory as used in sociological and poverty studies.[5] Both of these perspectives emphasize the actions of individuals and families within communities—not as victims, but as actors. While Ortner envisions "practice" as a model of local social and economic activism, "social embeddedness" emphasizes the intrafamily economic relations that allow families to exist: reciprocity, exchange, and pooled income.[6]

I am interested first in how communities maintain and reinforce those core values that identify rural communities in general. Several anthropologists have made valuable theoretical contributions to our understanding of the shared core values that are often associated with rural communities in the United States. I have paraphrased some of these here, and we will return to them in more detail in later chapters. In her studies of rural communities in Illinois, Sonya Salamon has contributed many insights into the concepts of shared community, but also into the distinctions that are relevant within and between communities. In describing the consistency that we find between rural communities, Salamon argues that there is an understood quality of rural life that distinguishes it from urban or suburban life, and that this lifestyle provides a desired quality of life and a beneficial environment in which to raise children.

In two of her studies, Salamon describes a "community personality" in which one finds certain indicators of a cohesive community:[7] ritual discourse (gossip and scandal) employed by those with vested interest in maintaining established order; mobilizing to achieve group goals: social capital, social networks, reciprocal trust; a sense of identity, defined as a context for self-characterization and belonging;[8] shared norms and values, with a density of social connections; and an idea of a friendly, inclusive community where new people are accepted.[9] Further, Salamon argues that in the rural community, status differences among people are downplayed; there is an ideal of egalitarianism, such as "those who make more should contribute more."[10] One's neighbors are like family and should be assisted in times of crisis. Anthropologists refer to this form of social reciprocity as "leveling."

These indicators are symbolic of community social relations that are embedded in, and reproduced through, certain central institutions that combine to maintain a collective identity—such institutions as community schools, churches, and local organizations and businesses.[11] The unique demographics, histories, and economies shape the community, forming what Salamon calls a "community effect."[12]

Janet Fitchen contributes to this list of indicators by arguing convincingly that the rural community is difficult to define, especially for the outsider. She notes that "the deeper meaning of community, while locality-connected, is of the mind: the ideational or symbolic sense of community, of belonging not only *to* a place but *in* its institutions and *with* its people."[13] In this way, rural residents define their community in terms of its opposite: the city. It is a place where people are safe, no one locks their doors, and core values are shared. These norms are threatened by those who invade their community from the outside: newcomers and transients.[14]

THE SHARED AND CONTESTED COMMUNITY IN CHIPPEWA TOWNSHIP

The perception of the ideal community outlined by Salamon is consistent with that of the descendants of the original farming families in Chippewa Township. However, the shared values of the farm community established since the 1800s are now crosscut by contested ideas of "community," evolving locally as young people leave the farms and as newcomers move to the township. Contested definitions of community force us to reconsider and reject the stereotype of rural communities as homogeneous and static. Salamon and others who have written about rural America warn us about creating stereotypes of *the* agricultural community, just as other anthropologists warn us about doing the same for the exotic "other" of Africa, Asia, or South America.[15] Like all communities, the ideal is reified in memory or in description. Early settlers came to the area with a variety of backgrounds. They came from Germany, Scotland, Ireland, England, Canada, and the eastern United States. Some came with only their most meager possessions and homesteaded on government land; others brought money they earned on the railroads, or arrived as speculators, or with professions, such as doctors. Indeed, some of the stories I have heard allude to tensions between the Germans and the Scots, and between the earlier settlers and those who came later, such as the Swedish.

Yet, the descendants of these settlers carry with them a collective memory of a community united against the vagaries of life in the wilderness: frozen winters, crop failures, and flu epidemics, as well as shared celebrations of successful harvests and social life. The descendants and those who have adopted the rural lifestyle express these same ideas as they describe what they like about their community today and what they feel is being lost: the sense of solidarity, neighborliness, shared experiences, mutual assistance, and collective values of hard work and kinship ties.

As I talk with residents of Chippewa Township today, the tensions between the idealized rural community and the reality of current economics and demographics are palpable. In longtime families (over thirty years), the stories of idealized community still dominate, and to some extent they shape my own perception of rural community. The idealized community, defined in terms of mutual assistance and shared activities, is still part of the daily lives of many farm families. They still count on their family members, even those who no longer farm, to help them seasonally or in times of illness. The community still has funeral dinners and benefit dinners, and there is a group of women who still have quilting bees.

The overall tenor of the community, however, is shifting. This shift is most disturbing to those who still imagine a community of interconnected lives and shared values. Increasingly, these rural families regret that their children are also part of the new world. Even though they may carry their family stories forward, young people today do not want to farm; if possible, they want to attend college, or at least learn a vocation or trade that will give them a well-paying job in a factory or business. They are still committed to the idea of family. They are prepared to help out on the farm, take care of family members, and maintain close ties to the homestead, but their vision is clearly outward from the community.

The contested community is further shaped by the role of the lake and the nonfarming village that abuts it. The lake has shaped the community from logging days to the present. Today, the lake area is by far the fastest growing region of the township, as more and more cottages and houses are being squeezed closer and closer together around the shoreline and on unpaved roads that spiral outward from the lake. The lake community, once defined primarily as summer vacationers, is evolving into a year-round residential lake as local families and those from other parts of the state upgrade their cottages to comfortable homes. These residents do not necessarily share the same values as the farm families who live a mile or more from the lakeshore. Rather, their goals are to live in the country and work in the city, or escape the factories of Lansing or Flint to the idyllic serenity of a lake community for their retirement. These residents become involved when local issues affect them: the condition and regulation of the lake, and proposals that might affect their property values or taxes.

Proximity of Chippewa Township to Big Rapids, and to some extent to smaller towns to the north, has beckoned a new population of residents, who desire the best of both worlds: rural living within commuting distance to jobs, shopping, and social services. These newcomers and nonfarming longtime residents are redefining community values and identity.

CONCLUSION

In general, my research focuses on the family as the unit of analysis. I hope to show that the community surrounding Chippewa Lake has experienced considerable disruptions due to the downturn of the national and state economies, and that the choices that families are making today reflect these larger issues. However, I am interested not in documenting the economic structure of the community, but in understanding what factors have allowed families to make a living and allowed the community to survive despite a weak economic base, and to examine the current threats to this community. To come back to the questions that I posed at the beginning of the chapter: Is the rural community lost? Is the rural family gone? My answer is "No . . . not yet."

CHAPTER 1

The Geography and Indigenous People of Mecosta County

[Delegates of the Ottawa] represent to me, that they have been to see the land this set apart, and say that it is not such as was represented to them nor such as they want—that a large portion of it is covered with pine and that much of it, is poor and sandy—, that they have been deceived in regard to it, and many of them declare that they will not go on to the land at all, much less accept it as their permanent home.

—OTTAWA INDIAN DEMANDS IN A LETTER TO ANDREW FITCH, MICHIGAN INDIAN AGENT, AUGUST 1857, LETTERS RECEIVED BY THE OFFICE OF INDIAN AFFAIRS, 1856–1857

WEST-CENTRAL MICHIGAN IS BLESSED WITH AN ABUNDANCE OF RIV-ers, streams, and lakes that have provided a pristine environment for early Native American communities, European settlers, and modern-day sports enthusiasts. Three river systems, comprising 293 miles of rivers and streams, drain the county. The Muskegon River flows through Big Rapids and, with the Little Muskegon River, drains the western eight townships, including Chippewa Township, flowing ultimately into Lake Michigan at Muskegon. The Flat River starts in southeastern Mecosta County and joins the Grand River before it too flows into Lake Michigan. Finally, the Chippewa and Pine River system drains six eastern townships, including Chippewa Township. These two rivers form the Titabawassee River at Midland, Michigan, and join the Shiawassee River, which becomes the Saginaw River, which ultimately empties into Lake Huron.[1]

Mecosta County also boasts 328 natural lakes and ponds, covering 4,744 acres.[2] Fifteen of these are located in Chippewa Township, though Chippewa Lake, covering 790 acres, is the largest and most influential in the local landscape.[3] In addition to lakes and rivers, Mecosta County has an estimated 51,922 acres of wetlands, almost 30,000 of which are forested.[4] One of the largest protected wetland areas, the Haymarsh State Game Area, is located in Martiny Township, which abuts Chippewa Lake to the south. The abundance of marshy wetland surrounding Chippewa Lake and extending outward into nearby farmland adds to local beauty. Government-protected wetlands, a hindrance to farming and development, provide a haven for a wide variety of plants, birds, ducks, and loons.

Much of the topography of Mecosta County is formed by glaciers that completely covered the area during the Pleistocene. The present topography is largely a result of the Wisconsin Glacier, the last one to cover this area.[5] While glacial moraine formed the hilly landscape and the smaller lakes,[6] larger lakes such as Chippewa Lake and the Martiny chain of lakes in Chippewa and Martiny Townships were formed when large sections of ice broke off from the retreating glacier.[7]

The receding glaciers also left behind the soil deposits that still have an impact on forestry and farming today. Coloma, Remus-Spinks-Metea, and Marlette soils provide a combination of well-drained sandy soil, loamy soil, and clay that are well suited for woodlands, pasture, and grain crops, such as wheat and rye.[8] Today, Mecosta County still has approximately 163,000 acres of forested area, about 45 percent of total land use. As we will see, original forests were dominated by white pine, but now, forested areas consist predominantly of secondary-growth aspen, maple, beech, birch, oak, hickory, red/white pine, and spruce and fir.[9]

INDIGENOUS PEOPLE OF MECOSTA COUNTY

When I first moved to Chippewa Township in 1982, I harbored several assumptions about the indigenous history of the region, both of which proved to be mistaken. First, the preponderance of references to "Chippewa" in local designation of landscapes and locations led me to presume that the indigenous people associated with Mecosta County were Chippewa Indians, or Ojibway, as they are known in the literature. Thus, I was very surprised to learn that the people associated with the region were actually Ottawa (also called Odawa in other regions).[10] The fact that the indigenous people were misidentified is just one mystery that shrouds Mecosta County history.

The second misconception relates to their local settlements, as there exist few documents and little material evidence of their presence in Chippewa and surrounding townships. As one travels through Mecosta County, vacations at the many lakes, or hunts in the forests or wetlands, one can imagine that this area would have been a haven for Native Americans. One has visions of wigwams along the Muskegon or Chippewa Rivers and their tributaries, settlements at the lakes, and well-worn trails leading from the county to other areas of western Michigan.

However, despite a bountiful ecological system comprised of forests, wetlands, rivers, streams, and lakes, there is little evidence that indigenous people actually settled in the area permanently, or even semipermanently. The *Archaeological Atlas of Michigan* describes a few minor trails passing through Mecosta County.[11] One trail follows the Muskegon River for a short distance from the southwest, ending at hunting sites at Big Rapids. Other small trails are evident along the Chippewa River tributaries in townships south and east of Chippewa Township, and along creek beds that used to exist near Clear Lake and Rodney in Colfax Township, southwest of Chippewa Township. Mounds have been identified along the Chippewa River north and south of Barryton, east of Chippewa Lake, and along the Muskegon River as it flows into Osceola County to the north. The only village site identified for the county is at Pretty Lake in Martiny Township to the south and east of Chippewa Lake. It appears that instead of settling in the township, indigenous people forged trails along the major river routes to favored hunting grounds and seasonal camps elsewhere, without establishing permanent or semipermanent settlements on or near Chippewa Lake.

The Ottawa

The first indigenous people identified with the Great Lakes are believed to have followed the retreat of the glaciers from southern regions from approximately 12,000 B.C. to 8,000 B.C., hunting mammals, including the mastodon, using stone-tipped spears.[12] The period from 8,000 B.C. to 1,000 B.C. is known as the Archaic Period, and during this time, indigenous groups spread out over the Great Lakes region, adapting their technology and culture to diverse environments, and developed trade routes to take advantage of products produced elsewhere, such as copper from the Upper Peninsula. In the Woodland Period (1,000 B.C. to 1,000 A.D.) indigenous groups developed more stable communities; produced pottery, baskets, and complex tools; and cultivated local plants as well as corn, introduced from as far away as Mexico.

It was during this period that several outside indigenous groups began to migrate into Michigan. The Hopewell mound builders from the Midwest moved into southern Michigan and brought with them their practice of burying their honored dead in earthen mounds.[13] But most significantly for this account, the Ottawa, Potawatomi, and Ojibway moved into the Great Lakes and established the Three Fires Confederacy, which defined indigenous culture in the region. Referring to themselves collectively as the Anishnabeg, the three tribal groups spoke dialects of the same language, Algonquian, and identified with each other using kinship terminology: the Ojibway were the older brother, the Ottawa were the next older brother, and the Potawatomi were the younger brother.[14]

The Ottawa position as the middle brother seems to apply geographically as well as symbolically to numerous aspects of Ottawa life and culture. The Ottawa lived in a transitional ecological zone, located between mild climate and hardwood forests of southern Michigan and Ohio, inhabited by the Potawatomi and the Huron (bands formed from larger Potawatomi populations), and the colder coniferous forests to the north, inhabited by the Chippewa.[15] Their kinship system was also flexible, exhibiting characteristics of the Chippewa patrilineal system and the Huron matrilineal system. While all Anishnabeg subsisted on cultivation supplemented by hunting, fishing, and gathering, the Ottawa were also known for their trade. Birch-bark canoes were the defining characteristic of Michigan Ottawa Indians as they traversed the rivers and Great Lakes trading between tribal groups, and later, they provided the links between Indian fur hunters and the French traders establishing themselves in Canada and northern Michigan.[16] Ottawa traders traveled as far as Green Bay, Wisconsin, through the Straits of Mackinac, taking corn from central and southern Michigan to the northern Chippewa and returning down Lake Huron with animal pelts that they traded to the Huron Indians, who then delivered them to the French along the St. Joseph River, and east through Lakes Erie and Ontario and the St. Lawrence River to French trading posts in Montreal and Quebec. In this way, furs from Wisconsin arrived in Montreal.[17]

Contact with Europeans

This harmonious relationship did not last long before the Iroquois, whose territory spanned the current states of Pennsylvania and New York on the southern shores of Lakes Erie and Huron and the St. Lawrence River, took notice. The Iroquois had aligned themselves with British and Dutch traders, but soon began a campaign to disrupt the Ottawa-Huron trade routes. The conflict resulted in the Iroquois Wars (1640–1649), and this tumultuous era set the stage for later proxy wars between the British and French, pitting the Great Lakes Confederacy (including the Huron) and their French allies against the British, who were aligned with the powerful League of the Iroquois.[18]

These wars, bundled under the umbrella of several European wars, culminated in the French and Indian War, which was fought from 1754 to 1763.[19] When the British won the French and Indian War, they did not continue the symbiotic relationship that had developed between the French and the Michigan tribes. They considered the Indians a conquered people and proceeded to administer power over them and seize their land. The period between the French and Indian War and the War of Independence was dominated by numerous Indian revolts and significant rebellions, such as Pontiac's Rebellion, which united Indians from numerous Great Lakes tribal groups against the British at Fort Michilimackinac. After attacking and gaining control of numerous forts in the Great Lakes area, including Michilimackinac, Sandusky in Ohio, Miami and Ouiatenon in Indiana, and others in Pennsylvania, Pontiac's forces failed to conquer Fort Detroit and Fort Pitt in Pennsylvania. The Indians were worn down by general fatigue by this time, a sense of defeat exacerbated by the fact that the British had infected the blankets of the Shawnee and Delaware warriors with smallpox.[20]

During the American Revolution, the Ottawa again chose the losing side and supported the British, who were now making land concessions and supplying the Ottawa with goods. The American colonists, however, seemed determined to expand westward. The Ottawa maintained their middleman position of trading with both the British and the remaining French traders in the region. When the Americans won their revolution in 1783, the British lost their jurisdiction over Ottawa land in Michigan, but retained their forts at Detroit and Mackinac.[21]

The period between 1783 and the War of 1812 was characterized by a deadly series of treaties in which the Michigan Indians ceded land and sovereignty to the Americans. The tribes of the Three Fires joined with indigenous groups in Ohio and Indiana, forming a pan-Indian nativistic movement that promised a return to a life in which Indians once again controlled their own destiny. This movement was led by a Shawnee prophet called Tenskwatawa, who established a settlement on the Tippecanoe River at Prophetstown, Indiana. Tenskwatawa's brother was the famous Tecumseh, who maintained a force of warriors at the site. In 1811, the governor of Indiana sent his troops to Prophetstown to break up the settlement while Tecumseh was away. Despite orders not to engage the whites, the warriors attacked the troops, who then retaliated and drove the Indians away. The power of the pan-Indian movement was finally crushed during the War of 1812, when in retaliation for the American aggression, the Michigan Indians once again tied their hopes to the British, who were soundly defeated by the Americans.[22]

Promises Made and Broken

The years following this military defeat were characterized by a new stage in the subjugation of the Indians, the process of ethnocide in the guise of civilizing the "heathen Indian." Missions were established along river settlements, and the Indians were encouraged or lured to these settlements with tools, oxen, plows, and other material goods. Chiefs were promised monetary and other resources to bring their people to the missions, and the chiefs in turn gained favor with the missionaries. Intertribal unity disintegrated into intertribal tensions and conflict as the Indian groups competed for American goods and political favors.[23]

Simultaneously, Native Americans were being alienated from their land. Two major treaties irreparably altered the indigenous landscape in Michigan.

The first was the 1836 Treaty of Washington between Henry R. Schoolcraft, the commissioner for the United States, and the Ottawa and Chippewa Indians, in which the Ottawa and Chippewa ceded all of their land to the U.S. government, with the exception of several large tracts of land awarded to indigenous groups in lieu of reservations: 50,000 acres at Little Traverse Bay; 20,000 acres on the north shore of Grand Traverse Bay; 70,000 acres along and north of the Pere Marquette River; 1,000 acres near Cheboygan; 1,000 acres located on Thunder Bay River; and numerous small tracts of land in the Upper Peninsula. While these regions are among the most beautiful and valuable in Michigan today, these lands represented reservations, and more unfortunately, they did not provide permanent residency. According to the treaty, the lands would subsequently return to the United States after five years unless otherwise allocated. The indigenous people retained hunting rights on these lands until such time as they were inhabited by settlers. The treaty provided yearly annuities from the government, as well as access to certain services, such as schools and missions, and supplies, such as vaccines, tools, salt, and other commodities.[24]

According to McClurken, the period between 1836 and 1855 was characterized by a new commitment of the Ottawa to reshaping their lives and establishing themselves in their new surroundings. They used their annuities to purchase available land and learned to grow crops, which they sold to their white neighbors. They continued to hunt and fish and made handicrafts that they also sold for income. They formed relationships with missionaries who opposed the Indian removal from Michigan. In return for attending church, missions opened schools for children and assisted the Indians in obtaining land and farming supplies. New ties to the white community through intermarriage opened avenues of kin obligations that both reinforced traditional kinship ties and expanded networks across racial, social, and economic lines.[25] Meanwhile, Indian agent Henry Schoolcraft's attempts to initiate the Ottawa removal from Michigan were thwarted when he was replaced by Robert Stuart in 1841. Stuart was opposed to removal, preferring the natural progression of the Indians to a farming lifestyle and assimilation into the local culture.[26]

The process of assimilation was hindered by the incompatibility of indigenous and European American agricultural practices. In indigenous culture, the women farmed, gathered berries, and made home implements such as baskets, while the men hunted, fished, and conducted their water trade. Western agriculture was a male activity, and Ottawa men were expected to abandon their hunting and fishing to concentrate on farming and maintaining livestock. Women's status in the community as farmers eroded, leaving them to earn their income in other ways, such as handicrafts or collecting berries for sale. Traditional obligations for sharing food with kin were also shifting in this environment as the new farmers had to sell their produce in order to pay their taxes and purchase items necessary for their new lifestyle.[27]

The second major treaty, the Treaty of Detroit, signed in 1855, further limited the land available to Ottawa and Chippewa bands. This treaty was signed by George W. Manypenny and Henry C. Gilbert, commissioners for the United States, and the Ottawa and Chippewa tribes, who were party to the 1836 Treaty. In general, the terms of the treaty were to "withdraw from sale for the benefit of said Indians as hereinafter provided, all the unsold public lands within the state of Michigan embraced in the following descriptions . . ." This treaty opened up lands, delineated in the 1836 Treaty, that had not been claimed by white settlers. Ottawa and Chippewa heads of households would be deeded 80-acre plots. Single individuals over twenty-one years of age, and families of orphan children received 40 acres of land. Yet these deeds were not permanent either. They were held usufruct for ten years, after which time a "patent" would be issued to the landholder. One of these regions, that in the area of the Pere Marquette River basin, included part of what is now Mecosta and Newaygo Counties. In addition to the land distribution, the government promised funds for teachers and schools, agricultural implements and cattle, blacksmith shops, and per capita annuities to the Grand River Ottawa in the sum of $35,000.[28]

As white settlers moved into north-central Michigan, they displaced Native Americans who were now being resettled in the designated areas of the state. As lands became available to Native groups through the various treaties, tribal leaders visited the areas to assess the lands made available to them. It is not surprising that the sections that had not been settled earlier by the whites were not the best lands for agriculture. Several letters sent to George Manypenny, the commissioner of Indian Affairs, indicated displeasure with the land available to Native Americans in this region. One letter indicated that representatives from the tribe who visited the county questioned the amount of land available for Native settlement. He argued that they could not find "four Towns [townships] in one body, that are vacant."[29] Not long after this, some lands in Mecosta County were withdrawn from the land available to the Ottawa through an amendment to the 1855 Treaty, and other lands were designated as available to them, where "the Indians will be more concentrated & will get better land with less interference from white settlers than if located in 'Mecosta.'"[30]

A later letter (August 14, 1857) from Andrew Fitch, Michigan Indian agent, to J. W. Denver, the commander of Indian Affairs in Washington, D.C., states that he had received a formal complaint from the Ottawa Indians in Michigan, arguing that the land set aside for them in Mecosta County was unsuitable for farming.[31] In this same communication, Fitch reported to Denver that the Ottawa wished to move to the Saginaw Reservation in Isabella County, where they had been invited by their brethren, the Saginaw, and where "they can be near together."[32] Andrew Fitch agreed in principle with this choice. He argued that "The land, from what I can learn of the Missionaries among the Chippewa's of Saginaw and from others, is of the very best quality and if they were to be located there, it would concentrate the Indians of this part of the state, a result much to be desired."[33]

Unfortunately an earlier letter from Henry Gilbert to George Manypenny, dated October 22, 1856, had already anticipated this desire of the Ottawa to live near their brethren in Isabella County. Gilbert decided that since the Ottawa annuities were not related to those of the Saginaw, that the Ottawa must settle in their designated counties (Mecosta or Oceana) in order to receive them. Further, they would not be allowed to receive their 80 acres of designated land in Isabella County.[34]

Despite the concern for land allotments, the reality was that few Ottawa actually gained access to land, and most who did own land lost it within six years. The best land was excluded from the allotments, and instead was allocated to white settlers. Indians often lost their land due to nonpayment of taxes, which were assessed at twice the rate as those of white settlers. Some lost their land due to deceit or fraud; others, often despite the assistance of whites, lost land to developers and railroad owners, who paid them far less per acre than their land was worth.[35] Indians alienated from land earned money by working at logging camps or selling fish. Once logging declined and white populations spread out along traditional fishing rivers and lakes, Indians lost their traditional sources of income. Instead they worked for others for wages and supplemented their income by collecting berries, fishing, and selling their traditional crafts.[36]

Resettlement and Pacification

As a result of the Treaty of 1855, the Ottawa dispersed throughout the allocated counties. Most congregated in three counties: Oceana (593), Mason (230), and Newaygo (130). Many settled in smaller groups in mid and northern Michigan, and still others settled in Ottawa, Kent, and Allegan Counties, where they associated with the Matchebanashshewish band of Potawatomi.[37] The last annuities distributed from the Treaty of 1855 were disbursed in 1870. The chief of the band that claimed territory in the area, including Mecosta County, was Metayomig. It is believed that he and another chief, Nonawquot, may have been brought from Grand River villages to the area around Pentwater to live on the reservations created under the Treaty of 1855.[38] Anglicized versions of his name are listed on several letters sent to Indian agents regarding land in Mecosta and Isabella Counties.

By the 1870s, the indigenous cultures were diluted as Indians were acculturated into the dominant society. Missionary schools were replaced first by tribal schools, and ultimately, in the 1880s, by boarding schools to which Indian youth were sent away from their families to learn American skills and values. One of these schools was the Indian Industrial School at Mt. Pleasant, Michigan, on the Saginaw Reservation, which opened in 1893. Ottawa children from elsewhere in Michigan were sent there to learn manual labor, the English language, and American ways. They were forced to cut their hair and wear Western clothing, speak English, and adopt American mannerisms. When they left the schools, however, the children had not gained any skills that would afford them well-paying jobs. Instead, many of them lived in poverty, with only part-time or seasonal employment. Others migrated to Grand Rapids to live with other members of the Ottawa, or moved further to Lansing or Detroit, seeking jobs in the growing manufacturing industries.[39]

In 1894, the federal government published a census report on the Indian populations in each state, with the exception of Alaska, based on the 1890 census of Indians taxed and nontaxed.[40] For Michigan, the 1890 census recorded 5,625 Indians, self-supporting and taxed. According to the census, there were 44 Indians in Mecosta County and 24 Indians in Osceola County in 1890. The largest populations of Indians were located in Emmet County (914), Chippewa County (441), Isabella County (355), and Mason County (335).

A report on the Ottawa and Chippewa Indians living in Mason County, included in the 1894 census, illustrates the conditions under which the indigenous populations lived, as well as disclosing the prevalent attitudes and stereotypes that government officials held about indigenous groups at that time. For example, the report states that most of the males could use English to converse, though "a stranger can get little information from them." Indian women were reported not to speak English. There had been no murders during the census period. Ninety families had houses, either log or wood-framed, and houses had a small patch of cultivated ground. They earned their living through a variety of "callings," including logging, laboring, fishing, hunting, trapping, picking berries and ginseng root. None raised food for the market. "They do not seem to know the first rudiments of economy." Consumption (tuberculosis) was the most prevalent disease, and "all are addicted to alcohol." Children attended public school, and most were Roman Catholic. Referring to a small group in one township, the author described them as unhealthy "pagan Indians" who lived in wigwams, believed in witchcraft, and worshipped imaginary gods.

Negative attitudes, based on the economic and social circumstances of Native American lives at the time, entrenched and then reinforced stereotypes that have persisted to the present day. Few of the settlers who moved into Indian country had any awareness of the complexity of indigenous culture before contact; there was no recognition of the integrity of their language or religion, and no comprehension of the vast economic, trade, and social networks that linked all of the indigenous groups of the Great Lakes with each other, and that connected them to indigenous and nonindigenous cultures beyond the Great Lakes as far east as New England and eastern Canada, and as far south as Indiana and Ohio.

The Grand River Band of the Ottawa Nation

Indian agent Horace Durant developed the most detailed census of the Grand River Ottawa in 1908, based on the 1870 annuities. This register is still used as a reference guide for Ottawa genealogies today.[41] This 1908 census not only records the descendants of those who received annuities in 1870, but also lists their ages and dates of birth when available. The registry further includes copies of intriguing notes that were sent out to descendants of the 1870 recipients, requesting additional information. One such note is handwritten by Horace Dumont himself and signed with his official stamp of office. Some of these genealogies are remarkably detailed and go so far as to list street addresses for several Grand Rapids descendants. For Mecosta County and its environs, the registry lists families residing at Chippewa "Station," including the descendants of Jacob Keyocush, Awbetawseqay, and others. The grandson of Jacob Keyocush, age sixteen in 1870 and a resident of Chippewa Station, is listed as being a student at the Mt. Pleasant Boarding School. According to Richard Santer, local historian, Chippewa Station is located in Osceola County.[42] The 1908 census also collected genealogical information on descendants of other local Ottawa in Clare (Clare County), Weidman (Isabella County but part of the Chippewa Hills School District), Remus (Mecosta County), Big Rapids, and as far as South Bend, Indiana.

The lineal descendants of the current members of the Grand River Band of the Ottawa include over 680 members who are descended from those people on the last annuity payroll of 1870, based on the signatories of the 1855 Treaty of Detroit.[43] In 1948, current Ottawa/Chippewa organizations included the Northern Michigan Ottawa Association. In the 1960s, the Grand River Band of the Ottawa Nation (GRBON) was formed, with Ron Yob of Grand Rapids as the leader.[44] Since 1950, the areas in Michigan with the largest populations are in Muskegon, Kent, and Ottawa Counties.[45] Few of the Grand River Band members migrated to the Detroit area; most have remained east of Mt. Pleasant and along the west Michigan shoreline to Traverse City.

CONCLUSION

The genealogies and histories are silent on what happened to the descendants of those 1870 recipients of annuities. Only forty-four Ottawa lived in Mecosta County in 1890, and there exists no ethnographic description of these families, or data on where they lived. Anecdotal stories about the Native Americans who coexisted with the early white settlers of Chippewa and Martiny Townships are limited to the scrapbooks collected by a local historian, Ms. Nettie Smith. I first interviewed Nettie in 1983 and had the opportunity to look through scrapbooks she had filled with local historical news items she had collected. Nettie, a prolific writer, had written many of the articles herself, including several based on her knowledge of a local Indian family who lived in Martiny Township in her lifetime. These articles had appeared in several local publications in the 1970s and gave me a glimpse into the lives of the community. Nettie has passed away since I first interviewed her, and I have no idea what became of her scrapbooks. However, I am glad that I had the opportunity to peruse them many years ago.

In one of these articles, Nettie wrote about her own childhood in Martiny Township and described the last Indian families to reside in the area. According to Nettie, the last Native Americans were James Shanwno and Moses John. James (called Indian Jim by the settlers) was a former chief of the Chippewa (Ojibwa) tribe who married a Dutch American woman, Sarah Fisher, the daughter of a college-educated trapper. Jim and Sarah had seven children and also raised two orphaned grandchildren. Moses John was a Potawatomi who married one of Jim's daughters. His Indian name was Wabeegamo. Nettie remembers, as a young child, seeing "Indian Jim" fishing on nearby Jehnsen Lake in his canoe, and watching him set traps in the marsh surrounding the same lake. According to Nettie, the last member of the related families alive in 1979 was one of Jim's granddaughters who had moved to Lansing. The other family members are buried in the Martiny Cemetery, in the Indian burial plot.[46]

These two indigenous families represented not the Ottawa, but the other two tribes of the Three Fires. However, regardless of band affiliation, there were still indigenous families in the county in her memory. These may have been the last descendants of the band, who decided to stay in the county rejected by the Ottawa in the Treaty of 1855, living and fishing on the land that they did not want.[47]

CHAPTER 2

Locating Chippewa Township in Time and Place

I was born in a log house about a mile and a half east
of here [Chippewa Lake] . . . At that time nearly everyone had the
floors of their home covered with rag carpet. The rags had to be cut in
thin strips and sewed together and woven . . . How well I remember
the good times we had sewing the rags for our carpet. A lot of young
people would gather at our house in the evening and sew rags,
eat popcorn and sing. When the rags were all sewed and wound into
balls, mother took them to Mrs. Foot and she wove our carpet.
We covered the floor with straw and put the carpet over it and
tacked it down . . . We thought it was just beautiful. I have seen
oriental rugs in later years that didn't look nearly as beautiful
to me as that rag carpet did then.

—VIRGINIA TABER BALL, "A STORY OF
THE HISTORY OF CHIPPEWA LAKE"

CHIPPEWA TOWNSHIP IS LOCATED IN NORTHWEST MECOSTA COUNTY. It is one of the northernmost townships, bordering on Osceola County. Chippewa Township contains ten lakes, with Chippewa Lake being the largest and most significant economically in the history of the township. Because Chippewa Lake is located in the southwestern corner of the township, the focus of this study is on those sections that surround the lake itself. The survey population did not include the northernmost sections of the township or those on the eastern edge. The former are distant geographically from Chippewa Lake and more aligned to Osceola County to the north; the latter are separated geographically from the rest of the township by the Martiny Lake system and are more closely aligned with Fork Township to the east. However, by limiting the scope of this research to Chippewa Township, I am forming an arbitrary boundary with Martiny Township that abuts Chippewa Township to the south. Many families who figure into the history of Chippewa Lake reside in the northern sections of Martiny. Several of the oral histories that I collected in 1983 are of families who were associated with Chippewa Lake, but who farmed land just south of the township line. Thus, when I am discussing the historical context of the lake and township, I will often refer to families in Martiny Township, as their history and contact with the lake community are often greater than those of families who live in the northern sections, and their experiences reflect life around Chippewa Lake more than those further north and east.

HISTORICAL DATA ON CHIPPEWA TOWNSHIP

The material I have collected on the history of Chippewa Township comes from various sources, some of which I have not been able to accurately document as to publication and date. Specifically, I have relied on two local historians, now deceased, both of whom I first met while conducting interviews for the 1983 Chippewa Lake Centennial. The first of these women is Nettie Smith, whose articles and scrapbooks provide insights into the daily lives of local families and the last indigenous residents of the area. Much of what we know about the history of Chippewa Township comes from the documentation of another local historian, Virginia Taber Ball, who was born in a log cabin just east of Chippewa Lake in 1897. During her marriage, she and her husband lived in Grand Rapids and elsewhere, but returned to Chippewa Lake, where they stayed. When she got older, and after her husband died, she began to write stories about the history of Chippewa Lake that have since become the official history of the area.[1] Information in her essays is also found in other local histories and published accounts, but it is unclear whether she did the research or used the sources of others, as she did not use citations. That the same informational tidbits are found in different sources indicates that historical information has freely cross-germinated among local storytellers, and the provenance of the information is not always clear. However, her lively and entertaining biographical sketches provide us with an articulate and revealing glimpse into early life in Chippewa Lake.

Virginia's family also had links to the White House, as she was always proud to relate. Her brother, Edward Taber, was a recognized interior designer who was chosen from a field of two hundred competitors to refurbish the executive office wing of the White House for President Herbert Hoover, after a fire. He designed the Oval Office, including the desk and chair used by the president. He evidently also went shopping with Mrs. Hoover to pick out items for the suites. Virginia had a copy of the letter written to her brother by President Hoover in 1930, thanking him for the work in redecorating the Oval Office. The story is that he liked the chair so much, he took it with him and had a replica made for President Roosevelt; she did not know what happened to the desk.[2]

EUROPEAN SETTLEMENT OF CHIPPEWA TOWNSHIP

Although the United States government acquired Chippewa Township from the Ottawa Indians in 1836 as part of the Washington Treaty, the first European settlers did not arrive until after President Abraham Lincoln passed the Homestead Act of 1862.[3] The first recorded European settlers were Mr. and Mrs. Pollock (first names unknown), who settled in one of the northernmost sections of the township in 1865.[4] They may not have stayed long, as their names are not found on the 1879 plat map, the earliest one that I have discovered.[5] The majority of settlers arrived in 1867 and 1868, and many of these family names are still prominent in the township today: the Sparks family (believed to be the second family to settle, in 1867), McCallums, Smiths, Jamiesons, McCormicks, and Sears. In 1868, the Eatons, Wylies, and Bovays arrived. With few exceptions, these first settlers staked their claims in the northern sections of the township, though some eventually bought additional land closer to Chippewa Lake later on, or their descendants did.

Early settlers can be traced from numerous regions in Scotland, particularly Argyllshire, as well as from Ireland and England. Many arrived in Michigan through a complex route from County Cork to Canada, and eventually to northern Michigan. Some members of the first families were born in Canada as their families made their way from Great Britain. Other settlers came from Germany via New York, Vermont, Pennsylvania, and Ohio.

Chippewa Township was incorporated in 1868, and John Sparks was named the first supervisor at that time. An interesting anecdote from Nettie Smith's scrapbooks reveals the settlers' acknowledgment of the small indigenous population still residing in the area at that time. Some people thought that the township should be named after Mr. Sparks, the first supervisor (Martiny Township was named in this way), while others suggested that it should be named after the previous indigenous residents. Thus, however misinformed, the township came to be called Chippewa Township. Chippewa Lake itself was not platted until 1883, and I have found no record of its indigenous name.

The earliest settlers purchased or obtained land through the Homestead Act, signed by President Abraham Lincoln in 1862. These parcels were normally 40 or 80 acres, but could be as much as 160 acres, more than sufficient for family subsistence. Later arrivals purchased land from the railroad companies that had purchased the odd-numbered sections for speculation in the logging industry.[6] Virtually everyone who settled during this time farmed for a living, growing crops and raising enough cattle, pigs, and chickens for family consumption—and perhaps extra to share or barter. The early families settled in clusters of related families, forming tight networks reinforced by daily interaction and economic and social exchanges. These kin-based communities still exist today.

The current plat map locates the Carmichaels, McCallums, and many other families concentrated in the same section or adjacent sections. Only those here for many years can locate Sparks Corners, Stockwell Corners, Cowden Hill, or the Hahn Farm—famous landmarks that are not on any map. When asked where someone lives, residents sometimes have a difficult time describing it. "Well it's . . . let's see . . . 115th or 120th Ave . . . you know, where old man Brigham used to live." Some locations maintain their name long after the last family member has passed away, and in some cases the house no longer exists, or has been occupied by several families since the original settler's.

ETHNOHISTORY OF THE FIRST WHITE SETTLERS

As I visited families to conduct oral histories, I sorted through boxes of photographs and pored over those intricate genealogies that I have discussed earlier. During this process, I learned that not only are families avid collectors, but they continue to pass information down orally through the generations. Some of these stories came from letters and other written materials saved over the years. Others are part of family lore, undocumented, but part of local legend. These stories have two themes: the first theme includes personal achievements and accomplishments—surviving challenges and hardship; the second theme is a romanticized version of social life in a time when cooperation and neighborliness were essential survival skills.

Stories of the first genre acknowledge the challenges of early life in Chippewa Township. One of the early settlers was Malcolm McCormick Jr., whose parents arrived in Canada from Argyllshire, Scotland, in 1831. Malcolm Jr. came to Big Rapids in 1865 and worked for six months on the Grand Rapids and Indiana Railway. In 1866, he became a sailor on Lake Michigan, quit, and ended up in Muskegon. In 1867, he walked from Muskegon to Big Rapids (about seventy miles), staked a claim in Mecosta County, and with a friend walked to Ionia to legalize their claim.

Malcolm purchased property from the Flint and Pere Marquette Railway in Section 22, where he settled with his wife, Margaret McCallum, and where all of their children except the oldest were born. Their second child, Mary, is listed in the *Album of Mecosta County* as the first (white) child born in Fork Township.[7] Malcolm was an integral part of the organization of the township, being among the first elected officials, serving as justice of the peace.[8] This particular office seems humorous and ironic to all local residents who know of the reputation of the McCormick "boys" of those early years, several of whom can be found in the inmate records at the Mecosta County Jail, where they frequently spent the night for such infractions as drunkenness and fighting.

Debra Carmichael Zielinski, who kept her family name so that it would be carried on, tells a story about how her great-great-grandparents came to the area. Alexander Carmichael left his pregnant wife in Canada while he came to Mecosta County in the 1870s to work in the lumber industry. After Debra's great-great-grandfather purchased land in Chippewa Township, he returned to Canada and brought his new family to their Mecosta County homestead. Debra relates the family legend of how her great-great-grandparents arrived in the township on foot, carrying their infant daughter in their arms. This infant was Debra's great-grandmother, Catherine McCallum.

It was not unusual for some of these early settlers to speak Gaelic, despite their immigration route through Canada. In his history of the Brigham family, Elden Brigham notes that the McCormicks and McCallums, all from the same region of highland Scotland, spoke Gaelic among themselves, separating themselves from the lowland Scots and their neighbors who identified themselves with more lofty ethnicities.[9] In fact, not all immigrants to Mecosta County were poor Scottish farmers. The original Brigham ancestor, Thomas, came to the United States from England and settled in Cambridge, Massachusetts, in 1635. The original homestead is now the home of the Radcliffe College campus of Harvard University. In Vermont, the Brigham family married into the Ryder family, whose ancestors were passengers on the *Mayflower*.

Elisha Brigham came to Mecosta County via Grand Rapids, Michigan, where he married Celia Baxter, whose family was well established. One brother was the editor of the *Grand Rapids Eagle*, and another was the assistant secretary of the Interior in charge of the U.S. Land Office. In 1867, Elisha purchased 40 acres in a section north of Chippewa Lake where another lake was located. He and Celia moved north with their family.[10] According to Brigham, Celia named the lake in their newfound section as Emerald Lake.[11] In Chippewa Township, Elisha is listed as a lumberman,[12] but the history describes their life as farmers. Both Elisha and Celia were also talented writers; Celia wrote poetry, and Elisha wrote articles for *The Pioneer* in Big Rapids, Michigan.[13]

Not all immigrants were from England or Scotland. In 1983, Ernie and Evelyn Nott (then in their eighties) told me of Ernie's grandparents who lived in Ithaca, New York, where Ernie's father was born. Ernie's grandfather hitchhiked to Pennsylvania to volunteer for the Civil War. He sent $300 to his grandmother, who then joined him in Pennsylvania. They decided to move to Michigan to homestead and traveled here, even though his grandmother was pregnant at the time. They arrived in Martiny Township in April, and Clara, Ernie's aunt, was born in the fall of that year.

In 1881, Emil Schröder, twenty-one years old, faced mandatory conscription into the Prussian army.[14] As a pacifist, he decided to leave Prussia for America. He left his fiancée, Augusta, behind and joined 750 other passengers on the *Polynesia*, working off his passage in steerage, and on May 4, 1883, he arrived at Castle Island, Port of New York. Meanwhile Augusta's family also emigrated to the United States; somehow, they met up in Brooklyn, and married in 1886. While in Brooklyn, Emil and Augusta maintained communication with their friends in Germany. One of these families, the Landgrafs, asked them to "walk over to Michigan" to see how their relatives were settling into their lives in Chippewa Township, Mecosta County.

Emil, discovering that walking to Michigan was impractical, took the train instead and located the Landgraf family. During his visit, the Landgrafs introduced him to the local Lutheran minister, and Emil decided he would like to settle here. The minister assisted Emil in finding a farm, which, incidentally, had been owned by relatives of Ernie Nott. Emil fetched his family from New York and settled in Chippewa Township. Later, they moved to another township, but kept their farm in Chippewa Township, renting it out to tenant farmers; today, Emil's grandson, Allen Schroeder, lives and works on that same farm.

The second genre of stories highlights incidents of family life that shaped the pioneer spirit of those earliest families. Elderly women whom I interviewed in 1983 related stories of the lives of their mothers and grandmothers. Several women told how their grandmothers had made soap and candles, and had tapped the trees for maple syrup. Their stories emphasize the importance of neighborliness and cooperation: stories of childbirth and helping neighbors in times of need or tragedy. Some of the stories are comical. One such story relates how a family member was walking from Big Rapids to northern Chippewa Township, carrying supplies. When he got about two-thirds of the way home, he remembered that he had forgotten to purchase something important, and he had to turn around and walk all the way back to town.

Other stories relate deaths and accidents. The most tragic community-wide event that was part of nearly every oral history is the flu epidemic of 1918, which killed hundreds of people, wiping out entire families. The local cemeteries all contain many tombstones engraved with the tragic date. I was directed to one cemetery in which the tombstones of an entire family were lined up, parents and four children, all of whom succumbed to this terrible plague in the same year.

Stories of both shared challenges and triumphs reproduce ideas of community and identity among the descendants of the earliest settlers. One such story is recorded by Elden Brigham.[15] It relates to Malcolm McCormick, who went to visit a young couple who had recently moved into one of the less populated sections of the township. When he arrived, he learned that the young wife and her infant child were in the house all alone. The husband had left the house two days earlier for provisions and had not returned. The wife did not know her neighbors and was afraid to leave the house alone because of her fear of the Indians nearby. She and her child were without food, so Malcolm left to seek food and provisions from the closest neighbors and gave them to the woman. The story does not say whether the husband ever returned, but indicates that he suffered from epilepsy that "reduced both his mental and physical effectiveness."[16]

Because the settler period is far distant in the minds of many of those I interviewed, their stories of community originate primarily in the 1900s, when their grandparents were farming. For insight into earlier years of settlement, I explored some of the documents compiled from Virginia Ball, as well as interviews conducted in 1983 when some of the grandchildren of the first settlers were still alive. From Virginia Ball's articles, we can identify several institutions that were of importance during the settlement years. The first of these was the Grange Hall, organized in 1874. The Grange is discussed in Virginia Ball's "Story of the History of Chippewa Lake" and in various oral histories.[17] It was organized as an informational group for farmers, but also as a social organization. In the earliest years and into the twentieth century, the Grange Hall provided men with a meeting place to discuss farming issues, set up threshing schedules, and socialize. On weekends and in the winter months, dances and social gatherings were held there.

Another community-based institution was the local church. The Chippewa Lake Church was built by the Chippewa Lake Lumber Company in 1885 on land the lumber company donated. The Chippewa Lake Church was not the only church in the area. Residents of other sectors of the township built their own churches, such as the Lutheran Church, so that churches and schools identified neighborhoods and ethnic groups, and bound related families into multi-stranded networks. Schools also provided continuity and community.

Local schools have always been critical in forging social networks and reinforcing community identity. Chippewa Township had several one-room schoolhouses, and many residents have photographs of these schools as they existed into the twentieth century. The first schoolhouse in Chippewa Township was built in Section 8 in 1870; the second school was established in 1871 at Emerald Lake, Section 3, in one of the northernmost sections of the county.[18] Later schools were established at Sparks Corners, Eaton Corners, Chippewa Lake, and in Section 27 east of the lake. Schoolteachers, if they were not local, came to live with families. These were young girls, often from neighboring communities. Once local girls completed their schooling, they were eligible to become teachers themselves, and teachers with local names begin appearing in the oral histories in the late 1800s—Sparks, Whaley, Eaton, and McCallum.

During the early settlement years, the population of Mecosta County grew steadily: from 1,017 in 1860 to 9,132 in 1874, according to the *Atlas of Mecosta County*.[19] Chippewa Township grew from 140 in 1870 to 291 in 1874.[20] In 1879, most of the early settlers were subsistence farmers,[21] but by 1900 the residents who were listed in the 1900 plat book for Mecosta County held a diverse mix of occupations: engineer, blacksmith, and cooper; wagon maker, butcher, livery owner, physician, and stock buyer.[22] Two women listed in the plat book were Delila Scofield, moneylender and real estate and securities agent, and Mrs. Christina Wylie, proprietress of the Dewey Hotel. What happened to Chippewa Township between 1870 and 1900 can only be described as revolutionary economic development, centered on the special attributes of Chippewa Lake, and the river system that flowed from it to larger cities and to Lakes Michigan and Huron.

LOGGING AND THE LUMBER INDUSTRY

Michigan, with its pristine forests, vast river systems, and its location surrounded by the Great Lakes, provided numerous opportunities for exploitation of natural resources, from the fur trade to the lumber industry. According to Willis Dunbar, the Saginaw valley was the first forested area in Michigan to be exploited for lumber.[23] The riverine system that threaded the valley facilitated the floating of logs from the forests to mills and to Lake Huron.

The logging industry did not suddenly appear in Chippewa Township. As early as 1870, logs were floated down the south branch of the Chippewa River to mills in Saginaw.[24] Before the first mills were built around the lake, dams were constructed in Chippewa Lake Creek to make the river navigable for logs to float to the Saginaw mills.[25] In 1872, the first township sawmill was built on Emerald Lake,[26] and two additional sawmills were built on

Chippewa Lake that same year.[27] In 1873 a steam-driven sawmill and grist mill were built at Emerald Lake,[28] and by 1882, two more mills appeared on Chippewa Lake, one of these relocated from Big Rapids.[29] The Chippewa Lake Lumber Company was organized by Charles Wyman in 1880, and by 1883 it controlled most of the land that now makes up the village of Chippewa Lake. In that year, the lumber company oversaw the platting of the village into the pattern that still exists today.[30]

As the logging industry grew, the railroad companies also expanded into the area. In fact, according to the 1879 township plat map, the railroads anticipated the development of this area, and large tracts of land in the township were already owned by various railroads at this time. At least two railroads cut through Chippewa Township during the late 1800s, carrying lumber east to Detroit and south to Indiana.[31] The logging boom in Chippewa Township resulted in an economic explosion in the new village of Chippewa Lake. At least five logging camps sprouted up around the lake to accommodate those who came to work as loggers and mill workers. While most families came to take advantage of the Homestead Act, others first learned of the opportunities during their employment as loggers or railroad workers in other regions of Michigan. My husband's ancestors came to Chippewa Township in this way, ultimately obtaining land through the Homestead Act.

Mill workers earned $26 a month and room and board. This was more money than families could earn in agriculture, and many young men joined the ranks of wage laborers. Logging camps were made up of a cook shanty, where food was prepared and served, and bunkhouses that provided bunk beds for up to sixty men per house. Camps also had a barn for the horses that pulled the trams from the forest to the lake, a granary for horse feed, blacksmith and carpentry shops, and the company store for the workers.[32] Logging companies hired local laborers for many positions in the camps, and hired women to work as cooks and laundresses.

Logging also opened opportunities for many other entrepreneurs, including livery stables, hotels, taverns, and dry-goods and clothing stores. Many families came to Chippewa Lake specifically to open hotels or taverns. Others, already living in the township, took advantage of the boom to start businesses in town, such as hotels and dance halls. At its height, Chippewa Lake had eight saloons, four hotels, several boarding houses, three grocery stores, two hardware stores, a roller rink, a shingle mill, and a creamery depot.[33] Chippewa Lake was a booming town.

In 1885, the lumber company provided the land and the lumber to build the first church, a Congregational church.[34] The church, along with the Grange and the schools became the core institutions for a thriving community. As it grew, the village also drew other professionals to fulfill the needs of the workers and the local population. After the first doctor came, and then left due to lack of business, Dr. Patterson arrived. People still talk about old Doc Patterson, and anyone who has lived here for some time can point out his house, which was the second house built in the village. Doc Patterson was also a pharmacist, so he and the third doctor to arrive opened a pharmacy to accompany their private practices. At this time, a veterinarian, blacksmith, and engineer also arrived in town, as well as a minister for the church.

Chippewa Lake also grew as a resort town during this time. Although the lake was used primarily as a means of transporting logs from the northern sections to the town and railroad tracks, it was also used as a resort for many city families. One enterprising man purchased a steamboat, named the *Reveille*, which he used to haul supplies and passengers from Evans Lake, southeast of Chippewa Lake, to Chippewa. On weekends, riding on the boat became a popular social activity for locals and tourists.[35]

Almost as quickly as it began, it all crashed to the ground—or more correctly, it burned to the ground. Because of the lumber and the fact that everything was built of wood, there were many fires in the 1800s and early 1900s. It is difficult to keep them straight, as the stories have become blurred over the years. However, from the late 1800s to 1906, nearly every building had burned down at least once, including the church. When the primary mill burned in 1894, loggers continued to move logs by rail, but when the lumber company itself burned down in early 1900, it was never replaced. By then, the white pine had been decimated by clear-cutting anyway. In 1906, so the story goes, the railroad was dismantled after the last train came through, very early on a Sunday morning in October. Later, when people arose, they found the tracks gone, and that was the end of the logging days.[36]

CHIPPEWA TOWNSHIP AS A FARMING COMMUNITY

Once the lumber industry collapsed, Chippewa Township returned to its agricultural roots. The impact of lumbering on the economic and social success of the community is evident in population figures during this era. According to the 1880 census, when the logging industry was in its early stages, the population of Chippewa Township was 445.[37] By 1890, it had more than doubled, reaching 1,000. However, by 1930, when logging was only a memory for local subsistence farmers, the community had shrunk to 1880 figures, recorded as 510 people.[38] The township population would not reach 1,000 again until 1980, ninety years later.[39]

The family farm characterizes the period from 1900 to World War II. The huge tracts of land owned by the railroad were divided into 40-, 80-, and 120-acre plots, and the rural landscape took on the appearance of a settled agricultural community. This period of Chippewa Township history lives in the memories of many old-timers, particularly those I interviewed in 1983. It was in these interviews, and also several of those conducted in 2004, that I heard many of the stories that reflected the second genre of anecdotes: of the strength of the rural community values.

Until World War II, most farming in Mecosta County was subsistence-based. Each family owned its own milk cows, chickens, and pigs and was economically self-sufficient. Chippewa Township farmers did not obtain electricity until 1931,[40] so all farm and household chores were labor-intensive, and all family members participated in such chores as milking the cows, pumping water from the well, collecting eggs, and feeding the farm animals. Households earned some cash from selling eggs and butter to storekeepers; others bartered their farm products for dry goods and other supplies, such as kerosene. Some families I interviewed remembered taking the cream from their milk to the nearest storekeeper, who then sold it to creameries located in neighboring towns. Women, with the assistance of children, made their own soap and were responsible for the care of domesticated animals, collecting eggs, and maintaining food gardens. These activities were in addition to the everyday care of the house, including child care, cooking, laundry, and cleaning.

Women, however, were not relegated only to the domestic realm in farming. Several families highlighted stories of their mothers or grandmothers on the farm. While women usually did not "drive tractor," some knew how and would drive them from time to time if necessary. Responsibilities of women were diverse and time-consuming. Several women remembered their mothers going out to the pasture to walk the cows back into the barn in the afternoons, milking them and collecting the cream. Women were also the family accountants and inventory keepers. It was often their responsibility to keep track of expenses and income, and to budget the family finances.

One woman I interviewed, Mabelle, told me how one day, while she was helping her father-in-law, Roy, plant potatoes, she caught her fingertips in the potato planter mechanism. One fingertip was completely severed. Mabelle's daughter Ilene ran to the fields to tell her grandfather what had happened. When he found his daughter-in-law holding up her bloody fingertip, Roy tossed the tiny piece to the ground and then fainted dead away. Ilene recalled that her mother, bleeding profusely, then sent her to the barn to get her father, Delmer. When Delmer saw his wife standing in the field with a fingertip in her hand and another dangling, he rushed her to the doctor, hoping they could be reattached. This was not possible, and her fingers had to be sewn up without the tips.[41]

Mutual assistance is an important element of all societies, but is particularly critical for the survival of communities that are distant economically or socially from cities and government services. Every family I interviewed shared stories about the importance of neighbors and the spirit of cooperation that existed in the early days. Women were more isolated than men and relied on other women for favors, such as bread starter, or starter coals for cooking and heat fires. Women provided more substantial services by sending food over to another farm when a neighbor woman was ill or postpartum and was unable to cook for her family. Women all gave birth to their children at home. Sometimes a doctor was present, but at other times he was not. Women learned to take care of each other and themselves.

Perhaps the most intriguing story I heard about what neighbors would do for each other was related by Irvin Austin in 1983. In 1892, Irvin's family homesteaded on a parcel of land in Martiny Township, one mile south of the Chippewa Township line and five miles from the lake. In 1917, Irvin and his wife built a new house on the land, but were unable to afford to build the kitchen. So, for $75, Irvin purchased a house on Chippewa Lake that had an intact kitchen. He then solicited his brothers and several neighbors to help him haul the house from the lake to his farm, five miles away. They made a huge platform from logs, somehow moved the house to the platform, and pulled it the entire distance with a team of fourteen horses. There is a high hill on a mile-long stretch of the route, which is still a hazard today, and when the horses had difficulty climbing that hill, they had to attach two more horses to the front of the team to get them to the top. Irvin laughed as he told this story, but added that no one would accept any money from him.[42]

Farmers grew crops primarily for cattle feed and for household consumption. Grain production, even on a small scale, required machinery to cut and thresh the grains so they could be transported to the silos for storage. At harvest time, farmers took turns hiring a thresher and hosting threshing parties that brought farm families together for a day of shared labor and socializing. The farmers' wives and children met at the farmhouse where the threshing was being conducted, and the women prepared the food for the workers. These parties were an opportunity for women to socialize, and according to stories, were also often seen as competitions among women as they prepared their best meals.[43] Curtis K. Stadtfeld, in his enlightened book *From the Land and Back*, describes another rural community in Mecosta County, Remus, where he grew up.[44] He relates many examples and stories of the cooperation and neighborliness that defined farming during a time when farm equipment was shared and the farming calendar was such that intense efforts needed to be focused on crops at critical times. According to some, this philosophy is still intact today. I asked one man how he defined a "neighbor," and he replied: "Around here neighbors is about any distance you're willing to drive."

Although Chippewa Lake condensed into a smaller community after the collapse of logging, it was still a thriving community in the mid-1900s. Hard work was tempered by many social activities related to the church and neighborhood get-togethers. For men, the Grange, and later the Farm Bureau were farming organizations that doubled as social groups. There was animosity between these two groups as the Farm Bureau came to be seen as a more scientifically based organization that could assist farmers in getting more from their fields as cash crops began to become more important. The Grange allowed men to get together to plan threshing activities, share advice on new crops, and socialize.

Both men and women socialized together in many ways during those days. Several people discussed card parties that moved progressively from farm to farm. The dance hall, and later the roller rink became important centers for activity and socializing. There was at least one local musical group of fiddlers, led by Stuart Carmichael, that performed in Chippewa Township and elsewhere. Virginia Ball, in her "Memories of an Old Timer," remembers fall community celebrations leading up to deer-hunting season where neighbors got together and chose up sides for a hunting contest.[45] In the late afternoon of opening day, the hunters all brought their kill to the village center, and the side who had killed the least number of deer had to put on the wild-game supper that was held in the town hall. Afterwards, the local fiddlers would perform and there would be a community dance. They made the best of hard winters by having sledding parties and sleigh rides for the children, and ice skating on the lake.

Chippewa Lake continued to be a popular social center into the 1950s, until the last of the dance halls burned down in 1963. For several years the dance hall was moved to the old potato-storage building on the town's main street, but the owners closed it down because it drew too many outsiders, some of whom were selling alcohol and drugs to kids behind the building.[46] Since the 1970s, the community itself has stagnated. Few new businesses have come to town, and those that have been established have not been successful. The resort community has not had the type of development that one would expect for a lake of this size. The reasons for this inertia are many, and we will look at this issue as related to the overall tension and conflicting definitions of community identified by the various groups that share this small piece of rural real estate.

ECONOMIC RESTRUCTURING AND POST-WORLD WAR II FARMING IN THE UNITED STATES

There is a vast literature in political economics and sociology on the economic crisis of the 1980s and its impact on rural America. In this section, I will briefly summarize some of the issues involved in this restructuring in order to present a context in which to understand the transformations in American agriculture, and specifically in Michigan, in the post–World War II period.[47]

The Rural Sociological Society Task Force on Persistent Rural Poverty outlined three phases of the process of economic restructuring that occurred between World War II and the 1980s, when it culminated in the rural economic crisis.[48] The first phase, from 1945 to the 1960s, was characterized by postwar growth in the industrial sector that resulted in urban and urban-fringe development at the expense of rural development. Returning soldiers and rural residents abandoned their rural roots to seek well-paying jobs in the manufacturing sector.

Phase 2 (1960s–1970s) was characterized by a revitalization of rural communities and concomitant new optimism in rural life. As cities expanded to absorb small towns, manufacturing followed, seeking inexpensive labor in rural areas and resulting in a stabilization of rural population growth. In phase 3 (1980s–1990s), the growing national and international economic crisis led to spikes in unemployment and underemployment, increased interest rates, and ultimately to widespread poverty in urban and rural areas. Many people can remember the horrific scenes on the evening television news of farmers forced into bankruptcy, weeping as their farms were being auctioned off. Books, films, and concerts such as "Farm Aid" highlighted this tragic era of American farming.

ECONOMIC RESTRUCTURING AND POST–WORLD
WAR II FARMING IN MECOSTA COUNTY

While there is little ethnographic data indicating that the experiences of
Michigan mirror those of other Midwestern states, it is clear that the farm
crisis affected all farmers in the United States. Likewise, it is clear that farming is on the decline as more and more farmland is being converted to rural
industrial parks and suburban housing complexes and shopping malls.
According to the National Agricultural Statistics Service, between 1982 and
1992, Michigan lost 854,000 acres of farmland, acreage that equals the size
of Rhode Island. This decline represents decreases in both size and number
of farms. Between 1992 and 2002, the average farm size decreased from
205 acres to 151 acres.[49] The decline in the number of farms is evident in
Mecosta County, where the number of farms has decreased from 1,890 in
1947 to 794 in 2002.[50] According to the Mecosta Conservation District
Resource Assessment, 110 of these farms are dairy farms.[51] In Chippewa
Township alone, four dairy farmers within one square mile of my house
have quit dairy farming since 2004. Three of these continue to raise beef
cattle and starter calves for sale. The Amish community holds about 90 of
the 794 farms in Mecosta County, which average between 40 and 120 acres.

The importance of agriculture to the county cannot be ignored, however.
Agricultural data for 2007 from the Michigan State University Extension
Service indicate that agriculture still has an important impact on county
economics. In 2007, the economic value of agriculture in Mecosta County
topped $41 million dollars, almost $20 million of this from milk production.
In other townships, larger dairy farms still prevail, and one dairy operation
in particular in southern Mecosta County produces over 110,000 gallons of
milk per month from 440 Holsteins. Agricultural income also derives from
a large pig farm in the county, and the production of wheat, hay, and corn
from farms of various sizes. The $41 million figure does not include a large
potato producer in Martiny Township that supplies Frito Lay, or Leprino
Foods in southern Mecosta County that provides cheese for Pizza Hut.[52]

None of these large enterprises reside in Chippewa Township, and in
general, Mecosta County is feeling the consequences of the death of small
farm agriculture. According to the U.S. Census Bureau, 4 percent of the
county population was employed in agriculture, forestry, fishing, and hunting in 1990 (616 people); in 2000, this percentage had dropped to 2.5
percent (435 people). According to the Mecosta Conservation District data,
21 percent of farmers in Mecosta County were working second jobs in the
1950s; by 2000, the percentage had increased to 45 percent.[53] Further, for

those who remained on the farm, their income dropped 16 percent between 1996 and 1999, while the average personal income of nonfarmers in that same period increased 17 percent.

IMPACT OF CITIES ON THE RURAL COMMUNITY

It is likely that the present city of Big Rapids was a popular spring camp for the Ottawa Indians. They camped along the swiftly flowing river to fish and to tap the maple trees for syrup and sugar.[54] European settlers discovered the area as the logging industry began, and the swift waters of the Muskegon River became a main artery moving logs from Houghton Lake to the mills in Muskegon. Permanent settlements began to develop along the river. The village of Big Rapids was platted in 1859, the same year that Mecosta County was established. Big Rapids was incorporated as a city in 1869.[55] The year 1859 is also auspicious because in that year, Anna Howard Shaw's family moved from Lowell, Massachusetts, to the Big Rapids area. Her autobiography, *The Story of a Pioneer*, relates her life in this county and how she later earned both a medical degree and ordination in the Methodist Church, and ultimately became one of the group of women, along with Susan B. Anthony and Elizabeth Cady Stanton, who fought for women's suffrage.[56] A statue of her stands in front of the Big Rapids Public Library.

Those years were characterized by rapid economic change, as Big Rapids and Mecosta County were experiencing rapid development due largely to the expansion of the lumber industry. Its location on the Muskegon River and access to railroads guaranteed its economic and political success. Between 1870 and 1880, three railroads were built that established Big Rapids as the local center of the logging industry and the economic center for the county. During this time, a second distinguished resident came to Big Rapids. In 1884 Woodbridge Nathan Ferris arrived and established a technical school that has become Ferris State University, a major educational institution and employer for Mecosta County. Woodbridge Ferris later became governor of Michigan and served as a U.S. senator .[57]

When the logging industry collapsed, so followed the economy of Mecosta County. By 1907, Big Rapids was suffering an economic depression that was felt throughout the region. In 1933, however, the discovery of oil and gas in the county resulted in an economic revival. The Austin gas fields today are a huge underground natural-gas storage facility. This discovery resulted in an economic upturn and a new era of affluence and growth.

Thus, Big Rapids has always been an important economic and political center. It has also served as an important geographic link between Grand Rapids and northern Michigan towns, such as Cadillac. US 131 (first a two-lane highway, now an expressway) served as a major link in the developing route from Grand Rapids to the Upper Peninsula. Impressive mansions still line the major thoroughfares in the city, as well as the river bank, and attest to the affluent history of this city, when logging barons, and later oil and gas barons, controlled the ebb and flow of industry. Today many of these mansions are still occupied, but many have been divided up into apartments or belong to fraternities for the local Ferris State University.

When the logging industry waned, as did oil and gas in later years, Big Rapids still thrived as the county seat of a predominantly rural county. For many years it housed the only hospital, center for law enforcement and governmental services, and major business district. Many of the oral histories include stories of journeys to Big Rapids, located fifteen miles from Chippewa Lake. The route, taken on horseback or in a carriage, was arduous, cutting through woods and wetlands. Stories of horse-and-wagon teams stuck in the swamps that separate the farming communities and the county seat abound, and in some low-lying locations, the current road still has to be rebuilt frequently as the protected wetlands continue to claim it, sinking the pavement into the swamp.

Today, Big Rapids has a population of nearly 11,000 and is a growing center for manufacturing.[58] The largest employer in the city, and in the county, is Ferris State University. Big Rapids was recently designated as an "enterprise zone" by the state of Michigan, so it will be able to offer numerous incentives to businesses and manufacturers seeking building locations. Residents of Big Rapids are proud of the small-town feel of this main street, where people know each other, and where local family businesses pass from parents to children, shaping a community with continuity and community values. Outsiders come to the town as university students and faculty members. Others are drawn from the surrounding rural communities to seek jobs in the various factories in and around the city. Since the US 131 expressway was extended past the city, giving it two exits, the access road has experienced rapid development of retail and restaurant franchises, which also employ both city workers and commuter workers from surrounding rural communities. With the exception of the university, K-12 schools, government, and several other employers, most of the manufacturing and retail employers provide nonunion but highly coveted jobs.

Beyond Big Rapids, employment opportunities also draw local workers. Many men from the Chippewa Lake area work for the gas fields that are located in Mecosta and surrounding counties; others work for the county road commission and for other businesses located in surrounding towns. Increasingly, people are seeking jobs in towns and cities as far away as Grand Rapids, seventy miles south of Big Rapids and eighty-five miles from Chippewa Lake. There are men who have commuted for many years, making the daily round trip from Chippewa Lake or Big Rapids to Grand Rapids, where they work in automobile factories or manufacturing companies that supply the automobile industry in Detroit. Since the expressway has facilitated the commute, this phenomenon has increased, and Big Rapids as well as the surrounding rural communities have increasingly become bedroom communities feeding the expanding manufacturing zones of Grand Rapids.

Chippewa Township is connected peripherally to the larger national and global communities. Residents are linked through wage labor in those subsidiary factories that provide parts for transnational corporations. Dairy and crop farmers are dependent upon farm subsidies and the vagaries of the marketplace for their farming income. They are also increasingly linked to the global market through their reliance on transnational corporations for fertilizers, oil, and gas, and the consumer markets for groceries and other necessary items. They pay taxes on large tracts of land without reaping the infrastructure benefits of their taxes. Economic pressures on the county budget have resulted in retracting squad cars and emergency vehicles from rural areas, as well as cutting back on snowplowing and other services, and rural people pay extra for other services provided to city dwellers as part of their tax payments: trash pickup, recycling, sewer (septic). They are of the world, yet distant from it in many ways.

CONCLUSION

We have examined the history of one particular community within the context of a larger economic milieu: the migration of immigrant families from Europe and the eastern United States, the economic pull of logging and ample land that promised new possibilities in the expanding nation, and the national impact of war and economic downturn. We have also begun to look at how some of these early settlers came to be in this small area in north-central Michigan, how their lives became intertwined, and how they formed a community. More importantly, Chippewa Township, while rural and isolated from urban centers, has never fit the idea of bordered communities, insulated and static. The history of Chippewa Township is one of immigration from various European nation-states, each group bringing traditions that at first differentiated them from their neighbors, but later diminished as the community grew and established itself. Chippewa Lake and the township surrounding it maintained a subsistence-farming worldview while adapting to loggers and other entrepreneurs. And finally, members of the community linked themselves to towns and cities beyond the township—Big Rapids, Evart, and Barryton—expanding their economic and social spheres beyond the homestead, setting themselves off from the "city folk" while taking advantage of the opportunities available to them elsewhere. This same ability to take from the city what one needs and reject the rest still benefits modern residents of Chippewa Township today.

CHAPTER 3

Farm Families in Transition

When Darryl McCallum's dad died, now this was before I
was born, the neighborhood took care of Ginger and the kids.
[Neighbors] got their crops off, anything they needed done . . .
When my dad was sick with cancer, I hardly had to take him
to radiation to Butterworth [hospital in Grand Rapids].
Everybody was more worried about me taking care of my
family, taking care of my mom [who had multiple sclerosis],
than going back and forth with Dad. Now, Dad had people
scheduled to take him . . . These neighbors . . . Dad called
them "the girls" . . . they went to high school together—they
took him a couple times, and they just had a blast, you know?
And you know how tiring radiation is, but it was good for
him too. And he was in control of his life, up until the
last week of his life. He wasn't really a burden to anybody.

—DEBRA CARMICHAEL ZIELINSKI, 2005

WE START OUR STORY OF MODERN CHANGE AND STABILITY IN THE
rural areas of Chippewa Township, as this is where the majority of residents
reside. This is also the area that best identifies the history of the community
since the 1800s, when the railroad tracks were ripped up, leaving the isolated farms behind. Descendants of these early farm families still live here,
often on the same land their ancestors settled, perpetuating the promise of
the idyllic rural lifestyle.

Born in the city, I have always had ambivalent feelings about my new life
in rural Michigan. I miss the activities and the opportunities for entertainment in an urban area, and most of all, I have hated the long commute that
my job requires, driving through four counties, two rush hours, and two
NPR radio broadcast zones.

On the other hand, I have become accustomed to the cycle of rural life. One knows that it is spring when the farmers can be seen and heard as their tractors move up and down fields of muddy spring growth, turning the soil and fertilizing in the heavy muck of the April thaw. The fresh smell of newly budding and leafing trees and flowers compete with the pungent odor of freshly applied manure. The apple trees along our fence line fill with apple blossoms, and the smell of lilacs is heavy in the air.

Conversations with my friends are punctuated by exciting news of a new foal expected or arriving. We chatter with spring-like optimism about our future gardens. While we in northern Michigan dare not plant too early because of late frost, we are not deterred from speculating about our gardens: how big they will be this year, how much we will plant of which vegetables, and when it is safe to plant. One May, I complained to my friend that my green pepper seeds never sprouted, and two days later, there were three pepper plants on my front porch when I came home from work. My friend had more starts than she needed and generously shared with me. Women are the primary gardeners in my circle, but I know some elderly men who have immaculate and very productive gardens that they tend individually or with their wives.

Summers are lush in the country, with the aromas of trees and flowering shrubs. It is impossible to feel depressed when one drives down country roads, surrounded by fields of corn stalks inching upward and the grasses waving majestically in the breeze. The smell of hay is strong as farmers take their cuttings and huge round bales appear mysteriously in fields throughout the area. Gardens are blooming, and one learns not to leave one's car door unlocked at work. Failure to heed this warning will result in finding a grocery bag full of zucchini or cucumbers on your back seat. I have learned to prepare zucchini grilled, baked, sautéed, and in Alfredo sauce, and now bake both zucchini bread and cookies. Summer events in the community and on the lake remind me of what rural living must have been like in the old days: children's T-ball and softball leagues, bonfires, parades, and Fourth of July festivities. People are outdoors and are able to reconnect with neighbors they have not seen for many months.

Fall gives us the warning of things to come, especially for those of us who do not welcome the winter snow. The change of colors is astonishing in the country and never ceases to amaze me. Gardens are cleared, and activities move indoors as women can or freeze their produce. There is a bustle of activity in the fall as farmers make last-minute preparations for the long winter: piling baled hay into barns, replacing/repairing heated water troughs for their animals, and bedding stalls to assure the safety of their animals during the winter months.

With the fall comes deer-hunting season, and today, as I write this section, our neighbor who lives a half mile north of us has just called me. He has wounded a deer and wants permission to cross our farmland to track it. He knows that he does not need to ask, but it is safety etiquette to do so just in case a member of our family is in the same field and not expecting someone to walk through. I was very much anti–deer hunting when I moved here, in my urban naiveté; now I understand the importance of the deer harvest, not only for venison, which everyone eats, but to cull the herd that has no nonhuman predators and that would otherwise overrun fields of corn, vegetable gardens, and fruit trees.

The Sugar Bush

Maple syrup was another of the gifts that the Native Americans gave to the European settlers. It was used as a sweetener for indigenous diets, as well as for barter in exchange for the white man's goods. Syrup became a staple of the colonial diet in areas where the sugar or red maple trees prospered.[*] Sap originates as starches that collect in the trees in the fall and remain stored in the tree during the winter. The starches convert to sap in the spring when the temperatures hit 40 degrees during the day but are still very cold at night. Sap is collected by tapping the trees in the early spring. Depending on the spring weather and the size and age of the tree, a single tap hole can produce as much as forty to eighty gallons of sap per year. It takes about ten gallons of sap to produce one quart of syrup.[†]

Several local families produce and sell maple syrup as a supplemental source of income. Wynne Nellis was one of these producers. When I had interviewed Wynne during the winter months, he told me that he had started tapping sugar maples for syrup when he was in high school. He bought his first syrup pan for $10 from a neighbor. He started with a small stand of maple trees in Fork Township, but now has a larger stand on his own property. At the end of our interview, he promised me that he would take me to his sugar bush in March when they tap the trees, but March came and went and no invitation came. It was a cold day in early April when Wynne finally called. He apologized that he had not called sooner, but he had been in the hospital. He was not able to make the trek to the sugar bush, but I could go with his son Tim and daughter-in-law Cheryl, who were tapping for him this year. That an eighty-four-year-old man, just out of hospital, would remember his promise and call me to apologize is an indication of his generosity.

I knew Cheryl Nellis well, as we had children the same age and had participated in community events together. I called her, and she invited me to the sugar bush on the following Sunday. It was a typical northern Michigan April—cold, but with a glimpse of sun that both teased and promised better weather ahead. When I arrived at the Nellis farmhouse, I was met by Tim, who motioned me toward Wynne's quad (four-wheeler) that was going to be our transportation for the trip. Fields in late March and April are either snow-covered or heavy with muck as winter reluctantly retreats. Today it was muck, and Tim did not want to get his truck stuck in the bush. So I hopped on the back and was immediately grateful that I had worn warm clothes and my farm boots as we took a harrowing ride off the tractor path into a wooded area that served as their family hunting grounds and sugar bush.

It was very quiet there, with a variety of deciduous trees; the maple trees were in their starring role with buckets nailed onto their bark. In a clearing, we came upon a group of small buildings and a rusty travel trailer that now serves as the "hunting cabin." During tapping season, one or two people will stay in the trailer and work around the clock to get it done at the right time. The area surrounding the structures is strewn with old equipment, sap buckets, and logs. A huge holding tank that contains the raw sap feeds into one of the sheds where the syrup is cooked. As the sap enters the shed, it flows into a new evaporator—a long table-shaped pan divided in two sections across. A wood stove sits under the right side of the table, but heats the other side to a rapid boil, because of tubes that extend along the bottom of the left side. A large elevated tank sits next to the table on the left, where the sap is dumped and then drained by a tube into the table cooker.

The cooker is a rectangular plate about 4 × 5 feet, with troughs that circulate the sap from one side to the other, moving up and down four longitudinal sections of trough that resemble a Disney World waiting line. The sap is heated and it boils as it works its way up and down the furrows until it reaches the last row. At this point it has thickened and is drained from the evaporator into buckets and transported to another building, where they funnel it through two filtering cloths into sanitized whiskey bottles.

Before buying the evaporator, they had to cook the sap in huge pans over a fire. This was a very tedious and time-consuming process, as it took around forty gallons of sap to make one gallon of syrup. Cheryl laughed that sometimes they would bring the sap to the house to cook on the stove, but Helen, Wynne's wife, got mad because of the sticky mess and demanded that they take their mucky business elsewhere.

They don't sell their product widely. They primarily sell to neighbors, and their profit depends on the quality and quantity of the sap, which in turn depends on the spring weather. If there is an early thaw and then a cold snap, the production of sap can shut off and affect the quantity and quality of the syrup. This year threatened to be a bad year for the Nellises' syrup. They had only gotten fifty gallons of sap two days previously, and twenty the day before my visit. The day I visited would be the last day of production. Before returning to the farm, Cheryl took a picture of Tim standing in front of the machinery. This year, they planned to have a label for their syrup.

*GEORGE Cornell, "Ojibway," in Clifton et al., *People of the Three Fires: The Ottawa, Potawatomi, and Ojibway of Michigan* (Grand Rapids, MI: Grand Rapids Inter-Tribal Council, 1986), 82.

†UNIVERSITY of Maine Cooperative Extension, "How to Tap Maple Trees and Make Maple Syrup," Bulletin #7036, 2007, available at http://www.umext.maine.edu/onlinepubs/pdfpubs/7036.pdf.

Winters are difficult. There is a certain stark beauty about winter here, but also the problems of unplowed roads and isolation. With the exception of dairy and beef farmers, people retreat to their homes. Farmers have no such luxury. Animals need to be fed and watered, equipment and outbuildings maintained. Dairy cows don't take vacations from producing milk, and dairy farmers don't take vacations either. Although we had horses for several years, we have been peripheral to many of these farming activities, watching as our friends make these preparations, and remembering why we sold our horses when our kids graduated from high school and moved to college towns.

The winter isolation is broken up by holiday events and socializing indoors; card parties and circulating dinners allow friends to keep in touch. This picture I have drawn is an accurate one—but yet, not really, as the reality of rural life is much more complex than I can portray in a survey of the annual calendar. My description outlines an ideal rural life where friends share and families cooperate, where everyone looks out for everyone else, and no one is violent or mean or deviant. It is difficult to separate the myth of rural life from the reality. My description is true, every word of it has happened, but rural life is more than this, and through a more detailed analysis, we can appreciate the complexity of rural life today, and probably in the past.

RURAL STEREOTYPES

In the classroom, especially in my introductory-level classes in anthropology, I try to instill in my students the idea that no cultures or categories of people can be stereotyped or generalized, whether we are discussing Mayan peasants or "women" in cross-cultural perspective. All societies, whether small- or large-scale, exist within a historical context and a political and economic system that shapes daily lives and local discourse. Within each society, individuals and groups act and respond in relation to their own position within that larger milieu, according to gender, age, occupation, religion, social class, and interests. This is certainly true for Chippewa Township.

Housing in the township ranges from mobile homes and modular homes to centennial farmhouses. Some of these centennial farms conjure up the most nostalgic vision of the ideal rural community—with picket fences; large, multilevel farmhouses with colorful flower beds and vibrant vegetable gardens; brightly painted barns and outbuildings; and the requisite number of horses and cows grazing, chickens pecking, and dogs frolicking. Others are stark visions of the reality of many farm families. Bare boards or aging vinyl siding convey a life of families who do not have the finances or the time to paint their houses. Dilapidated cars and pickup trucks collect rust behind barns in dire need of fresh paint, and farm implements are scattered around the yard where they were left after their last use. In the township, pickup trucks outnumber SUVs and sedans, and everyone owns at least one gun or hunting rifle. Rural residents are as perplexed about the suburbanites' fear of guns as I am about mud runs and tractor pulls. Schools are closed on the opening day of deer season, and in the winter, a shanty village develops on Chippewa Lake as locals stake out their spots for ice fishing.

Likewise, the stereotypes we use to describe rural America—such generalizations as "redneck," NASCAR dad, and farmer—do not accurately describe the lives of many of the people I have come to know, though many use such terms to describe themselves. For example, I have friends who define themselves as rednecks and proudly spell out the alternate meaning of the acronym NASCAR (Non Athletic Sport Centered around Rednecks). They listen to country music and wear boots and jeans as their everyday attire. Yet, some of these same people who joke about NASCAR and call themselves rednecks have college educations, own businesses, and have attended NASCAR races. One couple I know has attended the Kentucky Derby and sipped mint juleps.

During my research, as I interviewed one farmer, Lawrence Worth, about his life in the township, his wife reached into an antique dresser and pulled out a weathered photo album, presenting it to me. The album held page after page of fading color Polaroid shots of families and children in the Philippines, where Lawrence was stationed during World War II. I never knew he had been in the war, and he probably would not have told me about his wartime travels on his own. He is not the only township resident who has traveled widely because of war. Yet, I also have many neighbors who have never been out of the country, or even the state. Some rarely leave Mecosta County, and others, because of their dairy farms, never take vacations at all. Thus, as it is with non-Western societies and urban neighborhoods, so it also is with rural communities. It is likely that some of the stereotypes that we assign to rural America have kernels of truth, and many, in general, are descriptive of an earlier time; but even broad historical brushes are risky.

COMMUNITY PERSONALITY AND COMMUNITY EFFECT

Despite the diversity of origins and lifestyles, it is likely that the majority of the early settlers shared a particular worldview. Today, the descendants of these early settlers use the same ideas to describe what they like about their community and what they feel is being lost: the sense of community identity, neighborliness, shared experiences, mutual assistance, and shared values of hard work and kinship ties.

These same values are echoed in ethnographies written about rural American communities.[1] That there is consistency in these varied accounts indicates that there is an undercurrent of rural life that distinguishes it from urban or suburban life, and that also provides a beneficial environment in which to raise children. Research in various North American farm communities sheds some light on these themes of rural life that seem to permeate communities wherever they are found. Sonya Salamon, in her various works, describes a "community personality" in which one finds certain indicators of a cohesive community.[2] In addition, Janet Fitchen examines the official and local definitions of what constitutes a rural community as newcomers force these communities to renegotiate their identities.[3] There are various characteristics that shape a rural identity.

Ritual Discourse (Gossip and Scandal)[4]

In all bounded communities, gossip and scandal serve to maintain the status quo and to define accepted behavior. This is very true in small communities, where people keep close tabs on their neighbors. People talk about the behaviors of others' children, about the condition of their houses, their personal behaviors, and often make harsh judgments. No family is exempt, and often the most prominent families get the most scrutiny as a means of leveling, or equalizing social relations in the community.

Mobilizing to Achieve Group Goals[5]

An important part of all communities is reciprocal trust and mutual aid. This is accomplished through benefit dinners for special projects or to assist families with medical bills or other emergency expenses. On a daily basis, people help others with farm chores, fixing cars or machinery, snowplowing, and child care. Such mutual assistance reinforces social networks and builds social capital. The shared experience of survival in northern Michigan resulted in the development of a system of mutual support. As one informant said, "It was not so much that everyone got along or wanted to be best friends with everyone, but it was a matter of survival—you helped someone and they would help you." This system of mutual support allowed the community in Chippewa Township to survive. Consequently, it resulted in a community with dense, overlapping networks of family and social ties.

Sense of Identity[6]

Communities are often defined by physical boundaries within which families share a common history, and often livelihood. The physical space and the emotional unity that defines those who share that space create a sense of identity. While shared identity as "farmer" or resident of Chippewa Lake shapes behavior and cements social relationships, it also erects psychological boundaries that exclude outsiders who are viewed as threats to the unity and strength of the community. Outsiders are marginalized through labels (transients, newcomers, outsiders) and excluded from the social and emotional life of the community.[7] Conventional wisdom (though not necessarily reality) states that thieves are usually from out of town or from the less-established families. Those individuals who do violate the laws or the local mores are sanctioned through gossip or ostracism as a means of maintaining the community as a "reference point" for appropriate behavior.

Shared Norms and Values

Shared values and norms also provide a context for belonging to a community and developing a self-characterization as a member of a community. As an illustration, I would like to examine two seemingly contradictory norms to illustrate both the complexity of rural culture and the power of norms to shape and reinforce acceptable behavior. Kathryn Dudley describes a paradox of rural living that is apparent in the lives of these longtime farming families, the successful as well as those that are struggling, and that is the paradox between the ideal of independence and the reality of mutual dependence.[8]

Dudley argues that competitive individualism is admired in farming families: having the best corn crop or the largest herd are sources of pride, but at the same time, farmers are not supposed to brag or display conspicuous consumption.[9] Everyone can see whose corn has grown the most, and whose is still languishing after the Fourth of July. Neighbors can observe the number of cows or horses one has, and the condition of one's barn and farmhouse. A sense of friendly competition is apparent in Chippewa Lake at several social events that take place in the summer, such as tractor pulls, where huge slabs of cement are pulled and the distance measured, and horse pulls, where farmers pit their draft horses against each other. One farmer lamented the paving of the road in front of his house because he would no longer be able to practice pulling loads with his horse on the pavement as he had done on the gravel road.

This competitive spirit is tempered by the necessity of social solidarity and mutual assistance as we saw above. The spirit of cooperation was particularly critical in the past when cooperation was paramount to survival, but even today, farmers and others depend on one another. Farmers hire neighborhood kids to help them during the haying season or for "picking stone"; people may share equipment or labor, and families in need will realize the strength of the community when a benefit dinner is given in their honor to help them pay a medical expense or recover from a fire.

Egalitarianism[10]

The paradox of competitive individualism and interdependence is apparent in yet another shared value in rural communities: egalitarianism. This is not the same as "equality," where every person is exactly the same in economic and social qualities. This ideal is impossible in any society, no matter how homogeneous. Rather, the goal is to avoid overt competitiveness, greed, envy, and other qualities that can breed conflict and tension in small-scale societies. In egalitarian societies, status differences are downplayed as people project a façade: "We're all the same here." The egalitarian façade is maintained in several ways.

First, leveling mechanisms balance the differences between more and less affluent families. Again, gossip is a very effective mechanism of moderating behavior and minimizing conspicuous consumption. Neighbors speculate when they see a farmer or a member of his family driving a "new" (usually pre-owned) pickup truck or tractor. They wonder how the farmer could afford to buy a newer vehicle—where did the money come from? In this way, "community norms act to regulate private consumption practices by establishing a vision of the collective good over and above the interests of the individual."[11]

Thus, where the conflicting values of competitive individualism and egalitarianism clash, a community member must tread a delicate balance between achievement and maintaining a reputation as a generous neighbor and a social equal. This tenuous balancing act differs markedly from the worldview of many of the newcomers to Chippewa Township who take pride in the accumulation of material goods; modern, extravagant homes; expensive vehicles and boats. Their conspicuous consumption and lack of commitment to the cooperative spirit engrained in the community leave them open for social criticism and ostracism.

Second, the collision of worldviews between farmers and newcomers is also evident in the dual values of self-reliance and interdependence. Farm families in general have a deeply embedded suspicion of government and big business. Welfare is avoided at all costs; people turn to each other to find jobs and to solve their problems. In their view, those who depend on welfare, or expect their government and employers to take care of them, are weak or lazy. Older farm families are living products of the Depression, when families took care of each other, shared food and services, and survived. They received very little from the government. In fact, farmers fed the country as well as themselves during these years, and they are proud of their independence.

Those of us raised in cities have an expectation that government or our employers will take care of us. We expect bus service, welfare if necessary, electricity, natural gas and water, child care, health insurance, and a myriad of other services that few people in the rural areas take for granted. This gaping fissure in expectations and experiences between rural and urban, farm and nonfarm, and different generations all compound themselves in this clash of cultures in a small village.

The Inclusive Community[12]

Locals see themselves as a friendly community, where everyone is welcome; yet, newcomers, as we will see, don't always agree with this self-assessment. Misunderstandings of the local cultural norms foment feelings of disgruntlement within the newcomers, who find it difficult to breach the invisible yet impermeable boundaries of the community. Longtime residents, in stereotyping newcomers as "uppity city folk," are overly critical of their attempts to participate in local debates.

The Community Effect

The above indicators are symbolic of community social relations embedded in certain central institutions that combine to maintain a collective identity, such as community schools, churches, and local organizations and businesses.[13] "Community effect" is the culmination of the process by which social behavior in a community is shaped by its history, demography, economic opportunities, social norms, and social networks. This is a useful concept in understanding how towns develop their personalities, and how individuals within these towns define themselves.

In Chippewa Township, the community effect has evolved through the complex history of logging, farming, and summer resort community. It has only been in the past thirty years that the regional economy has shifted from the farms to the manufacturing towns and suburbs, and twenty years since the lake has evolved from a summer resort to a year-round retirement community. As such, the township offers a unique example of how community personality is affected by economic and social change. It is within the context of economic change that the tensions develop between the established "community effect" and new economic and social pressures that threaten it. The extent to which community members and leaders can reinterpret and rethink community will shape the future of the community and its ability to negotiate new realities and shape a new worldview.

CHARACTERISTICS OF RURAL FARM COMMUNITIES

The failure or success of farm families is influenced greatly by the structure of the household. The community effect is held together by a complex matrix of interrelated and intergenerational families. Historically, intergenerational families facilitated the division of labor on the farm and in the household, and assured the passing of property from one generation to the next.

Men, Women, and Farming

Jessica Pearson distinguishes four types of farm women: the supportive homemaker who might have a job off the farm, the seasonal helper, the farm partner who works alongside her husband, and the matrifocal farmer, women who own and run farms independently of male farmers.[14] Historically, the first two categories most accurately described the farm families in Chippewa Township. Because families were large and farms were passed from father to son, there existed a strong core of farmers, related by blood and marriage. Women kept the home, but also were responsible for the care of domesticated animals, egg production, and growing and preserving vegetable, fruit, and berry crops. These symbiotic family structures fulfilled the subsistence needs of the family.

All of the farm families that I interviewed had stories of their mothers or grandmothers working on the farm, driving tractor, taking the cattle out to the fields or bringing them in, maintaining the vegetable garden, or managing egg production or the care of small domesticated animals, such as pigs or chickens. Women's primary responsibilities, however, were in the home. Here, they cared for the children, prepared meals, canned the produce from their gardens, sewed clothing, and cleaned. They also prepared meals for community dinners and church events, and visited kin and neighbors. I found that women were often the farm bookkeepers and managers, organizing the labor pool and running errands. These chores were dispersed somewhat in extended households where a larger pool of labor was available for daily chores and occasional emergencies.

The role of the women in these families was one of supporting the enterprise, but these women were not considered farmers themselves. Their role was perceived by their husbands, and perhaps themselves, as homemakers and "kin-keepers"—those who maintain the family and other social ties through participation in church, family rites of passage, and mutual assistance. In this sense, they also illustrate the first two types of female farmers outlined by Pearson.

Over the years, the traditional relationships that existed between husband and wife and parents and children have been transformed. First, increased technology and mechanization has allowed women to perform farm labor that was too difficult or time-consuming for them previously, such as milking cows and driving tractors. As women are able to do these chores, their responsibilities have shifted imperceptibly in some families from farmer's helper to farmer's partner. This has occurred in several farm families we will discuss below. Unfortunately, in several of these families, where children are unwilling to take over the farm, the wife has no choice but to share all of the farming chores with her husband. In families where the sons take over the farm, the parents have the freedom to retire and become involved in other activities, such as public service, volunteering, or becoming "snowbirds," traveling to Florida or Arizona in the winter months.

Today, in addition to informal income, women in farming families supplement farm income by seeking off-farm employment, or pursuing formal self-employment in the home. In dual-income families, women have a variety of occupations—from factory workers, to teachers and nurses, to self-employment. One woman bakes cakes for special occasions, and with her husband follows one of the local auctioneers with their lunch wagon in the summer. Women's income, whether formal or informal, all contributes to the household economy.

Children and Farming

Historically, children were a critical component of the family farm, as their labor was necessary for the overall survival of the family. Early farm families were quite large, with five to seven children and three or four generations of kin living on the same homestead. Life on a farm required cooperation from everyone in the household. Children of all ages were important sources of labor—from gathering eggs, to feeding chickens, to helping with the household chores. As children got older, their chores expanded, and they were able to work in the fields or use the mechanized farm equipment. The earliest field chores might include walking along the tractor-pulled wagon picking stones from the field and throwing them on the wagon, or later emptying the wagon onto the huge stone piles at the edge of the farm. Later, they might learn to drive the tractor or assist in the plowing, baling, or working with the heavy equipment. These chores increased in responsibility and in danger as the child became older and stronger.[15]

Today, on working farms, it is not unusual to see young children working on the farms before and after school. I often see young boys driving tractors (farm children can get special driver's licenses for farm purposes) and hauling hay. Girls help around the farm, taking care of the animals and doing other chores. They have lives very different from their peers in non-farm families, who have the leisure time to participate in sports or music, attend after-school functions, and enjoy snow days by playing video games or hanging out with friends. Farm kids spend their summers working with their parents and perhaps, for leisure, taking care of their 4-H animals or working on 4-H projects.

Although both sons and daughters contribute to the family subsistence, there was a historical preference for sons, as they were more likely to stay on or near the farm to help their fathers. Daughters moved away to live with their husbands and contribute their labor to another household. There was always some pity for the farmer who only had daughters, and in reality, their farms often struggled. In many cases, the daughters became proficient farmers themselves, learning to drive tractors and help in many of the daily chores. They often learned to hunt and became proficient in many aspects of farming life. In cases where the farmer had no sons, he and his wife might try to convince a son-in-law to live and work on his farm, offering his daughter and son-in-law the farm in inheritance.

Traditionally, most adult sons continued in farming, following a pattern that is quite consistent among the oral histories I collected. When a young man married, his new wife lived with his family and they worked the family farm cooperatively—he working with his father, the young wife working with her mother-in-law and sisters-in-law in the home. Later, the father often assisted the son in purchasing his own farm, where he and his wife would raise their own family. In most of the oral histories I collected, it was the expectation that at least one son would carry on running the family farm.

Sons who purchased their own farms usually remained in the same area, which allowed them to receive assistance, borrow equipment, and have female kin nearby to assure the social networks within and between the joined households. In this way, family farms were expanded over the years as each son, or sometimes daughter, obtained her or his own farm. It was often the youngest son who inherited the original farm, being the last person to work with the parents. The youngest son and his wife often established themselves on the original farm as the elderly parents retired and took on a secondary role in the household. The mother-in-law continued to be an integral part of the family, assisting with child care, cleaning, or cooking, and it was important that the wife and the mother-in-law could get along.

Endogamy

In anthropology, endogamy refers to the practice of marrying within certain social or kinship categories. In the United States, there is a tendency for young people to find their spouse from within the same racial and ethnic group, religion, social class, and even region of the state. In many peasant communities, there is a tendency for people to marry someone from the same village. This practice allows parents to have input into their child's marriage choice, and reduces the risk that their child will marry someone who has different values, or who might be abusive or irresponsible. Further, parents are assured that their daughters will move no further from home than their neighbor's farm, or at most, to the next township over. Community characteristics such as gossip, shared values, and similar life experiences bring young people together who already understand each other's motivations and goals.

In the days of the early settlers, opportunities for marriage were limited to those families who lived close by, or to new families moving into the area. Thus, the genealogy of all settler families is a tangled web of intermarriage, with at least one case of brothers marrying sisters. This is particularly true for the Scotch Irish families, where there are complex ties between the McCormicks, McCallums, Carmichaels, and Churches. It is this interweaving of settler families that proves the truism of longtime residents that "everyone is related to everyone else."

The role of community endogamy reinforces more than village ties. Ethnic ties were also reinforced through endogamy. Comparing the genealogies that I collected on families from the British Isles and from Germany in the township, I found only one case of intermarriage between these groups. Analyzing genealogies is beyond the scope of this book, but this is a curious finding, especially since these families lived in the same township. The answer may lie in several factors, including geography, chronology, and culture. Some of the Germanic families I interviewed came into the area later in time than those from the United Kingdom, and tended to settle south of the lake, while the earlier settlers, primarily of Scotch-Irish descent, settled north of the lake. It is also likely that linguistic and cultural distinctions between British and Germanic heritage and history may have acted as intangible barriers to marriage.

Longtime residents know the genealogies of most families who reside in both Chippewa and Martiny Townships. Individuals from farm families (full and dual-income) are much more likely to choose their spouses from the same community. Five of the six men interviewed who are full-time farmers married women from Mecosta County; four of these were from Chippewa Township. The children of farm/dual-income families are also more likely to choose their spouses from Mecosta County than are the children of nonfarm families (46 percent compared to 30 percent). Husband and wife originate from the immediate Chippewa Lake area in only three of thirty-nine nonfarm families surveyed.

The Ideal and the Real in the Imagined Community

While the elements of history, culture, and the local "community effect" are deeply embedded in the worldview of rural residents, we must, as observers of behavior, be wary of applying them universally, as the subtle differences between the British and German settlers may suggest. We must also be wary about romanticizing the virtues of life in a small community, such as inclusiveness, egalitarianism, and mutual assistance. Even those who extol the benefits of a rural life recognize the drawbacks that accompany them. For example, the ideal that everyone knows everyone is a two-edged sword, with friendship and close kin ties on one edge and incessant scrutiny and gossip on the other.

In the real world, everyone is not equal. People know who has money and who doesn't and may resent it. In the real world, there is diversity of religion, norms, aspirations, and motivations, even in small so-called homogeneous communities. In the real world, not all homes are safe places for children to live in, and rural communities, like any community, can breed dysfunction and even instill in their children distrust for those unlike them. The same leveling mechanisms that assure that those who have the most give the most, and share with others, can also result in minor vandalism and criticism against successful families who, from their perspective, don't share enough, or who are "too good for us."[16] In addition, dependence upon neighbors often causes ambivalence toward them: family crises bring the community together to help, but also force people to admit that they are unable to handle their own problems.[17]

CONCLUSION

We have explored the stereotypes that many of us share about rural people in general and farmers in particular. These preconceptions shape our attitudes about rural lifestyles and prevent us from understanding the complexity and diversity of their lives. The research of sociologists and anthropologists has opened up this world to us, and has helped us to understand the characteristics and shared values that give meaning to their lives and that define them as members of a larger community. The principles of egalitarianism, shared norms and values, and the resulting community effect enmesh individuals and families together in a dense web of historic and ongoing relationships. In the following chapters, we will see how the rural community effect is challenged and transformed when confronted with diverse value systems and expectations. How do families and communities maintain their integrity at the intersection with newcomers with their own ideas about community and their own views about the quality of life?

CHAPTER 4

Chippewa Township as Rural Community in Transition

You see, you have to put so much money in [farming],
without the benefits, and you build equity, but you don't
see it. In a factory, you can see what you are earning; but
on a farm, you're building equity, and it's almost like
having life insurance—you have to die to win.

—ALLEN SCHROEDER, 2003

IN APPLYING THE CONCEPT OF COMMUNITY EFFECT AND EXAMINING how shared goals of rural communities are shifting, we can draw upon the factors that have defined the community personality of Chippewa Township in the past, and the changes that have occurred in the past twenty years. These factors include population growth and demographic factors, structure of households, economic factors and education, and historical factors. In this section we will discuss the first three of these and how they juxtapose with the rich tapestry of local history.

POPULATION GROWTH AND DEMOGRAPHICS

The population of Chippewa Township has more than doubled since 1960, from 543 to 1,239 in the 2000 Census. The rise in township population is not a response to increased job opportunities in the township or the village of Chippewa Lake, as there is neither manufacturing here nor any substantial business opportunities. Nor are these new residents coming to the country to farm. Rather, while some of this growth results from natural birth rate, substantial growth is attributable to two incoming groups: families coming from urban areas to combine a commuting lifestyle of work and a rural quality of life, and retirees seeking the solitude of a retirement cottage or home on a quiet lake. Chippewa Lake is a long way from the global marketplace, a fact that some people rejoice in and others rue.

The combination of an aging farming population and retirement community has resulted in a graying community, one which the younger people perceive as a gerontocracy. According to the 2000 U.S. Census, 63 percent of the township population are thirty-five years old or older, with 23 percent being sixty-two and older. The median age for the township is forty-three years. In contrast, for Mecosta County as a whole, 16 percent of the population are age sixty-two or older, and the median age is thirty-two years. The local generation gap serves to isolate younger families from the political and social processes of the community, and effectively, if not consciously, excludes them from the local debates. The perception of disenfranchisement was evident in our interviews with young people in the community.

Ethnicity is not a contributing factor in local political dynamics. The population of the township (indeed the whole county) is not ethnically diverse.[1] Mecosta County overall is 93 percent European Caucasian, and Chippewa Township is 97 percent Caucasian. The largest minority group in Mecosta County is African American (due primarily to families and students associated with Ferris State University); that of Chippewa Township is Native American. Diversity in rural Mecosta County is not defined in terms of ethnicity, but in such characteristics as rural versus urban, social class, and generation.

THE STRUCTURE OF THE FARMING HOUSEHOLD IN CHIPPEWA TOWNSHIP

The roles of men and women in modern farms is in some respects more complicated than in the past, because the demands on farm families extend beyond the needs of the family. Farmers today are producing for larger markets, so dairy-farm families form tight cooperative units assigned to the production and storing of the grain feed, moving of cattle to and from pasture, and milk production. In addition to these chores, increasingly complex machinery needs to be maintained, fueled, and driven; errands need to be run; and the needs of the children cannot be ignored—schooling, transportation, and care of their health and welfare.

Yet, this type of small-scale family farm does not support a family. Modern family farms require supplemental income to cover taxes, purchase and maintain equipment, and provide the necessities of life. Few farm families have health insurance for their families, let alone dental, vision, or other benefits that others might take for granted. Supplemental jobs sometimes will provide these benefits and thus provide farm families with some health security.

Children's Postmarital Residence

Continuity of family farms over the generations is a critical factor in the reproduction of rural community. Success in farming depends on the willingness of adult children to settle in the area and remain available to assist their parents on the farm. Since there is no data on postmarital residence of children in earlier families, it is impossible to make an accurate comparison. Data collected for farm and dual-income farm families indicate that fewer than one third (29 percent) of married children have left the county. The married children of farming families not only remain in the county (71 percent), but frequently they remain in the same household as their parents (four of twenty-four, or 17 percent), or in Chippewa Township (four of twenty-four, or 17 percent). Nonfarm families have reversed this pattern: 28 percent of married children remain in the county while 72 percent live elsewhere.

The Importance of Work off the Farm

With the demise of dairy farming and the lack of manufacturing, retail, or service oriented employment, Chippewa Township is clearly a community with no visible means of support. The changing economic structure of the township is evident both in census materials and in my own research. Comparing the 1990 and 2000 censuses for Mecosta County, the percentage of Mecosta County residents involved in agriculture, forestry, and mining shrank from 4 percent to 2.5 percent between 1990 and 2000. According to the 2000 Census, less than 2 percent of the township population were involved with farming, fishing, and forestry occupations.

The current economic downturn is particularly devastating to farmers, even those who are no longer dairy farmers. The cost of diesel fuel was more than three times as expensive during the summer of 2008 than it had been the previous summer, and with increased fertilizer costs, many local farmers did not plant corn that year. I asked one farmer why local farms aren't converting to corn production to take advantage of the high price of ethanol, and his response illustrates how small farmers are disadvantaged in many ways. In addition to the high cost of fuel and fertilizer, the local elevator will only take a specified amount of corn, and farmers must transport their corn to other towns in Michigan to sell it. The cost of transport and limits on production discriminate against these small family farmers and benefit large corporate farms that have the ability to shift their strategies and earn subsidies.

According to the 2000 Census, the median household income for Chippewa Township in 1999 was $33,800, nearly identical to that of Mecosta County as a whole. Only twenty-four Michigan counties (of eighty-three total, or 29 percent) have median household incomes lower than Mecosta County, and all of these are located in northern Michigan and the Upper Peninsula. The gender gap in earnings is notable, with female full-time workers in the township earning 62 percent of their male counterparts ($20,400 compared to $32,800), while in Mecosta County full-time female workers earn 70 percent of men's salaries, also likely due to the university salary structure. Women in Chippewa Township find jobs primarily in factories, the fast-food industry, or the informal economy, and their contribution to the family income does not significantly improve their standard of living. Rather, their income pays for special projects or to defray an ever increasing cost of living.

The percentage of Mecosta County residents living below the poverty line (14 percent) places it notoriously as fourth highest in the state, just above Lake County in central Michigan, Luce County in the Upper Peninsula, and Wayne County (Detroit Metropolitan Area). The poverty rates for Chippewa Township are slightly lower than the county as a whole: 10 percent of individuals and 8 percent for families. The fact that all members of rural families work in some way to support the family affects what might seem to be a low poverty rate. Supplemental income and extended families boost the total family income, resulting in a low poverty rate for township families. Rural families in general see shame in accepting "the welfare" and will instead seek other means of bridging the gap between income and expenses. In contrast to the above statistics, 27 percent of female-headed households are living below the poverty level. This statistic underscores the importance of an intact family for survival.

Learning a vocation is the preferable means by which dual-income families are able to achieve a better lifestyle for their children. While Bill Stein and his son farmed, Bill's wife, Ilene, worked as a bookkeeper for a local mill, and later, upon retirement, she was elected as the township clerk, a position she still holds today. Even before Ilene worked as a bookkeeper, her own mother did the same job at the same mill while her husband farmed with Bill, then a young man. This valuable skill, passed from mother to daughter without a formal education, supplemented the farming income. Learning a vocation is still an important component of education in the district today.

Others seek unskilled jobs to supplement farm incomes. Women often work in local restaurants or stores, or sell Mary Kay, Avon, or other home-sales items. Some women earn a substantial portion of supplemental income for their families from informal sources—what is known as the informal economy, including babysitting for family members or neighbors, house cleaning, or selling garden produce. Men may earn extra money fixing cars or boat motors, transporting boats to the lake, or snowplowing. In addition to supplementing income, the underground economy provides a flexible source of income for residents, especially women, who wish to stay home to care for children or grandchildren and prefer not to work in a factory. In this way, men and women maintain their independence and reinforce their social ties in the community.

CHILDREN AND THE FUTURE OF FARMING

The beaten path that takes children away from the farm is fraught with emotion, as both parents and children know that farming can no longer support a family and provide the quality of life it once did. In this section, I will look at some of the factors that shape the decisions to leave the farm, and the impact of the modern economy on these decisions.

Education

In settler days, small one-room schoolhouses provided the basic educational needs for farmers: basic reading, writing, math, and perhaps some history. Children walked to school, and many probably did not attend for more than five years. In later generations, the one-room schoolhouses were supplemented by a high school. In Chippewa and Fork Townships, the one-room schoolhouses fed into a high school located in Barryton, ten miles east of Chippewa Lake. As might be expected, full-time farmers in our survey had the lowest educational levels, with only two of twelve farmers or their spouses having more than a high school diploma or vocational training (one having a vocational degree, and another a university degree).

Today, Chippewa Lake is incorporated into a huge consolidated school district. Children from preschool to high school pile into school buses or cars and commute distances up to fifteen miles for elementary school, and up to thirty miles for middle or high school. The expectation that children will complete high school is still not universal, but most parents want their children to graduate, and high school graduation is a major rite of passage for most young people. Yet, while children in nonfarm families may participate in sports or other extracurricular programs, farm children are expected to work on the farm before and after school, on the weekends, and during all vacations.

The local high school provides an extensive career center that offers many vocational programs, such as cosmetology, computers, drafting, mechanical skills, and construction. Many young people who are not college-bound complete these programs simultaneously with their high school curriculum. In recent years, more and more young people are attending college or vocational school. Local community colleges offer liberal arts education, and students who cannot afford to live away from home will often start here, and the successful students will transfer to larger universities. Ferris State University in Big Rapids offers a liberal arts education, but specializes in occupational and professional careers, such as mechanical engineering, allied health services, plastics technology, etc. Students who continue their college educations leave the farm in the short term while they are studying, but also long term as they find employment in more fertile marketplaces.

As more recent generations have appreciated the importance of education, it is not surprising that dual-income farmers and their spouses are much more likely to have more than a high school diploma or vocational training than in the past. In fact, farm/dual-income women are more likely to have completed post–high school degrees than are men (39 percent to 24 percent respectively). Education gives husbands and wives considerable flexibility in their livelihoods, provides jobs with benefits, and allows them to be flexible in their farming decision making.

Darryl and Carla McCallum are both retired schoolteachers. Darryl is from a farming family, and he and Carla live on his family's farm. The family farmhouse is beautifully maintained and has an ambiance of an earlier time,

TABLE 2. Educational Levels by Occupation

Males

Occupation	Some high school	High school diploma	Vocational training	Some college	College degree	Graduate courses	Graduate degree	Total
Farm	1	5	1	0	1	0	0	8
Dual-Income	1	2	2	1	1	0	1	8
Non-Farm	7	15	6	4	1	2	1	36
Total	9 (17%)	22 (42%)	9 (17%)	5 (10%)	3 (6%)	2 (4%)	2 (4%)	52 (100%)

Females

Occupation	Some high school	High school diploma	Vocational training	Some college	College degree	Graduate courses	Graduate degree	Total
Farm	0	3	0	0	0	0	0	3
Dual-Income	0	14	2	2	1	0	1	20
Non-Farm	1	2	3	10	2	1	0	19
Total	1 (2%)	19 (45%)	5 (12%)	12 (29%)	3 (7%)	1 (2%)	1 (2%)	42 (100%)

filled with country crafts and family heirloom antique furniture. Before they retired, Carla and Darryl grew some crops with the assistance of Darryl's brother. They also raised some cattle, and their daughter, Leigha, was active in 4-H. Now that they are retired, they continue to farm and have expanded some of their agricultural pursuits, doing volunteer work with a regional wildlife conservation group. Leigha was valedictorian of her high school graduating class and earned a college degree from a prestigious private university in Michigan. She and her husband (from the same school district, and who graduated from the same university) have professional careers and live near Grand Rapids.

Off-Farm Employment

It is not only the profession-bound students who affect farm labor, but also those young people who stay in the rural area. As the costs of farming outstrip any profit, and as credit is more and more expensive, all young people must make the choice of seeking jobs "off the farm." Even young men who hope to take over the family farm cannot make a living on the farm in the short term. Rarely does a young man earn a paycheck from the family farm, unless he has an agreement with his father to share the milk checks. Consequently, if he hopes to marry and raise a family on the farm, the money he earns when he is young can be used later to invest in the farm enterprise. Consequently, jobs in local factories, the service industry, or the gas and oil fields allow the worker to assist in farm chores from time to time.

No intelligent young man goes into farming to make money. Farming is in the blood and in the soul. Men who describe farming to me today say that it is the only thing they know. Others say it is peaceful work: "No one can bother you when you're on your tractor." Nevertheless, peace and tranquillity don't pay the property taxes, and many farmers, given these realities, face an uncertain future. Some families accept the new future for their children. In fact, some families have encouraged and enabled their children to attend college with the knowledge that this opportunity will likely mean that their children will leave the farm forever. Poorer farmers feel the shift more severely. Unable or unwilling to support their children in higher education, their children face a future with few opportunities and meager choices. In the following section, we will take a look at some of these lives and the strategies that farm families in Chippewa Township employ to overcome the new realities of rural life.

STRATEGIES OF FARM FAMILIES
THROUGHOUT THE LIFE CYCLE

In my sample of fifty-five township (rural, non-village/lake) residents, only six (11 percent) of them were currently farming households, and eight (15 percent) households were involved in farming as part of a dual-income strategy. Several of these families have quit farming within the past few years. One of the farmers in our sample has retired and passed his farm on to his son, and another is in the process of doing so because of poor health. Several others have phased out of dairy farming (or are currently doing so) into general beef and/or crop farming. These latter farmers all expressed a tremendous loss, not only economically, but emotionally as they sell their cattle and move on to a different life. For many of these families, it is the culmination of a long process of letting go of a lifestyle, decreasing herd size as children find other employment and as retirement approaches. These families demonstrate very well the transition of farm families today as successive generations become disassociated from farming.

The full-time farmers in our sample were, with two exceptions, over sixty years old (one in his eighties). Only four of twenty (20 percent) children of farmers are currently in farming or farm-related occupations. The majority of children of this generation of farmers (in their forties to sixties) assist their parents during harvest and haying seasons, but they pursue other occupations as well. Several of these adult children have college degrees and have had professional careers. One dairy farmer expressed this dilemma very forcefully when he lamented that it is impossible to remain in farming if one's sons or sons-in-law do not farm.

The complexities of farm life, and the myriad of factors brought to bear on family decision making illuminate some of the misconceptions that outsiders, including anthropologists, have of rural people. Some of the strategies they employ nevertheless offer glimpses of the shared concerns of farm families. First, decisions are never made based solely on the needs of the individual, or even the nuclear family; all decisions take into consideration a larger circle of kin and the perceived future of their children and grandchildren. Second, all decisions are embedded in a shared identity with land and birthplace; the elder generation might sacrifice potential profit from sale or division of land so that their children can inherit or purchase it. The sale of land to outsiders, or the division of land into smaller sections, is done only as a last resort, and with great anxiety and sadness. A look into the lives of farming families can illustrate the diversity of experiences and the stages of farming intensity that characterize this region.

Passing the Farm On

Tom and Esther Hahn

Tom Hahn claimed that he could trace his family back to the Revolutionary War, so he was many generations from his European origins. His family moved to Chippewa Lake from a community in southern Mecosta County around 1915, when his father worked construction on one of the roads in the area. His parents bought the farm that lies on the north shore of Chippewa Lake, where they raised dairy cattle. Tom carried on the farm after his parents' death, and farmed this land until 2003.

The Hahn farm is a beacon on Chippewa Lake, their huge barn visible from the opposite shore. Tom's first wife was the mother of all of his children, and she was a partner in the farming enterprise. At one time they had 600 acres spread over several parcels, of which 250 were utilized for farming and grazing. Tom's first wife, Margaret, was the daughter of the Chippewa Lake minister, Reverend Zuse. Tom and Margaret raised four children—three boys, and a girl. All of their children live within a few miles of the farm, and the oldest farms what remains of the original 600 acres. Margaret passed away, and years later Tom married his second wife, Esther, whose father was a Russian immigrant from Belarus. Esther had settled on the lake with her first husband, who later passed away. When she and Tom married, she took on the role of the farming wife. The Hahns have had their share of controversy, as their farm received some of the blame for the contamination that the lake suffered from for many years, threatening the resort business and property values around the lake. The causes for the lake contamination were more complicated, however, involving substandard septic systems and poor drainage. Having invested in the sewer system, the Hahns continued their farming enterprise until 2003, when they sold the cattle and retired. They moved to a new house across the road from the farm and continued to be very active in the community. Both Tom and Esther passed away as I was completing this manuscript. Their oldest son has taken over the farm, which now encompasses only 400 acres and is solely an agricultural enterprise.

Wynne Nellis

The Nellis farm is located about two miles from our house and less than a mile from the village of Chippewa Lake. Despite its proximity to the village, the road is unpaved. To get to the farm, I drive slowly as my car finds each and every pothole. The principle that dairy farms have first priority for road improvements has no meaning here. The farm itself has the appearance of a well-worn enterprise. Tractors and farm implements huddle under a makeshift shed attached to the house, and a plethora of cats scurry under your feet. Since the original barn burned down many years ago, a pole barn now serves as the milking area. The farmhouse, situated in a spacious yard under a sprawling oak tree, is in its original state, in poor repair, and begging for paint. Inside, the living room is furnished with overstuffed furniture that swallows one whole and from which one cannot escape easily. On the walls hang old photographs of the Nellis ancestors, as well as photographs of the now-grown children and grandchildren. A piano dominates the living space, and the farmhouse has a cluttered yet comfortable feel, as Wynne and his wife Helen led very busy lives.

Wynne Nellis's paternal grandfather came from Germany in the 1800s with five of his brothers. They settled first in New York and then moved to Michigan after working on the Erie Canal. His maternal grandfather, James Wynne, came from Ireland to Michigan via Ohio during the same time. His parents met in Fork Township, and as far as my data show, this was the only instance of an Irish and German family intermarrying. Wynne, the youngest of ten children, was born in 1920. He purchased 160 acres in Chippewa Township while he was in the army during World War II, sending money to his sister to purchase the land. Before entering the service, Wynne had worked other farms, and he was also a trained mechanic. When he returned from Europe, he first worked as a mechanic for a car dealership in Big Rapids before going into farming full-time.

Wynne married a divorcée from Big Rapids, much to the dismay of his family, but Helen proved to be a powerful force in his life. She moved from a comfortable home in Big Rapids, where her husband, a pharmacist, had abandoned her and her young daughter. Helen and her daughter, Joan, moved to the farm, and Helen took over the household of a growing family, consisting of her daughter and the two sons she had with Wynne (a third son died soon after birth). Helen was a musician and earned money by playing the piano for the Chippewa Lake Methodist Church and serving as choir director. She also gave private piano lessons to many of the neighborhood kids, including mine. Helen died of cancer in 1996.

Until his illness and death, Wynne ran the dairy farm with his two sons, his daughter-in-law, and sometimes with the help of friends and his daughter-in-law's father. The Nellis dairy farm is one of the few still operating in the township, perhaps the last one. His older son is Tim, who is married and lives with his family in a home directly behind the farmhouse. Tim and his wife Cheryl have three children, who also helped their grandfather on the farm as they were growing up. Although he has a full-time job "off the farm," Tim helped his dad when he could, doing the haying and "driving tractor." Tim told me that he could not be a dairy farmer like his dad, because "you cannot make a living at it, and if you have another job, you can't do the 24/7/365 job of dairy farming." In addition to farming, Tim, his wife, and his father-in-law assisted Wynne in tapping their maple trees for sugar each spring, setting up camp in their sugar bush, about one mile from the farm. For many years, Wynne supplemented the family income by selling and delivering propane gas to farms and houses in the area, suffering several bad burns in the process. When Wynne's health deteriorated in 2008 and he had to be moved to a local nursing facility, Tim and Cheryl, with the help of one of their sons, worked the farm, taking off hay and growing some crops. They are discouraged by the hard work and cost, especially with the gas crisis, but are determined not to lose what Wynne had taken so many years to build.

Wynne's younger son, Pat, never married and has carried on the dairy operations since his father's death. Pat is a quiet giant, tall and large, soft-spoken, with a shy demeanor and a continual look of dishevelment. His dirt-stained bib overalls barely contain his flannel shirt, and his unruly graying hair forms a matted fringe along the edge of his John Deere cap. I did not know when I first met him that hidden under the quiet, untamed exterior resided a passionate fiddler who had inherited a love of music from his mother, as well as a modicum of talent. His taste and talent for music, however, are not expressed in the measured style of church hymns, but rather in lively bluegrass and country fiddling. When the mild-mannered farmer exchanges his bib overalls for his dress jeans and bolo tie and escapes the dairy barn, his entire personality changes. Like early settlers who enlivened their leisure evening hours playing music and dancing, Pat takes his fiddle with him to any local event that might offer the possibility for music. His love of bluegrass music draws him out every fall to the Wheatland Music Festival in nearby Remus, Michigan. Sometimes we see him there, sitting in a performance tent or under a tree, jamming joyously with Appalachian fiddlers, elderly dulcimer players, and middle-aged hippie guitarists, among the thousands of bluegrass enthusiasts that congregate here every September—doubling, for one weekend, the population of the county. He has attended the Wheatland Festival yearly for thirty-two years.

After Helen died, Wynne and Pat lived in the old farmhouse alone, and it took on the appearance and ambiance of a bachelor retreat, with little regard for tidiness and a disinterest in the condition of the kitchen. Wynne and Pat were looked after by Tim and Cheryl and their children. Wynne's step-daughter Joan, who lives and works in Big Rapids, also visited often and took over some of the bookkeeping responsibilities that her mother had done before her death. Now Pat lives in the farmhouse alone.

The Preston-Stein Family

The Preston-Stein farm is located in the northern sections of Chippewa Township, far from the village and the lake. Like the unpaved road to Wynne's dairy farm, this distant road disproves another local truism that the road to the township officer's home is always paved. However, though unpaved, this road is in good repair, as is the beautiful farmhouse that sits up on a hill overlooking a stunning countryside.

The Stein farm is well cared for. The barn is painted bright red and the yard is maintained; flowers grow along the driveway and along the side of the houses. A vegetable garden is visible from the end of the driveway, and a clean though enthusiastic dog meets you at your car. There are two houses here also: a neatly painted and trimmed ranch house where Bill and Ilene live and where their children were raised, and the original farmhouse on the other side of the driveway, a short distance away. The farmhouse was constructed of fieldstone, a common building material in the old farming days; both houses are in good repair, with well-maintained exteriors and ordered interiors. The barn stands behind the old farmhouse.

Bill and Ilene run a four-generation farm that has an interesting history because it passed through maternal lines. Roy Preston was born in Chippewa Township in 1885. His mother died when he was young, and his father left him with his sister and brother-in-law, who also lived in the township. Roy's father eventually moved to the Upper Peninsula of Michigan, and Roy remained in the township with his aunt and uncle. Eventually Roy married Ida Mae Ward, a Mecosta County native, and they bought their farm in 1913. Their son, Delmer Preston, married Mabelle Morse in 1932. Delmer was very active in local politics, serving as township clerk and supervisor. They had three daughters, one of whom is Ilene, who married Bill Stein and moved to live on his family's farm in Evart. When Ilene's grandmother Ida passed away, her father, Delmer, offered Ilene's husband, Bill, a partnership in the farm, and they moved back to Chippewa Township in 1957. Today, their son, Marvin, is the fourth generation to work and be a partner in the 500-acre farm.

Delmer passed away in 1991, but until she was 99, Mabelle still lived on the farm in the warm months and spent her winters in Florida as an official "snowbird." Mabelle is now 101 years old. All of the Preston-Stein women worked on and off the farm. Mabelle milked the cows and was the woman who lost her fingertips in the potato planter. She was also a self-trained bookkeeper and worked for a mill in Evart. Her daughter Ilene also learned bookkeeping and had various jobs, including work at the same mill. Today, Ilene is the township clerk, following in her father's footsteps.

Two of Ilene and Bill's children, the daughters, have college educations. One is a teacher and the other works for a mental health organization. Neither lives in the area, but they both come to visit and help out during busy seasons. Another son, Dick, worked in construction until his death in 2007, and the last son, Marvin, has taken over the farm and lives there with his wife, Ireta, who works in Big Rapids.

Besides being township clerk, Ilene is very active socially, in church and in the Emerald Lake Birthday Club, a local women's group. She still shares an image of a community embedded in familial and other interpersonal networks. When I interviewed this family, three generations of women sat at the kitchen table (Mabelle, Ilene, and Ilene's daughter Valorie), laughing, sharing stories and memories of Chippewa Lake at an earlier time. The old farmhouse, where Mabelle lives in the warm months, was immaculate, and reminiscent of the ideal farmhouse that all Americans carry in our heads—cozy, with country-style furnishings, handicrafts, and a small but neat kitchen. We sat at the kitchen table with a box of photographs and memorabilia, the story unfolding as each picture was fished out of the box, passed around, and put aside.

The women in these three families illustrate Pearson's category of supportive homemaker and farm partner.[2] Wynne's wife was the least involved with farming, as her interests were centered on music and her obligations to the church and household. She was also born and raised in Big Rapids and had not been socialized into farm life. Tom Hahn's first wife as well as Mabelle Preston and Ilene Preston Stein assisted their husbands on the farm and performed the gendered roles of farm wife and mother. Mabelle and Ilene, while embedded in the farm household, also had skills that provided their family with supplemental off-farm income.

When Children Don't Farm

Raymond and Judy Miller

The original Miller family settled in Chippewa Township east of my husband's family. Ivan was the family patriarch during my husband's childhood—a rough man with descriptive language and two sons, who were the terror of the school bus, and as young adults, of the local bar. The two sons, Raymond and Glen, ultimately bought farms near our house where they pursued dairy and crop farming. Despite their reputations, both families have been good neighbors to us. Unasked, Raymond or his sons plow our driveway after major snowstorms and bring us sweet corn in the fall, and Raymond and his wife Judy have always been very protective of our children.

Raymond and Judy bought a grand farmhouse to our west, but at the time I moved to the area, I had no idea about its former grandeur. I had never ventured past the kitchen and dining room of the house. From this area, and surreptitious peeks beyond into the living room, it was clear to me that here was a farmhouse where housekeeping was of low priority, and where husband and wife were both entrenched entirely in the farming enterprise. The front door opened into a small dining area where the floor was barely visible and there was no room on the countertop or table to put one's coffee cup. Coats, barn boots, shoes, and whatever entered the house were dropped at the door, and entering was a challenge. Outside, there are two barns, one of which is the milking barn and another is used for storage of equipment. The land surrounding the house is used for grazing of their farm animals, cows and Belgian horses.

Raymond and Judy were both dairy farmers until 2005. They have 200 acres of land that they used for grazing their one hundred head of cattle and draft horses, and raising grain crops and hay. They also use the fallow land of neighbors (including ours) for hay, and sometimes alfalfa and corn. Their younger son, Troy, lived with his wife and children in a trailer on the farmstead until several years ago, when they built a home to the south of us, but still on family land. He works at a nearby potash plant with his brother, Marty. Marty built a house on another parcel of family land and lives there with his wife and five adopted children. Both Marty and Troy work full-time off the farm, but help their parents with the haying and with other seasonal farming chores.

In their dairy operations, Raymond performed the duties related to the feeding and overall care of the animals, and maintained the field crops— planting, and harvesting. Judy milked the cows twice a day and ran the errands. She and the boys helped with the haying, baling, and those additional chores that require intensive cooperative effort. At times, they also hired neighborhood boys to help with the haying and other chores. Except for a short period of time when Raymond worked at the oil rigs, he has been a farmer all his life. Judy does not have a garden, lacking the time required to tend it or to put up the produce. Since selling their dairy herd, Raymond raises draft horses and beef cattle for sale. He continues to grow corn and other silage crops, though Judy is now incapacitated by Alzheimer's.

Glen and Claudia Miller

Raymond's brother, Glen, also had a dairy farm until 2005. He and Claudia (Judy's sister) worked both in the barn and in the house. Glen worked 200 acres and had fifty head of cattle. Claudia and Glen have two grown children, both of whom helped on the farm as children. Their daughter Renee is married with children and does not actively work on the farm, but she and her husband recently built a home on the Miller land within sight of her parents' house. Paul, though he has a full-time job off the farm, does help his father with seasonal chores. Like his sister, he has also moved back into the community, in a mobile home on family land near his cousin Marty. Claudia keeps a garden where she harvests potatoes, tomatoes, and cucumbers for pickles. She cans her produce and shares the food with her children. In both of these cases, the farmers are in a critical period of their lives as they ponder their future and the future of their farm investment. They are all in their sixties, and neither of their children were interested in taking over the farm at the time of my initial interviews, yet Renee and Paul have both moved back to the township since that time. Raymond and Glen sold their dairy cattle in the same year.

Neither Claudia nor Judy was involved in community organizations during their years as farmers, and their contributions qualify them as farm partners, using Pearson's criteria. Their days were spent totally in farm or family-related activities. Since they did not have extended family or children actively working on the farm, both families relied on their strong husband-wife partnerships to succeed. The Miller brothers and their wives farm separately. Their situation is further complicated by the fact that there has been a long-standing estrangement between them that has lasted well over thirty years. Their farms are one mile apart as the crow flies, but they seldom speak, and the feud has also alienated the two sisters. Where cooperation and mutual assistance would have benefited both farms, instead each family has struggled to keep their farm intact.

Peter and Jada Nellis

Peter Nellis is the nephew of Wynne Nellis. Peter's father, Ed, passed away in 2006, leaving Peter the 220-acre farm that his parents had owned since the end of World War II. Ed and his sons raised dairy cows and various crops. Ed had returned from the war with a disability and depended on the assistance of his children as he got older. Ed's wife, Myrna, however, was not a farming partner. Rather, her role fit more closely in the supportive-homemaker category discussed earlier. Myrna always had a job or a number of income sources on and off the farm, formal and informal.

Ed and Myrna had five children—three daughters and two sons. Two of the daughters married and eventually moved away; the third lives several miles away in Martiny Township. One son, who was estranged from the family, passed away, leaving Peter to work the farm. Peter married and had four children. He and his wife were the primary workers on the farm, Ed being older and more disabled with age, and Myrna working off the farm. When Peter and his wife divorced, she took two of the girls with her, leaving the two older children, one son and one daughter, on the farm. Peter remarried, bringing a new wife and her children onto the farm. Jada was a strong partner with Peter on the farm until multiple sclerosis slowly disabled her.

Eventually, relations between Peter and Ed went downhill, even as Ed's health deteriorated. Personality and other issues in the family resulted in estrangement between father and son, which resulted in conflict over the inheritance of the land. This in turn threatened the financial stability of the farm. After Ed's death, Peter sold the dairy cattle, and they subsist on multiple sources of income, including selling on eBay and the very popular biannual mud runs.

Since our initial interviews with Peter and Jada, their situation has improved. Peter's lifelong experience maintaining farm equipment qualified him for a position at a Big Rapids factory, where he now works as second-shift head of maintenance. This job gives Peter full benefits, which have greatly improved their economic standing as Jada's multiple sclerosis continues its course. Jada, for her part, now trains people who want to sell on eBay. She has clients and is thinking of expanding into a business enterprise. Peter went to auctioneering school and is a very popular auctioneer. He has a dream of being a full-time auctioneer and opening up a local auction house.

Meanwhile, Peter's children have grown and are becoming aware of the importance of the land in their family's heritage. Jim, the oldest, is married and has bought a house near the farm, helping his father when he is not working at his off-farm job. Jordan, the third youngest, is living on the farm. She has taken an active interest in the farm, raises horses, and also works full-time at the same factory where Peter works. The second child, Jenny, lives in southern Michigan. She has finished a tour of duty in Iraq and has been accepted into a special program for veterans where she has been awarded a scholarship to study social work. She hopes to work with veterans diagnosed with post-traumatic stress disorder. The youngest of the four Nellis children, another daughter, is living out west with her mother.

Peter told me that he himself had an opportunity to attend veterinarian school at Michigan State University when he was young, but his father had pressured him to stay on the farm, invoking ideas of family and the importance of land. Because his father was a veteran injured in World War II, with a large family to support, Peter turned down the scholarship and became a partner in the dairy farm. Peter told me that he does not want to use guilt and shame to keep his kids on the farm, but he has inherited the same sense of sadness that it might someday be sold off.

This story illustrates what happens when several generations of family become estranged and factionalized. Yet, even here, there is hope that the farm might be saved, and the land remains connected to the family name. Peter told me that he is committed to not making the same mistakes his parents did. He wants to keep the lines of communication open with his children and let them all feel that they are part of the family heritage on the farm. He wants to instill in them the pride of being a landowner and carrying on the family heritage.[3]

Peter provides his children with a good example of the importance of community. Despite their difficulties, Peter regularly volunteers his time to work charity auctions throughout the area, and his extraordinary ability to encourage even the tightest wallets to open for a good cause is legendary.

The Retired Farmer

Allen and Lois Schroeder

The Schroeders represent families who farmed at least part-time during their younger years, and who have returned to small-scale farming after retirement. Allen's father, Charlie Schroeder, was three years old when their family moved into the community from New York. This was in 1905. Allen's grandfather, Emil, was a stonemason by trade, but took on the farming lifestyle that is still in the family today. Charlie was the only one of Emil's seven children who remained on the farm, and when he was stricken with arthritis, he rented out his farm to others and moved his family to Grant Township, where his wife's family owned a store. Allen was born in the house attached to the family store.

Allen met his wife, Lois, in Grant Center, and in 1957 he brought his wife and children to the family farm. They raised crops while Allen studied at Michigan State University and also worked for a tractor supply company in Reed City. After several years, they returned to Grant Center and then back to the farm again in 1996. Allen and Lois are retired now, but he breeds and raises starter calves for dairy and beef farmers. They have a strong attachment to the 160-acre farm that kept drawing them back. When I asked Allen why he got back into farming after so many years, he told me that there is something relaxing about getting on a tractor and riding around, not working for someone else in a factory or selling on the road. Speaking on farming, Allen uses similes to describe his feelings: "Farming is like life insurance—you have to die to win . . . you have so much money into it and the only way to get your equity out is to pass it on to your children or sell it, but if you sell it, you don't have anything left." In another analogy, he says that "farming is like having a tiger by the tail . . . you don't dare let go, because you'll get bit."

Allen and his wife, Lois, have three children—two boys and a girl. The children all helped on the farm when they were young, and today one of these sons continues to help him from time to time, though all of them have jobs "off the farm." The two sons are married, and their daughter is unmarried but lives on her own. They all visit the farm often, but none are planning to take on the farm in the future.[4]

CONCLUSION

Modern farming cannot be examined through the same lens as farming of the nineteenth century or even the mid-twentieth century. The days of the romanticized farm family with father and sons working together in the fields, and mothers and daughters working together in the home, quilting with grandmother, and tending a garden, are unrealistic today, and may even have been unrealistic for earlier generations. Nor can American agriculture or rural communities be viewed as synchronic, homogeneous systems. Farmers and farming communities, though marginal to the global economic system, are sensitive to the vagaries of the global economy. Their responses to economic shifts are varied and related intricately to their location in that global system, their location in the rural community, and in their own families. Likewise, the options open to small farmers depend on their skills and education, and on the value system that informs their decisions.

We must be wary of applying social-science definitions of rural community to the reality of the lives under review. It is likely that our descriptions are based on those same romanticized images. Janet Fitchen argues that although social scientists have a difficult time defining "rural" and "community," residents understand what it means to them; they believe in its existence, and they are certain of their own presence within it. According to Fitchen, "The deeper meaning of community, while locality-connected, is of the mind: the ideational or symbolic sense of community, of belonging not only *to* a place but *in* its institutions and *with* its people."[5]

Rural people define their community using such criteria as its physical boundaries, political jurisdictions, socialization, social participation, and mutual support systems. It is this complex network of relationships embedded in history and locality that newcomers cannot achieve. Their idea of community, even after many years of residence, lacks that deeply ingrained, densely packed history and genealogy characteristic of the original settlers. Instead, the sense of community that newcomers bring with them is based on their own individual expectations of what rural life is like, and the values that they place on social position and social interactions.

CHAPTER 5

Township in Transition

My parents honeymooned at Chippewa Lake and bought a cottage here. They brought us kids up here every summer from Lansing where we lived. I hated coming up here when I was young. There was nothing to do. One summer after I graduated from high school we came up here and I met [Dave] and I never left . . . Sometimes I miss Lansing. There is nothing here for kids to do. But I could never raise my family in Lansing. I'm not worried about drugs here. I know where my kids are and I know that people are watching over them.

—KRISTIN, 2005

I FIRST MET HARRY DODGE WHEN HE WAS RECOMMENDED TO US FOR a major home renovation. Everyone in Chippewa Lake calls Harry "Junior," but my husband and I could not bring ourselves to use that nickname for a man who was, at that time, in his mid-sixties. I still remember the perplexed look on Harry's face, and the soon-to-be-familiar gesture of removing his baseball cap and scratching his head with the same hand, as we described to him how we wanted to add a two-story addition to our small one-story house that would form an L-shaped structure. His look of bewilderment turned to amusement when we insisted that the addition have a cathedral ceiling and skylights. I must admit that I doubted that this soft-spoken, lean sexagenarian was up to the task, especially when nearly every sentence he spoke started with "Well, now, I don't know about this . . . ." Harry, however, amazed me with expert skills and a perfectionist's eye for detail. The deadline for the project was the birth date of our third child, who would have nowhere to sleep otherwise. Harry beat the deadline by two weeks, and we were moved into the addition before I went to the hospital.

When I arrived at the home of Harry and Marilyn Dodge to interview them for this project, Harry offered to take me on a tour of the village of Chippewa Lake. He claimed to know the names of the original owners of the houses in the village. I took him up on his offer, waved hello and good-bye to Marilyn, and off we went for the grand tour. Harry loves to talk, and his role as tour guide and local historian is just another of his passions, along with construction and gardening.

Harry's grandfather came to Chippewa Lake in 1896 from Adrian, Michigan—drawn to the area by the logging industry. His father had a small farm on the lake and ran a resort, with cottages and boat rentals, on the west side of the lake. Harry served in the Pacific during World War II and then moved to Flint, where he worked in the automobile industry. In the postwar era, there were few jobs in Mecosta County, and employers in Big Rapids paid only 75 cents an hour. In Detroit and Flint, they were retooling the assembly lines from the production of war machines to automobiles, and there were lots of well-paying jobs. After three years at Buick Motors in Flint, Harry returned to Chippewa Lake, where he learned carpentry, and he has been a self-employed carpenter in the area for many years. Marilyn's family lived in the Detroit area, and her family had a cottage on Long Lake. They met at Chippewa Lake, which was the center of social activity for the entire region. Marilyn and Harry married in 1951 and lived in a log cabin that Harry built, overlooking the lake. Marilyn jokes that she has lived in Chippewa Lake for fifty-three years, almost long enough to be considered a native.

As I rode with Harry through the village and on the gravel roads along the lakeshore, I discovered that he has built or remodeled most of the homes and cottages in the area, including ours. Harry could name all of the original owners of the old homes in the village, and tell stories of who lived there, what they did for a living, and who bought the houses when the old folks died. Now, at age seventy-six, he has a solid memory of all of the families of his youth, yet he laments to me as we drive down these streets today that he doesn't know who lives in most of the houses anymore.

Harry offers us an excellent example of the perception held by many of the old-timers that community identity has somehow been lost. Harry's recollections of the "old days" illustrate the contested community, the idea that an era of shared values has evaporated or decayed over time. The nostalgia expressed by many old-timers neglects the reality of those earlier days, when there were logging-camp owners, entrepreneurs, loggers from distant places (like Harry's own grandfather), and farmers struggling to eke out an existence from mediocre soils. The rural community he remembers from the stories and recollections of his youth are refined and redefined over time. Harry's story, related to me, draws upon several dichotomies that shaped his description of the ideal community: the rural ambiance far from the city, close-knit families living in the same community, and the appeal of knowing one's neighbors.

Janet Fitchen, in her book *Endangered Spaces, Enduring Places: Change, Identity, and Survival in Rural America*, discusses the difficulties that social scientists often have in defining a "rural community."[1] She argues that rural residents themselves formulate their own definitions—a self-definition that exists over time and space and consists of physical boundaries, political jurisdictions, institutions, social participation, and mutual support. The self-definition is often expressed in opposition to what they perceive as "urban." For example, they may define their own town in contrast to other places: "Here we don't have to lock our doors."[2]

In the same book, Fitchen addresses the tension that occurs when community identities are challenged, primarily by the influx of newcomers from other places. When this occurs, local residents set up boundaries that allow them to preserve their self-identification as homogeneous: "We are all alike here." These boundaries include compartmentalizing outsiders into various categories such as newcomers, transients, or vacationers. Individuals in these groups are treated differently from "old-timers" through exclusion from social events or the political process, or by labeling or stereotyping. Old-timers blame changes in their community on these newcomers, lamenting that "now we have to lock our doors at night," and that "we don't know everyone anymore, like we used to."

Donna, a woman whom I know well, expressed the tension that long-time residents feel when newcomers move into the community. She lives in the village of Chippewa Lake, in the house owned by the locally famous Doc Patterson. She is related to one of the settler families in Martiny Township, and is the designated genealogist for her family. She is famous for dressing in full costume on Halloween night, sitting motionless on her porch as a scarecrow or clown, giving the children a great scare as they approach.

During our interview, I asked her how the community has changed over the years, and she related a story of how her son, when he was younger, rode his bike through a neighbor's yard. "In the past," Donna said, "that would have been considered 'boys will be boys' behavior. If it was more serious, the parent of the house would yell at the kid or call the parents, but this man, who was not from here, called the police. He never came and talked to me first. That would never happen in the old days." She continued, "It's not that my son didn't do anything wrong, but in the old days, we all took care of each other's kids. We had long-term friendships, and we all felt responsible for their good behavior. Now, people watch the neighbor kids judgmentally and want them to be punished for wrongdoing." This concern focuses on a shift in philosophy about children in rural communities, who were once seen as an integral part of the community, linked to the past and future; children are now perceived as threats to that idyllic community.

CHIPPEWA LAKE AS RURAL VILLAGE IN TRANSITION

The Village

The village of Chippewa Lake, located south of the lake, has been called by some a sleeper town, one that seems quiet on the surface, with little to commend it. Indeed, a tour of the village, especially in the winter, seems to support this impression. When one enters the community from either the south or the east, one first sees the lake, an unexpected sight, a beautiful gem, in the midst of countryside. Driving through the town, however, one is struck by its disorder and feel of abandonment. Coming from Big Rapids in 2007, one passes small bungalows and a few large homes on both sides of the road, attesting to a grander past. Millett Park, on the left, is flanked by a boarded-up diner and roller rink, a newly closed stained-glass shop, and a home built as a military bunker, surrounded with litter, old cars, and yard ornaments—without the yard. On the right stands the abandoned gas station/video arcade, and the grocery store.[3]

At the T in the road is the only stop sign. Here, directly in front of you, is the laundromat and large-equipment repair shop, now closed, that was converted from an old barn many years ago. Recently, an impromptu used-car lot appeared in the front yard of the old shop/barn. Turning left, toward the lake, one sees the post office, the township office, and the volunteer fire department. To the right, high on a hill, is the church. The main road continues past the church, then it curves to the right and the lake glistens on the left. Now, on the right, on the same ridge where the church stands, is a row of well-maintained cottages and homes, with a view of the lake, and lake access across the road. Further on is the cemetery on the right and the small township park on the left; beyond are the marina, gas station, a restaurant, and resort cabins.

Turning right at the T takes one to the village proper, comprised of several blocks directly south of the main road that cuts through the town. The landscape of the village has changed considerably over the years. As we have seen, during the logging days Chippewa Lake was a thriving community, with hotels, bars, blacksmith shops, and dance halls. Later, in the 1940s, though condensed somewhat, it was still an important population center, with dance halls, stores, and a thriving school and church.

Being the center of the business district and the resort community, the more affluent nonfarm residents lived here, such as the doctor, veterinarian, hotel and store owners, and other established families. As such, the homes here were very large, by local standards. Many of these houses still exist, though some are in disrepair. Others were lost in one or more of the fires that swept the town over the years.

Where the original houses still stand, they are surrounded by large yards with majestic trees and neatly tended garden plots. Donna's family, whose son rode his bike on a neighbor's lawn, is one of the families who have lived in the village for many years. Six of the nine families we interviewed in the village had lived there for at least sixteen years, but four of the families reported that they had no relatives who lived in Chippewa Township.

Over the years, other large lots have been divided into smaller parcels, interspersed with small bungalows and mobile homes. The village looks neglected—especially in the winter, when houses are closed up against the cold and wind, looking almost abandoned. The mobile homes, an inexpensive housing option for the young and the elderly, contribute to the impoverished appearance of the village, according to some. While some families maintain their mobile homes and spruce them up with "skirts" and landscaping, others allow theirs to deteriorate into metal tenements, rusted out, with old machinery and off-season storage underneath. Because of the inexpensive rentals in the village, families or individuals often pass through or seek temporary housing on their way to a separation or divorce, or because of temporary unemployment or homelessness.

The Township

Moving away from the village to the north, east, and south, one finds the rural township, with the same ambiance of fifty years ago. In the rural areas of the township, farms are still widely spaced, with acreage surrounding each farmhouse. Most sections (each section takes up one square mile) have no more than one farm per one-mile length of road, or perhaps five farms per section. As I drive down the dirt or sometimes paved roads to visit these farms, I see stately farmhouses and large barns. Grazing cattle and horses, or corn, bean, or alfalfa fields fill the acreage between the houses and the next corner. Dogs run free around the yard, running up the drive as my car passes and barking excitedly if I pull into the driveway. Farms are separated by fence or tree-lined borders, and I have a sense of openness and space.

The rural landscape represents in a sense the personality of the families who live here. Most farmhouses display a pride of place. The farmhouses are well tended; the yards are mowed and often landscaped with trees or flowers. Vegetable gardens are often located at the side of the house, well weeded and planted in neat rows. They demonstrate a pride of place that is not evident in many of the residences in the village.

This well-ordered world is not universal, however. Several of the dairy farms in the township feature disheveled homes in dire need of paint and repair. As these farmers transition from farming to wage labor, the barns weaken and collapse from disrepair, and abandoned farm machinery rusts in the yard along with old automobiles and trailers.

Today, few township residents are active farmers, though many are the children or grandchildren of farmers. They no longer use the property for farming but continue to live in the family farmhouse, or they have built homes on farm land, as we did. Some families have moved to the community from cities or towns throughout Michigan, following jobs in the larger population centers, but seeking homes in the rural setting. These commuters include local business owners, blue- or white-collar workers, or professionals.

Nonfarm families in the village and township are more diverse in their histories and experiences than are the farm families. As a group, they run the gamut from new arrivals to those who have been more than forty years in the area. It is more difficult to find the essence of the families who have stopped farming, never farmed, or have chosen to live in Chippewa Township for its atmosphere. Yet, it is this population that is contributing to the reshaping of the local identity—setting itself up against shared norms and expectations characteristic of earlier epochs. This community, along with the retirement community on the lake, will represent the "contested community" that is emerging from the ashes of the farming past.

While these various categories of residents share some experiences and overlap in some characteristics, their values and sense of community differ in important respects, and conflict with those of long-term farming families. To highlight the differences between farm and nonfarm families, we will compare their general demographic characteristics. For these comparisons, "nonfarm" includes township, village, and lake residents who are not involved in full- or part-time farming. (Specific characteristics of the lake residents are explored in the next chapter.)

CHARACTERISTICS OF NONFARMING FAMILIES

Years of Residence

The data on Chippewa Township in 2005 indicate that the definition of longtime residence is indeed relative. Nearly half (46 percent) of those in nonfarming families have lived here for more than thirty years, and 63 percent have lived in the area for more than twenty years. Yet, thirty years does not compensate for not being descended from pioneer families, as Marilyn Dodge attests. Many, but not all of these longtime families are descendants of farming families, so their roots trace back many years, though they no longer farm. Others are descended from the logging families who also trace their descent deep into local history.[4]

Of fifty-two households (farming and nonfarming) we interviewed, 25 percent of the sample households have lived in the area (Martiny, Chippewa, and Fork Townships) for three or more generations: eight were third generation in the area, four were fourth generation, and one was fifth generation.[5] The remaining thirty-nine households (75 percent) either came to Chippewa Lake as children with their parents (five), or came here as married adults (thirty-four). The latter group is most likely to reside in the village itself or around the lake.

Marcia Ulrich is just one example of a nonfarm resident who has deep roots in the township. Marcia is the sister of Darryl McCallum and, like her brother, was rooted in the rural farming community. She met her husband, Michael, at Ferris State University (then Ferris State College), where they were both students. Michael's family lived in the nearby town of Mecosta, but it is unlikely they would have met had it not been for their common university experience.

Michael's father owned a gas station and marina, and his mother was a real estate broker. He did not get involved in part-time farming until he and Marcia purchased property two miles from Marcia's family farm. Although Marcia did not finish college, Michael earned a BS degree and worked for many years in public health. Their farming consisted of selling corn and raising some beef cattle. Marcia bakes cakes as a home-based business and has provided extraordinary cakes for many special events in the community, including birthdays, graduation open houses, showers, and our daughter's wedding.

Most of their energies were expended on their only child, Wendy, who was an excellent student who participated in 4-H. She attended a Michigan public university and earned her B.S. and M.A. degrees in accounting. Wendy currently lives and works in northern Michigan. In their retirement, Michael and Marcia had a traveling food wagon for a while and accompanied one of the local auctioneers; today they still do some farming, and Michael has recently completed his dream project—building and flying his own airplane.

While multi-stranded kinship and social ties form the backbone of shared identity, many longtime married couples, such as Marilyn and Harry Dodge, came together because of the lake itself. Others, like Kristin (introductory quote), are in marriages that were sparked by summer romances. Others like the Ulriches live here because of family ties, but their perspective is outward-looking, not inward. Many of these marriages have resulted in strong, rural-based extended families, though without the emotional tug that might compel their children to raise their own families here. Our own family fits this model.

Louise's family came to Chippewa Lake every summer from Grand Rapids. Her family's cottage was next door to a permanent resident, Doug Christiansen, and his parents. Louise and Doug laugh today as she remarks that she used to hate him when she was a young girl, because he always chased and teased her. Later, dislike turned to love and they married. They settled in a home near the lake and her parents ultimately retired to the lake, so both sets of parents were neighbors. Louise and Doug have been married over forty years and have two children and several grandchildren. One son married a young woman from Chippewa Lake, and they now live on the same lot in the village where Louise's parents lived. The other son met his wife in college and they live and work in Grand Rapids. Until his retirement several years ago, Doug traveled daily to the General Motors plant in Grand Rapids, a three-and-a-half-hour commute each day.

Julie Austin provides another example of how a summer resident becomes an integral part of her adopted community. Julie also came to Chippewa Lake as a child with her family. Her father was a farmer in the Lansing area, but when her parents divorced, she moved to Oklahoma with her mother and step-father. However, she returned to Michigan during the summers and spent time at her grandmother's cottage on Chippewa Lake, and it was here that she met her future husband, Mike Austin, whose grandparents were among the early settlers in Martiny Township.

Mike, Shelley, and Patricia Austin are the grandchildren of Irvin and Edna Austin, who were profiled in chapter 2. Their parents did not take on farming, but instead purchased property on the north side of the lake. One of the daughters married and moved away for twenty years, but has now divorced and is living on the same property. Mike and Julie also built a house on the same lakefront property and raised their three children on the lake. In fact, they joke that all three of them lived with their parents as adults at one time or another—while houses were being built, or while recovering from a painful divorce. Today, all three children have houses side by side on the lake on what is called the Austin compound.

Their mother, Shirley, a member of one of the other founding settler families, married James Austin, and they ultimately settled in Chippewa Township. Shirley owned an H&R Block franchise in Big Rapids and was one of the community's primary volunteers. She also served as township treasurer, supervisor, and clerk, and was one of the founding members of the Merry Circle Club. Julie Austin has taken after her mother-in-law by becoming township treasurer. She was also the first woman to be accepted into the Chippewa-Martiny Volunteer Fire Department.

Endogamy and Children's Postmarital Residence Today

While many nonfarming young people came to Chippewa Township to marry, raise families, and retire, it is less likely that their children will continue the pattern. Many young people may like the rural atmosphere when they are young, but later find that their community sets limits on their opportunities. Those who earn a college degree or learn a vocational skill are most concerned about finding jobs for themselves and their spouses, and they follow those jobs to the city. Likewise, children are more likely to find spouses at college than from the local community, and it is often difficult for him or her to convince the spouse that Chippewa Lake is *the* place to live. Local parents lament, as parents do everywhere, that their children have jobs and families in far-flung regions, and that they are too busy to visit them regularly. There are a few exceptions where college-educated children have returned and found professional jobs in the Big Rapids area, and as Big Rapids expands and grows, there will be more opportunities for children to return to their community.

The extent to which local young adults are leaving became really clear to me during one of my interviews for the oral-history component of this project. At the end of an interview, Julie Austin and I were discussing our children and what they were doing. In the process of comparing educations and jobs of local children who are now in their twenties, we listed at least fifteen who were attending university or had already earned college degrees and who are living in other cities and even states, pursuing careers in law, medicine, accounting, pharmacy, business, and even anthropology. It is unlikely that many of these will return to live in the area, unless jobs become available or the rural lifestyle draws them back.

Other young people, especially those in multigenerational local families whose ties to the community run deep or who have not pursued higher education, are more likely to remain in the area, close to home and life-long friendship and kinship ties. These young adults seek jobs or careers within commuting distance, choosing the quality of life over higher salaries or more opportunities elsewhere.

Income and Occupation in Chippewa Township

As families transition away from farming, family members are seeking employment in a wide range of jobs, depending on their educational level and their willingness to move away from home.[6] According to the 2000 U.S. Census, current residents of Chippewa Township are employed in a broad spectrum of occupations, such as manufacturing (33 percent); education, health, and social services (18 percent); and retail (14 percent). Because full-time farmers had the lowest educational levels, they have had the most difficulty finding work off the farm. Household heads of dual-income families had more variable educational levels, which offered them the option of working both on and off the farm.

For nonfarmers, there are challenges in finding jobs in the rural areas, as most of the available opportunities are unskilled or semiskilled jobs that offer poor wages and few benefits. Few of the local factories or businesses have unions; indeed, rural America has the optimum economic climate for manufacturing, and west and northern Michigan have drawn many of the automobile-related industries to the area.[7] On the other hand, the lower cost of living in the area also reflects the economic base, and those who have professional careers or union jobs in the university or elsewhere are able to live very comfortably in the community.

Local women have a high level of employment. Over half of the non-farming wives in the sample (twenty, or 54 percent) have jobs, and most of these commute to work at the university, retail stores, restaurants, or factories. If we consider pre-retirement occupations, 71 percent of women in our sample have some source of income in or outside of the home.

One local woman illustrates how the pull of career and family obligation affects women in particular. Deb Carmichael's mother started showing the symptoms of multiple sclerosis when Deb was six months old, and spent many years in a wheelchair. While Deb's father was alive, she studied nursing at a local community college, and worked as a geriatric nurse in various hospitals and nursing homes in Michigan. When her father's health deteriorated, she gave up her job and returned to the farm to care for her mother. Deb's husband had a job that kept him on the road, and she raised their children, cooked and cleaned for her father, and cared for her mother for many years. Despite her incapacity, her mother outlived her father, and when her mother died, Deb did not return to nursing, but remained on the family farm, where she and her husband raised their two children. When I asked Deb, now forty-five years old, if she missed nursing, she said, "I got kind of burnt out by twenty years of working out [of the home] and then I had my mom [to take care of]. My whole reason for being a nurse was my mother, so it's like—do I want to start another kind of job? I might be happy flipping hamburgers at McDonald's." In fact, Deb is very busy. She is a member of the board of elections for the township; she gardens and is a member of the Emerald Lake Birthday Club.

Commuting

Since the township offers few opportunities for jobs, most of the available jobs require commuting at least ten miles. According to the 2000 Census for Chippewa Township, 95 percent of working adults commute to work, with only 5 percent working near or at home. The mean travel time to work was nearly thirty minutes, slightly more than the amount of time it takes to drive to Big Rapids.

In our survey, we found that 30 percent of those who have jobs travel fewer than eleven miles to work, each way, and about 70 percent commute more than eleven miles, each way, with about half of the commuters travelling between eleven and twenty-five miles (approximately the distance to Big Rapids or Evart). Those who work in the community are employed in a variety of ways—as owners or employees of local businesses, or as skilled laborers such as builders or mechanics.

In households where one family member commutes, the household division of labor adjusts to the routine of late dinners and absentee parents. I remember a conversation I had with my good friend Louise, discussed above, whose husband commuted to a General Motors plant located south of Grand Rapids, daily for thirty years. Louise was a stay-at-home mom who had raised their two sons, helped care for her parents, and volunteered for many local organizations and events. She also earned income from time to time, making and selling crafts. As a commuter myself, I remember remarking that I didn't know how Doug was able to make that long commute daily. My own commute was of comparable distance, but I only made three round trips a week and had a place to stay in Grand Rapids to limit my driving. She replied that she took good care of him. "When he comes home, I have supper ready and all he has to do is relax and go to bed early. I put the kids to bed and do the chores. I know he is really tired when he gets home." This comment made me really envious and desirous of having my own "wife" who would have the meals ready for me when I returned from work. Because I am the family cook and came home to children and their activities, a husband who also worked full-time and commuted, and the ubiquitous stack of papers to grade, the luxury of a cooked meal and early bedtime was not in my paradigm.

The prominence of female labor and commuting also has important implications for local development, and for female participation in local organizations. Working women are more likely to shop in the city and participate in social activities that relate to their professions or jobs. These activities diminish the economic support given to local businesses. In our survey, only two households, both comprised of retired couples, indicated that they did their primary shopping in the village, and that it was a conscious choice for them to do so. I suspect, however, that they no longer do this, as the only grocery store in the village closed around the time of the interview segment of this project.

Because of jobs, women become more reliant on relatives for child care and for other assistance around the house. Working women also have little time for activities that once regularly added to the rural family diet, like gardening or canning. While all but one of the full-time farm families also harvest vegetable gardens, only half of the dual-income and nonfarm families do so. Unless working women and their families have access to garden foods through relatives, they become more dependent on store-bought produce. This not only increases their cost of living, but takes them another step away from the self-reliance goal of rural living.

CONCLUSION

The lifestyle of the majority of township residents differs markedly from that of settler families. Although many longtime residents hold within them the memories (real or handed down from their elders) of a past community, they currently live in another world, far removed from the remembered or imagined past. The philosophy of many of their elders—that reading and writing are the only necessary educational skills—is no longer viable in the modern world of computers and other technology. Those families who have adapted to these new demands, or encouraged their children to learn twenty-first-century skills will simultaneously prepare their children for the new world and separate them from their traditions and roots. The young people who are compelled by tradition or inclination to remain in the community and not pursue additional skills may sacrifice affluent lifestyles but find fulfillment in working locally, and find contentment in remaining close to kin and friends.

CHAPTER 6

Chippewa Lake as Resort Community

> *I bought this cottage at Chippewa Lake because I love to [water] ski and the lake does not have restrictions against water sports. I am against all associations and lake restrictions . . . It is the old ladies of the town who want to restrict the use of the lake . . . I wish the township officials would force people to fix up their trailers and property . . . the mess just proves the mentality of the old Chippewa Lake locals.*
>
> —INTERVIEW WITH A RECENT TRANSPLANT
> AND YEAR-ROUND RESIDENT OF THE LAKE

ELEANOR ERLENBORN'S FAMILY HAS BEEN COMING TO CHIPPEWA Lake since the early 1920s, when she was just a baby. She told me a wonderful story of how her grandmother, Louise Rosander, borrowed a boat from someone and rowed around the lake, looking for the best location to build a cottage. At that time, there were only a few cottages on the lake, and she found a beautiful spot on a small peninsula called Birch Point, and their cabin still sits there today, all alone, with a large yard and beautiful beach. Eleanor's grandfather was a tailor in Chicago; he was first invited up to the lake by a local judge who loved to fish on the lake. After building the cottage in 1907, the family came up yearly for vacations. Eleanor's mother met and married a local man from a prominent farm family, but they settled in the Grand Rapids area, bringing their family up every summer. When I interviewed Eleanor, she was eighty-three, and was staying at the cabin with

97

her daughter, son-in-law, and grandchildren. Since our interview, Eleanor has passed away.

The one-story cabin with a stone fireplace has a homey atmosphere inside. There is a long screened-in porch along the back of the house, where we sat drinking ice tea while she told her story of many summers at the lake when she played with Tom Hahn and his siblings, who lived at the nearby farm. Tom and his wife were sitting there with us, all of them reminiscing about the old days.

The lake has undergone tremendous change since Eleanor Erlenborn's family built their cabin. Early cabins like hers were small bungalows, built as getaways, rustic and cozy, with few amenities. As families grew, people added rooms, updated the plumbing, and made other improvements to make them more comfortable and "modern." Later, in the 1950s and '60s, the new postwar middle-class families purchased lots and placed mobile homes on them. Lack of ordinances allowed a wide variety of structures to be built or placed on the lots.

In recent years, a transformation has begun to alter the appearance of the lake. More affluent families and retirees began to upgrade their cottages as permanent or nine-month homes. Over the past ten years, some very beautiful homes have been built across the road from the lake (having lake access), and on the lake itself. These new homes or rebuilt cottages have multiple stories and modern-design windows and roofs, manicured lawns, well-built storage buildings, and built-in grills. These homes, like those in the village, are now interspersed with the more modest cabins and rusted trailers, giving the lakeshore a crowded, cluttered appearance in some areas.

Today, the lake area is by far the fastest growing region of the township. There are 628 cottages and homes around the lake; at least one-third are inhabited year round. Some of the remaining two-thirds are summer cottages or cottage/homes inhabited for nine or ten months by "snowbirds," or retirees who leave Michigan for warmer climates during the winter months. There are also two cabin resort businesses, one at the East Bay area of the lake and the other at the southwest area. These latter cabins have access to small "beach" areas that actually comprise only a dock and small shallow area for children to swim. The cabins at East Bay don't really have a swimming area at all, as the docking site is very marshy.

Chippewa Lake has always drawn serious sports fishermen for its bass and walleye. Many of the older longtime residents like to fish in both summer and winter, when the ice-covered lake is littered with small ice-fishing shanties and pickup trucks. Patricia Lovell is one of those for whom the peaceful fishing waters represent the lifestyle she desires. Patricia was raised in a farming family in a nearby county, and when she married, she and her husband raised their family in the same community. Her husband owned several lots on Chippewa Lake, so they retired here twenty years ago, following the snowbird migration to Florida every winter. Since her husband died, she has stayed in her house on the lake year round.

Patricia still fishes for blue gill on the lake. For her, the major problem on the lake is the abundance of Jet Skis and water skiers who disrupt her fishing at all hours. Currently, the designation of the lake as an "all-sports lake" is the major source of tension between lake residents and townspeople, and among lake residents themselves. The "all-sports" designation means that there are few restrictions on the use of leisure craft on the lake, nor are there local wake restrictions or quiet hours other than those imposed by the state. In recent years, there has been a proliferation of Jet Skis and jet boats that compete with the fishing boats for space. This has resulted in some conflicts in recent years, as quiet hours established by the state are not regularly enforced, and those who value the lake for fishing often find that their opportunities are limited to the very early or late hours of the day. Indeed, on some of the holidays or weekends, speed boats are on the lake from sunup to sundown, while the fishing boats are huddled against the shoreline, bobbing up and down with the wake, and pontoon boats dare to come out only in the early morning or early evening hours.

Linda and Darrell Schmidt represent many of the residents on the lake. Linda was raised in a farming family (not in this area) and decided early on that she would not continue in that lifestyle: "Twenty-four hours a day and I don't care for it—if you weren't driving a tractor to feed the cows, you were feeding the cows, and if you weren't feeding the cows you were cleaning up behind them."

She moved around the state quite a bit when she was young, living in various towns and cities. She and her husband had both lived in Lansing, but they met in Mecosta County, and they have lived in their cottage on Chippewa Lake since 1989. None of their six grown sons lives in the area, but they come to visit with their families. Darrell is retired, but Linda works at Ferris State University. Like most other lake residents, their concerns are primarily about lake issues. They are glad that there are no wake rules on the lake, indicating that the township board meeting where such regulations were discussed was "the biggest township meeting ever." They use the lake primarily for boating. Their cottage is often "party central" on the lake— their huge bonfires inviting both their friends and neighbors, but also the fire department from time to time.

CHARACTERISTICS OF LAKE RESIDENTS

Length of Residence

The lake residents, with some exceptions, do not have the historic or kin-ship linkages to the community that the village or the township farmers have. In our survey, 42 percent of the lake residents (and four of the nine villagers) stated that they had no family members living in the area, com-pared to only 15 percent of the township residents. More than half of the lake residents have come to Chippewa Lake from other areas of Michigan. They have chosen to live here because of their interest in fishing, boating, and other lake activities, and thus their concerns and complaints are directly related to issues surrounding their lake experience and their property values.

In other characteristics, however, lake residents are similar to their village and township counterparts. For example, they are likely to be longtime resi-dents. Seventy-two percent of those surveyed have lived in the community for at least sixteen years (compared to 80 percent of township residents and 66 percent of the village residents). Nearly half of the household heads are retired, though several have postretirement occupations. The Hahns and the Austins are the two families who have lived the longest on the lake.

Social Class

In the ideal community, differences in social class are minimal, and con-spicuous consumption is discouraged. Historically, Chippewa Lake was a "working-class" or "blue-collar" lake, in that the people who came here as vacationers or retirees were drawn to this lake because of the inexpen-sive housing costs, low cost of living, and low taxes. The lake residents, at least those who are not lifelong residents of the township, were likely to be retired from the automobile industry in the Lansing or Detroit area. Afflu-ent retirees, executives, and professionals from the automobile industry were attracted to the more prestigious lakes in northern Michigan near Traverse City and Petoskey. Many are drawn to the Canadian Lakes community in southern Mecosta County.

This demographic is changing, however, according to the members of the township board. Today, many of those who are currently purchasing and remodeling older cottages and building homes in the area represent a higher economic group: managers or small business owners. This shift began when the sewer system was installed, with two results: a higher cost to cottage owners on the lake in sewer assessments and maintenance fees, and a concomitant increase in property values and taxes. Tax rolls for the township also indicate this shift. Between the mid-1980s, when the sewer was installed, and today, there has been a striking turnover in lake property ownership. Few of the lakefront properties today are owned by the same families as in 1985, according to the township board members. The encroaching resort and retirement community with their Jet Skis, jet boats, and expensive houses exemplifies the contrast between the working-class and the middle- to upper-middle-class lifestyle.

Today small lots with only a lake view sell for more than the cost of lakefront lots twenty years ago (still inexpensive at $12,000). An example of this is one lakefront property with a 20 × 20 cabin and 100 feet of lakefront that sold for $169,000; two years later, it was resold for $255,000 (2007 rates). Although the 2008 financial crisis has affected house prices here as everywhere in Michigan, current prices are still prohibitive for the middle class. Further, these valuations place lake houses out of the reach of most families who are looking for a summer home, or even most retirees with fixed incomes.

As this shift occurs, people begin to differentiate themselves from their neighbors living in the village or township. Because Chippewa Lake has a combination of year-round residents and summer vacationers, the tendency to categorize one's neighbors is just too tempting. Once a couple decides to retire on the lake and remodels their cottage, they begin to judge their neighbors and the condition of their property. Those who own small trailers and come to the lake as weekenders or vacationers come under the scrutiny of those who have expensive homes and cottages. I was often led to a window of a lake house and asked to look at a yard across the peninsula or next door, to witness the lack of care that others took in their summer residences.

Consequently, like the village and township residents, permanent lake residents also named the temporary summer people as what they liked least about living in the area. As retirees from primarily urban areas, these lakeside "hovels" are clear evidence of "trailer trash" in their eyes. One man, who is employed by a Lansing-based company but works at his home on the lake, believes that the old and rundown trailers and cottages are an extension of the "mentality" (his words) of old Chippewa Lake locals.

DEVELOPMENT OF LAKE AND VILLAGE

Despite its size, Chippewa Lake has only one nice beach area that would invite day-trippers, though it has various shallow swimming areas. Unlike other large lakes in Michigan that have wide beaches and picnic areas, Chippewa Lake has only a tiny township park that consists of a small clearing on the side of the road, protected with trees, but with no improvements. It is used primarily by local families who have no other access to the lake. Another small beach area, where swimming lessons were given years ago, has become overgrown with weeds from lack of use, resulting from ongoing conflicts with the cottage owners on either side who complained about the noisy kids and the walking traffic up and down the dead-end road leading to the lake.

The nicest beach area is at the public-access and boat-ramp, where people can picnic and park their cars for the day. Although it has a roped-off swimming area, its appeal is hindered by the commotion of boats being unloaded, the noise of motors starting, and the dangers inherent in having children and boats in the same vicinity. These areas are not conducive to the development of a summer beach resort that would draw people from the city or small towns to spend the day, shop, and eat in the restaurants.

Despite the growth of the lake community and the increased population of the township generally, the village has not developed as a shopping district that would support a local population or draw tourists. One resident had a stained-glass shop in the village for several years. Her combined stained-glass and Avon business was the only shop that had the potential to attract a tourist clientele, but during the research phase of this project, she and her husband decided to sell their house in the village and the business and move south. Until the 2008 renovations, it was one of the abandoned buildings, boarded up and for sale.

The local bar is also a microcosm of the changes in this rural community. For many years, when the roller rink was open, the bar was an integral part of the community. In those early years when I started coming to Chippewa Lake, the bar, though dark and heavy with the pungent odors of grease and cigarette smoke hanging in the air, drew local farmers and families. Locals came to the bar to socialize or play pool, have a hamburger and beer, while their children or grandchildren were at the roller rink. Video games and a dance floor added to the appeal, and bands often came in the evening to add to the family entertainment. Kids ran in and out of the bar touching base with their relatives and begging money for snacks or ice cream from the ice cream parlor down the street. The bar was always a different place later at night, but afternoons and early evenings, it was full of people, families and friends crowded around large round tables, sharing pitchers, catching up on gossip, and re-creating community.

The bar has a different feel today, though it still draws some local people during the day. It is no longer a family bar, despite the attempts of recent owners to convert the bar into an Irish pub/sports bar. The addition of large televisions, live music, and karaoke has brought in more patrons, especially in the summer, but the reputation is still such that few locals admit to patronizing it in the evenings. The struggles of the local bar represent the struggles of the community at large: the necessity of running a business that depends on nonlocals and seasonal clientele for its survival, while maintaining the ambiance and feel of the local tavern.

The community continues to depend on the summer people to keep their businesses alive throughout the year. The bar, restaurant, and marina store rely on their summer business to make it through the year. In actuality, however, summer people do not contribute to the local economy as they once did. Most weekenders stop at Walmart on their way to the lake, purchasing their food and supplies before coming to the cottage. They may eat one or two meals at the bar or restaurant and purchase a few groceries from the marina store, but these contributions to the community are not sufficient to maintain these businesses year round. With the closure of the village grocery store during the research period, the community has lost an important source of revenue and jobs.

The loss to the community in tourist dollars is exacerbated by the lack of activities that might draw vacationers or residents from neighboring communities. Chippewa Lake has not been able to offer the amenities that accompany a vibrant community for locals or vacationers. Many families remember the crowds of kids on the weekends enjoying the roller rink. The music from the building could be heard all through the community. Even earlier, from the 1940s to '60s, there was a dance hall (actually two, as the first burned down and the second was built elsewhere) that drew resort people and rural residents from the entire county. Older people have good memories of Chippewa Lake as a thriving resort town.

Lake Activities

Without the roller rink or other activities for young people, there is no draw from surrounding communities, so in recent years, the town seems empty, even during the Fourth of July or Chippewa Lake Days celebrations.

The lake is the busiest during the week between Chippewa Lake Days and the Fourth of July celebrations. This is when many of the summer residents come to the lake. There are several events that occur over the holiday, the most recent being a boat parade on the morning of the Fourth, when people decorate their pontoon and fishing boats in patriotic colors, or follow other themes, and make a circuit of the lake.

The most popular lake event is the poker run. On the lake, many people participate in the poker run, promoting the dubious combination of alcohol and boats. People who own cottages at strategic locations on the lake are solicited to be the dealers. They are given envelopes, each of which contains a playing card, and they sit on the dock waiting for boats to come around and pick up their envelope. In order to participate, individuals must sign up at Millet Park in the village, pay a small sum, and receive several starter cards, all concealed in envelopes. During the specified hours of the day (usually two or three), the participants crowd on their pontoon boats or on their Jet Skis and make a circuit of the lake, collecting a card at each participating dock.

This offers an opportunity to socialize, as boaters will joke and converse with those sitting on the docks—often passing beverages back and forth before moving on to the next dock. There is jovial banter as boats crowd around a dock and try to maneuver to get close enough to grab the envelopes. When they have made the circuit, they take their envelopes—unopened—back to the park. Game officials open the envelopes and make note of the best poker hand (five of seven cards collected). When all the participants have turned in their cards, a monetary prize is given to the contestant with the best poker hand.

The Chippewa Lake fireworks are very popular, as they are set off from a barge in the middle of the lake. People with pontoon boats start to congregate on the lake at dusk, armed with insect spray and alcohol. Others watch from their cottages. For a small community, these fireworks are quite impressive, and people who don't want to fight the masses of people and traffic surrounding the Big Rapids fireworks come to the smaller communities, like Chippewa Lake, instead—especially if they have friends with cottages on the lake. Events to raise money for the fireworks are continuous throughout the year, including a pig roast and Bowl-a-Thon sponsored by the owner of the East Bay Marina. On the weekend closest to the Fourth, and on the holiday itself, people visit all the cottages to collect donations for the following year.

Failed Development

The lack of development cannot be blamed on the businesses that are currently operating in the village. The local store and business owners are extraordinarily generous with their contributions to the community, such as food or other contributions to local events. Self-employed men with large mowers donate their time and machinery in mowing the abandoned lots during the summer and for the parade, mowing and repairing the softball diamond, and preparing the track for the tractor pulls. Those with tractors give hayrides for children for the Halloween party; those with snowplows clear out the driveways of elderly neighbors and the church. One self-employed man donated a pig for the pig roast organized to raise money for the new park. As mentioned above, the past owner of the marina was in charge of raising money for the Fourth of July fireworks every year, sponsoring a pig roast and a Bowl-a-Thon. He also sponsored fishing contests in the summer, and winter events on the ice, such as the ice races and a winterfest.

New owners of businesses come to the village enthusiastic about living in a small rural community. They contribute to events and bring new ideas to town. However, over time they begin to feel taken advantage of, as more and more is expected of them, and their returns are negligible. There is frequent turnover in many of the local businesses. The bar has had at least seven owners over the past twenty years, and the marina has had four. With a few exceptions, the owners of local businesses come from outside the community, and many, though not all, leave when they sell the business. Recent new business owners complained that they come to town to start a business, but people are not friendly to them; other business owners do not cooperate among themselves to enhance village life, and there is a resistance to forming business-based organizations.

One year, a man from the Lansing area came to town with deep pockets. He bought the roller rink; the old bait shop, which he converted into a restaurant (in fact both restaurants on the lake were former bait shops—and now the lake has no bait shop); the abandoned gas station, which he remodeled into a video arcade; and another building that he rented out as a beauty shop. Barney was a jovial fellow who immediately became the hero of the young people of the town. Kids hung out at the video arcade during the day, and the roller rink was in full swing at night. He sponsored other activities, such as dances, and contributed to many events. Unfortunately, within a few years, Barney lost interest and lost money on his investments, and he pulled out of town, leaving boarded-up buildings in his wake. He specifically drew the wrath of the community by tearing up the expensive wood floor of the roller rink and making it into a boat-storage facility. This assured that no one would ever be able to have a roller rink in there again. A mountain of land contracts further inhibited any potential entrepreneurs from investing in the businesses. Because all of these buildings were on the main road that passes through the village, they contributed to the dilapidated appearance that everyone lamented. The new supervisor tore down the roller rink, the stained-glass store, and other abandoned buildings on the main road, greatly improving the landscape, and erasing permanently any physical evidence of Chippewa Lake's lively past.

About fifteen years ago, a local entrepreneur planned and implemented the design of a housing development. His development was modeled after Canadian Lakes, an affluent year-round community in southern Mecosta County. He purchased over 300 acres of land in the northern sections of the township and hired local people to prepare the area for development— building roads and excavating artificial lakes, and clearing land for house lots. He had brochures and was selling lots when he was tragically killed in an airplane crash, leaving his dream unfulfilled. The township supported this project as it promised to contribute to a "rebirth" of the community. Today another developer owns the property, but so far has not pursued the completion of the project.

Dennis Love, another potential entrepreneur, started coming to Chippewa Lake twenty-five years ago with his parents when he was twelve years old. His family lived in Lansing, and Dennis remembers Chippewa Lake as a thriving place, with lots of things for kids to do. He always loved the cottage they rented, perched on an isolated peninsula that juts out into the lake. Dennis now owns this house.

Dennis has a real entrepreneurial spirit and hoped to be a part of the rebirth of Chippewa Lake as a vibrant resort community. He and his mother purchased the Chippewa Lake bar in 1979 and they owned it until 1986, sold and rebought it, owning it until 1989. He came to the community with many ideas for economic development. As local business owners, he and his mother promoted the village by sponsoring a softball team and contributing to the improvements to the field, bleachers, and scoreboard. Dennis also promoted two development projects, neither of which came to fruition. First, in 1984, he and several other business people tried to establish a local business association to promote local development, but the idea was ultimately struck down by local groups and the township board.

In a subsequent conversation with the members of the township board (not the same one that ruled on Dennis's earlier request), I was reminded of two important aspects of rural life—the importance of self-reliance and the fear of outsider control. According to the board, the idea of a community or a lake association (also suggested from time to time) will always be rejected by the community. Organizations that attempt to regulate business or housing threatens the individuality that is valued so highly here. That a small group of people would decide which businesses could come into the community, what their buildings might look like, and what they could sell, is totally unacceptable and contradicts basic community values. The fear of regulation and standardization also helps to explain local resistance to zoning boards, incorporation, and eyesore ordinances, as we will see in the next chapter.

Dennis's second venture was to build a campground for recreational vehicles and trailers. He owned a large tract of land on the main Chippewa Lake–Barryton road across from the lakefront cottages, where he hoped to develop the campground. His plans included a swimming pool and recreation building. The cottage owners, primarily summer people, bombarded the township meeting at which this plan was discussed. Dennis had hoped to get approval to pursue a zoning change that would allow the campground to be built. Cottage owners nearest the proposed site soundly rejected the idea, as they were concerned about kids running through their property to get to the lake or using their docks, as well as theft and vandalism. Local and full-time residents were (and still are) very disappointed by this response, as they saw the proposed campground as a benefit to the community. Nevertheless, it was the county zoning board that ultimately rejected the project, ruling that there was no safe walkway from the campground to the public access located about a quarter of a mile away, along a road that encircles the lake.

Dennis's frustration at the local resistance resulted in a disengagement from the community that he and his wife adopted, even though it was the county that ultimately rejected his plan. In our surveys, several respondents commented that they thought the trailer park/campground would have been a good idea, and they too blamed the "elders" for its failure.

Today, Dennis is a realtor in Big Rapids, owning his own business. His wife is a software consultant for a national corporation, with a local office. They now live in Big Rapids. Dennis is very disappointed that the community has not been open to new ideas, and argues that the community is economically depressed because of it.

CONCLUSION

The fault lines between the rural community and the resort community are starting to take shape in this small township. We can envision these fault lines as axes of contention between old-timers, newcomers, and transients. The longtime and farming residents desire to return to their "remembered" past where the community is busy with social activities, where the church is the center of social life, and where people congregate at the dances, the roller rink, and the local restaurants. Development, to these residents, means the reestablishment of businesses that benefit the community as a whole. Yet they resist the organizational structure that might facilitate this development as it violates a critical tenet of the rural community, individual freedom.

Lake residents and other newcomers have also come here for the ambiance, for the rural life, or more likely, for the lake; their idea of "rural" and "community" differ from that of the farmers and others who have lived here for many years. The newer residents, without this collective memory of past events, desire to shape the community in such a way that it resembles their perception of a rural village, but perhaps with the conveniences of their town of origin. They want paved roads, trash pickup, and well-stocked stores; they want a clean community and a lakefront that will improve their property values and not remind them that it is the local impoverishment that allows them to purchase an inexpensive cottage and pay minimal property taxes. They want to have the best of both worlds in their retirement, which they have earned through hard work and much saving. Rather than mutual assistance, they are motivated by self-interest and short-term goals. Instead of being embedded in a historic village, they are constantly reinventing an adopted community.

The summer residents are even further removed from the historic past and the local community. They arrive on Friday afternoons and leave Sunday, with perhaps a week or two of vacation during the summer. These families have the least invested in the community and participate marginally in the local social events. Their interests are limited to those things that have an impact on their enjoyment of the lake: the cost of maintaining their property, and issues that might compromise their enjoyment, such as a public campground and special lake assessments. We will now explore several issues that highlight these points of contention, that divide people on the basis of history and class, and that hinder the community from acting as one unified group for the benefit of the whole.

CHAPTER 7

Contested Identities

With all the out-of-towners moving into the area, Chippewa Lake is not as private as it used to be years ago. The old blood for the most part is gone. Now we have people with a different mentality who sever the ways of the old Chippewa Lake.

—PETER NELLIS, LIFETIME RESIDENT
OF CHIPPEWA TOWNSHIP

CHIPPEWA TOWNSHIP IS LIKE A MICROCOSM OF A CITY, WITH INTRIGU-ing dramas playing out in an area of 36 square miles. Critical points of contention that crosscut the occupational and geographical axes of Chippewa Township can be dramatized by examining two local debates. These debates exemplify the complexity of issues and opinions in this community, but also bring into focus the underlying differences in worldviews that shape the discourse of the divergent interest groups. The first debate, on chemical treatments recommended for the lake, is one that primarily pits the seasonal and permanent lake residents against each other, but has ramifications for all township residents; the second debate took place at a "Meet the Candidates Night" during the summer of 2004. During the second debate, several issues arose that highlight the conflicting discourses surrounding rural life.

THE AXES OF CONFLICT

In this section, I would like to outline three axes of tension in the township that define various loci of contested interests and ideas of community that emerged in the last two chapters: lake residents versus other township residents; transient and seasonal residents versus permanent residents; and newcomers and retirees versus longtime residents. These categories of residents are not mutually exclusive, as permanent lake residents and longtime residents share ambivalence toward the seasonal and transient residents, and these axes are crosscut further by such demographic factors as township versus village, generation, and animosities that exist between organizations and social groups. These three axes, however, will allow us to examine the most important arenas within which contested identities are acted out.

Lake Residents vs. Other Township Residents

This locus has several dimensions. The first centers on the uses of the lake itself and its designation as a sports lake. The lines between lake residents on this issue are not clearly drawn, but generally, lake residents prefer the lake to remain an "all-sports lake," while longtime township residents would prefer regulations, such as wake laws, that would protect the lake for fishing interests.

The second dimension exemplifies the complexity of the issues that divide the community, exposing the raw biases of social class and suburban ideas of orderliness and appearance. Lake residents, especially newcomers and retirees who have invested substantial time and money in their new homes and upgraded cottages, are critical of those whose cottages and mobile homes clutter up the landscape and threaten their property values. Those who complain are frustrated to find that nothing can be done locally to ameliorate these conditions because the village is not incorporated, nor does it have a zoning board that could restrict the placement of mobile homes among other homes and designate areas for rental and residential properties. These concerns pit the full-time and retired lake residents against the township and the seasonal residents.

Third, while the lake residents lament that their interests are not being adequately served by the township governance, the village and township residents often complain that township board meetings are dominated by issues regarding the lake, instead of issues that would benefit the township as a whole.

Transients vs. Permanent Residents

In our survey, when we asked what respondents liked least about living in Chippewa Lake, all residents named the summer vacationers as what they liked least. Because the summer vacationers were not interviewed for this project, their opinions have not been formally documented. Evidence of their perspectives often crystallizes at township and other meetings conducted to discuss such issues as the proposal for the campground, the lake, and tax assessments. Unlike permanent lake residents, seasonal residents are maintaining two homes; increases in taxes, increased maintenance costs of the sewer system, and the health of the lake affect them critically.

A second population of transients includes those who rent mobile homes in the village or on the lake, or apartments in the community's only apartment building. Because of inexpensive rents, college students, newly separated or divorced singles, and other low-income families relocate here from other small towns. Fairly or unfairly, this population is often blamed for the condition of the village. Indeed, the lawn of the apartment building located across from the church is often littered with dilapidated chairs, sofas, and toys, and the parking lot is cluttered with old cars, bicycles, and uncollected trash. They are less likely to take care of their property, but the blame for rental conditions can often be shared by property owners.

The transient population is also blamed, often unfairly, for much of the local crime. People remember that the only murder that has occurred in the village was committed by the estranged husband of a woman who moved to the village with her boyfriend. After a confrontation between the husband and the boyfriend, the former murdered the latter. This caused locals to ask why people come to their community to kill each other.

Newcomers and Retirees vs. Old-Timers

This locus embodies several points of contention, some subtle, others more tangible, illustrating well Fitchen's categories of insider/outsider groups in small towns.[1] First, in the opinion of many old-timers, the newcomers represent a higher social class whose members set themselves above the locals, displaying conspicuous consumption and a concomitant attitude of superiority. On their part, the newcomers and retirees feel spurned. Firmly entrenched in the middle class, they do not see themselves as arrogant, but as "regular people" who are only seeking their own rural and lakeside paradise. They see the locals as clannish and old-fashioned, unwilling to change with the times, perhaps a little unreasonable. Friction was evident in the "Meet the Candidates" event, where deeper meanings of community emerged in the guise of a debate on volunteerism and local participation. Volunteerism, embedded deeply in the local perception of the ideal community, became a major point of contention at the meeting, where, ironically, the newcomers accused the locals of lacking the idealized qualities that most identify rural culture: friendliness, inclusiveness, and neighborliness.

The second source of tension between these groups is more subtle and philosophical, and effectively illustrated in Salamon's description of how the suburbanization process is precipitated when outsiders begin to move in and reshape small towns according to their image of what they should be.[2] The rural community, in this idealized configuration, is often shaped by popular media in which the "quaint" countryside comes complete with all the amenities that they enjoy in the city: paved roads, trash pickup, mail delivery, water and sewer—all provided by tax dollars. Such assumptions reflect a lack of understanding of how services are provided (or not provided) in rural areas.

A township official expressed her frustration with this idealized view of rural community. She argued persuasively that many people retire to Chippewa Lake or have their summer residences here because of the relatively low cost of housing and low taxes. According to this official, "People come here from Lansing and they expect to get the same services here that they get in the city, but they don't want to pay higher taxes. They want to see 'eyesore' ordinances in the village, but don't understand the costs of enforcing these ordinances, or understand that to do so would mean that the same ordinances would have to be enforced around the cottages and farms as well." In addition, in Chippewa Township, unlike other areas, 87 percent of the taxes go to the school district. Residents from the city are accustomed to having tax dollars applicable to services and don't realize that the township only gets 1.25 mills from the taxes collected. "They don't understand why they don't have trash pickup or mail delivery. They don't know where their tax dollars are going, and they don't understand that they can afford to come here *because* of our lower property values and lower taxes."

This suburbanization of community is in essence what many local people criticize, and perhaps fear, the most. These loci of difference are defined in terms of general categories of behavior. For the longtime residents, the newcomers, lake retirees, and transients are stereotyped and lumped into a single category as urban, arrogant, self-important, and unfriendly. Likewise, the newcomers and lake retirees describe the longtime residents as old-fashioned, controlling, and cliquish.

DEBATED ISSUES OF LAKE AND COMMUNITY

Milfoil Treatment Issue

In general, my observations of the township board meetings confirm the township residents' contention that the board meetings are dominated by lake issues and concerns. However, it does not follow that the board is uninterested in the betterment of the entire township. Instead, the issues of the lake, weed infestations and sewer maintenance, are critical and ongoing concerns. Very few residents attend the township board meetings unless there is a major issue on the table, or if they have a personal complaint or problem. The few people who attend regularly are almost entirely lake residents and those who are employed by the township.

The two major issues that have dominated the local political arena are the sewer system and the Eurasian milfoil invasion of the lake. The sewer system has already been introduced and will be discussed in more detail in the next section. Here, I will discuss the debates over the milfoil.

In the past five years, Eurasian milfoil weeds have been introduced into the lake. These weeds are not local, and are not consumed by any local fish species. As a result, they multiply rapidly, taking over the native water flora that fish do eat. Many other lakes in the area have also experienced this invasion. It spreads as fishing boats are transported from lake to lake without having their propellers cleaned. This is an important point, for it indicates that the milfoil is brought to the lake by nonresidents or locals who fish in other lakes. It also means that, once eradicated, there is a strong likelihood that it will be reintroduced in the future.

There are two methods of eradicating milfoil. Introducing weevils into the lake is a nonchemical but less effective remedy that has the consequence of introducing another foreign species into the lake. The second method is a chemical that attacks only the milfoil and does not impact the fish or the native weed species, allowing them to reproduce. There was a lot of controversy over the efficacy and safety of this option, especially since the chemical treatment is expensive and more than one treatment is required.

The township board meetings that dealt with the milfoil brought so many lake residents that they had to be moved to the community building. As might be expected, the primary concern for all property owners around the lake was the cost of the treatments, as well as suspicion about the possible effects of the chemicals on fish and humans. Many property owners questioned the integrity of the board and its ability to make informed decisions. Heated discussion ensued at all meetings on the topic, even though representatives from the Department of Natural Resources and the state Department of Environmental Quality attended to discuss the options for eradication and their efficacy.

While most people recognized the need to eradicate the weeds, how the costs were assessed became the focus of debate—would it be by building, lot, or length of shoreline? Would those cottages off the lake have to pay the same as those on the lake? What about those who were likely responsible for the invasion—those who moved their fishing or speed boats from lake to lake? Eventually, a formula was devised that was similar to that drawn for the sewer, whereby those residents who had lake-frontage parcels, or parcels with deeded or dedicated access to the lake were assessed per "lot." Although many people are unhappy, the procedure was done. Unfortunately, treatments are still continuing as of 2011.

Increased assessments of the sewer system and chemical treatments are critical issues for all who use the lake. For those who live here full-time (one third of the residences), the cost is offset somewhat by the fact that the lack of foreign weeds protects the native plant and fish species, and it protects the economic value of their investment. For the summer residents, the costs incurred for these improvements can be an economic hardship, because for them, the cottage is their second home, for which they pay taxes, insurance, and upkeep. Unfortunately, these new assessments, especially for the milfoil, were unexpected, and occurred at the same time that the sewer assessments were increased. While summer residents want to protect their investment, it is more costly for them to do so, and they were very vocal about how the assessments were formulated and how payments were to be made.

The frustration of surviving on high overhead and low income was apparent at one township board meeting I attended in the summer of 2004, where the assessments on the Eurasian milfoil treatment were discussed. The owner of one set of resort cabins, located across the road from the lake in the village, complained about his assessment for the milfoil. He objected to paying an assessment as he does not have any lake frontage for his cabins, only an easement down to a dock. This grievance resulted in a long discussion of the history of that piece of land, and an unprecedented offer of the township treasurer to personally pay his assessment if he felt it was unfair.

Further, lake-property owners complained that people who live in the township and use the lake regularly are not assessed, and that since these same people fish in various lakes, they are likely to have contributed to the infestation in the first place. Pertinent questions were raised: how might future invasions be avoided? Can boats being unloaded into the lake be monitored or at least assessed to defray the costs of future infestations? How would this be accomplished and who would be responsible?

The ensuing debate, which encompassed many months in late 2003 and early 2004, offers a glimpse into the dynamics of life in a small community. The small animosities that otherwise are shared over coffee in farm kitchens, in the bar or local restaurant, or over a bonfire on the lake come into sharp focus in a debate over weeds. These animosities came into clearer focus during a "Meet the Candidates Night" held in July 2004.

Meet the Candidates Night

In July 2004, the local Lions Club sponsored a "Meet the Candidates Night" in Chippewa Lake. The purpose of the event was to allow the candidates for township offices to introduce themselves and discuss issues of importance to the community. This event was very instructive as it highlighted three additional issues that concern local residents, and for me, it underscored some of the most poignant differences between lake and township residents, and between newcomers and old-timers. The four topics that dominated the meeting were 1) the actual purpose of the meeting, to meet the candidates for township offices; 2) whether the maintenance and oversight of the sewer system should be contracted to professionals; 3) whether the community should have some kind of board or mechanism to develop laws to control eyesores and to keep the community clean; and 4) volunteerism and the perception that old-timers did not want or seek participation from new residents. The open discussion of these topics very clearly demarcated the differences among the various categories of people that reside in the township and around the lake, and will be discussed below.

Meet the Candidates

The township board has three officers: the supervisor; the clerk, who is in charge of the elections and acts as the secretary for the board; and the treasurer, who also is in charge of sending out and collecting tax assessments. There are also two trustees, who are elected and who serve with the board as voting representatives of the population of the township.

In Chippewa Township, the supervisor is also the coordinator of the sewer committee, along with the treasurer. A local man was hired by the sewer board to maintain the system, though he has not had formal training in this capacity. Certain township board members also serve on the sewer committee, a committee that also includes officials from Big Rapids, and that monitors the sewer system and assesses and collects maintenance fees for the sewer. In addition, members from the Chippewa and Martiny Township Boards also serve on the board of the Chippewa-Martiny Volunteer Fire Department, and various county boards.

The village of Chippewa Lake is not incorporated, so the township board is responsible for all business regarding the lake, village, and the entire township. Because it is not incorporated and because they do not have a local zoning board, the village does not have the authority to pass ordinances such as zoning restrictions or "eyesore" ordinances other than those regulated through the Mecosta County Commission. Because of lack of village taxes, they also cannot hire law enforcement officers to enforce county laws or provide full-time protection to the community. One of the ongoing complaints of many local people is the lack of police protection on the "east side" of the county and the long response time for emergency vehicles, which are spread thinly throughout the rural townships.

During the summer of 2004, the terms were expiring for the members of the township board, but only the supervisor and trustees had opposition. The candidates were campaigning for the August primary. Because all of the candidates for the officer positions were Republicans, the winners of the primary would serve as the new township board. Two of the trustee candidates were Democrats, so the trustee positions were not finalized until after the general election in November.

To provide an open forum, the Lions Club sponsored this event, which was held in the community building. The format was set by the Lions Club. Members acted as moderators and hosted a reception afterwards. There were over fifty residents present, excluding the Lions Club members (recognized by their bright yellow and orange vests) and the candidates. Of these fifty participants, I did not recognize any individuals from the major farming families, except those who were on the board. The vast majority of the members of the audience lived in the area immediately surrounding the lake or in the village.

There were three men who ran against the incumbent supervisor in the summer election. These men represented the various interests of the community, except farming. The current supervisor had been criticized by many as not very effective in his job—not attending to some of the problems of the sewer system, or to other issues that were important in the community. The supervisor has lived in Chippewa Lake for many years and was running for reelection. During his turn to speak at the meeting, he said only, "I do a good job and make difficult decisions. If you have questions, ask them."

The first candidate running against the supervisor lived on Chippewa Lake, but before retirement was involved in law enforcement in Ingham County (Lansing), where he had also owned a charter fishing business. He, like many others, started coming to Chippewa Lake when he was a child in the 1950s, and continued to come for many years before retiring here three years ago. In his written statement, he stressed his experience as a law enforcement officer and as a businessman and claimed that Chippewa Township should be run like a business. He indicated that he wanted to solve the problems of the community, and that he was not prejudiced by past events, nor did he have fixed ideas of how things should be. He made a slip of the tongue, saying at the meeting: "We like urban living . . ."

The second candidate had come to the lake from Detroit thirteen years previously, after having vacationed here with his family. He holds a bachelor's degree in business administration and had retired from General Motors. He also argued that the township should be run like a business. He complained about the condition of the village, and argued that some of the paid positions in the community should be volunteer positions instead. Village governance should be cost-effective. Yet, he argued in favor of the sewer system being put up for bids to outsiders.

The third candidate was George Griffes, a longtime though not life-long resident of the township; George and his wife have a house across the road from the lake. George had been a township trustee for nine years, and supervisor for three years of a four-year term. Because of family problems towards the end of his term, he did not run for reelection, but was interested in running again. In his letter to the community, he stressed that as supervisor previously, he had established a ten-year plan for the sewer system, which he claimed was not followed by his successor. He is also currently the chair of a committee to raise money to expand and improve the park at the community building. As a longtime member of the Lions Club, George has been linked very tightly into the community for many years, and he won the election.

For the township trustees, I will briefly summarize three candidates, as their candidacies shed light on some of the issues we will be discussing. Kristin Lytle is one of the youngest women in our survey, and she was a candidate for trustee. Kristin came to this area from Lansing, first visiting with her family during the summers. She met her husband here, and when they married, they settled in the community. Kristin and Dave have twins, who were five years old when we did the initial interviews. Kristin was a member of the Young Women's Club, but resigned in 2007 after serving thirteen years in the club. She and her husband currently serve on the fireworks committee, which is instrumental in raising money for a very impressive fireworks display every July 4th. In 2008, the committee put on an $8,000 fireworks display. Dave serves as the assistant chief of the Chippewa-Martiny Fire Department, and has served twenty-two years on the department as of 2008.

Kristin attended the township board meetings regularly, and in talking with her informally, she was very concerned about the fact that the elders do not want the younger people to participate. Her platform involved an appeal for people to get involved in the community, and for the community to provide local programs and events that will support children and teens who have little to keep them occupied. Kristin lost the election, but won the position when she ran again in 2008.

The second candidate for trustee was Pat Lovell, a woman who had come to Chippewa Lake seventeen years previously with her husband. They raised their children in Montcalm County, and retired to Chippewa Lake, where she has remained even though her husband passed away. She felt that her volunteer work qualified her for the position of trustee, and like Kristin, she promoted the development of activities for local families.

The third candidate, the only male, said very little in the meeting. He was also a recent resident, whose employment before retirement was electrical wholesale. He said that he was not set in his thinking about things, but didn't offer any suggestions for bettering the community. Although he seemed to offer the least in terms of platform, he defeated the two women who ran against him. The other trusteeship position was taken by one of the incumbents, a longtime female resident in the community, whose family was one of the farm families in the rural township. The township clerk, Ilene Stein, and treasurer, Julie Austin, had no opposition. Julie is much younger than her cohorts on the township board, and is known for her steady temperament and good judgment. It was she who offered to pay the resort owner's milfoil assessment.

After the candidates introduced themselves and gave their short statements, the floor was opened to comments and questions. Because I didn't know all of the participants and audience members, I did not always know the residence of all of those who made comments or asked questions. I often relied on my neighbor in the audience to help me to identify the various speakers. Most of the audience was comprised of lake and village residents. None of the farm families that I know were in attendance, except those who were candidates.

The Sewer System

In the 1980s, it became clear that the existing system of individual septic tanks set around the lake was no longer sufficient to maintain a clean lake, and the township began discussions on the installation of a sewer system that would connect all residences on the lake. Debates regarding the necessity of the system and how it would be funded caused so much tension in the community that one man had a heart attack during one of the township board meetings. Despite the fact that the township supervisor conducting the meeting was an EMT and tended to him, the man could not be revived.

The sewer system has been successful in restoring the quality of the lake for fishing and swimming, yet it continues to elicit tremendous emotional response as assessments rise and maintenance is a constant challenge. Now that the system is over twenty years old, costs of maintenance and repair increase, as do complaints about the sewer services. The issue of the sewer arose at this meeting also as the assessments had recently been sent out and residents were facing yet another increase. From the questions, it was clear that many people did not understand the assessments—one village resident complained about having to pay for the sewer, and the board had to patiently inform the person that he was not being assessed.

It was clearly the newcomers around the lake who were most verbose about contracting professionals to maintain and oversee the sewer system. There is widespread belief that the township board is not qualified to oversee it or assure proper maintenance. They felt that having a contract with an outside board or group would assure that the sewer would be maintained more adequately and inexpensively. Recent breakages and seepages proved their point, in their opinion. The board members responded to this complaint, arguing that the proposed solution would be very expensive, as the contractors would be paid on retainer. They also asserted that having a committee or board composed of nonlocals would not guarantee emergency service any more quickly than that currently provided by the local maintenance person, who is always on call.

Discussion then turned to Richard, the sewer maintenance person who responds to all calls regarding problems with the sewer and makes repairs. Several community members noted that Richard did not have the training or the qualifications to provide adequate service on the complex system. Richard's defenders responded that he has had training, and that he often must cobble together the system because of lack of funds or proper equipment. Richard, obviously irritated by the discussion, started to stand to defend himself, but was restrained by a friend of cooler temperament.

The expressed concern that the local officials do not have the expertise to monitor the sewer system frustrates the longtime residents and officials. Such statements reinforce the educational and social-class differences between the local government officials, longtime residents, and the newcomer retirees. Local residents are sensitive to the difference in educational levels between themselves and some of the new residents on the lake, and they perceive these comments as indicative of the newcomers' view of them as hicks and farmers. For example, in a later conversation with me, the new township supervisor, a very astute individual, felt compelled several times to preface his comments to me with "I only have a high school education, but . . ."

In their deliberations, the local officials are balancing the interests of the few with the needs of the community, and the possible solutions reflect local values that permeate the "community effect": keeping the sewer in local control instead of bringing in "big government" to regulate it, maintain it, and control it; considering the costs to the taxpayers; maintaining the trust of the community who votes for them. Here, a local issue of sewer maintenance becomes the nexus of an intersection where divergent ideologies meet: urban versus rural, tradition versus change, and historical multi-stranded relationships versus single-stranded/single-issue concerns. In this case and others, leaders are often forced to choose between the interests of people whose place in the community is marginal and those who are there to judge her or him for generations to come.

The lake residents, in their turn, understand the local customs enough to be suspicious of the motivations of the local leadership. They know that the local people will resist their suggestions, and they attribute this to clannishness and rural intransigence. In their turn, strategies for penetrating the wall of resistance elude them, and they are only able to make alliances with others who share their marginal status. They are reluctant to accept the idea that the local leaders are working for the community as a whole, believing instead that local leaders are too mired in tradition to appreciate the larger issues of the lake or to understand "modern" governmental structures.

Coming from urban areas, they are accustomed to a certain degree of political corruption. This was apparent when one member of the audience questioned how much and why the township officials were paid for their work with the sewer system. He even suggested that the time they spend should be volunteered and not reimbursed. It was interesting that the same man who made this argument was the one who argued most strongly for contracting this service to outsiders. If he were to attend the township board meetings and see the budget, he would see how little the township officials were reimbursed for the time and energy they expended on township-, sewer-, and lake-related business.

The Condition of the Town

The issue around which the villagers, township residents, and lake residents coalesced most decisively was the run-down condition of the town. In surveys, many residents lamented the lack of house and yard maintenance, abandoned buildings, and general clutter as both what concerned them most and what they thought should be remedied to improve the quality of life of the community. Currently, the county ordinances apply locally, but are rarely enforced due to lack of sufficient law enforcement officers to deal with these types of infractions. Here, many residents want the township to enact and uphold local ordinances regarding the condition of the village and lake, allowing the township to force residents to clean up their yards and maintain their mobile homes and lake property. This would require village incorporation. With incorporation, the village could pass ordinances and hire a law enforcement officer to enforce them. A zoning board would allow the incorporated township to regulate the location of businesses and set specific areas for rental units, trailers, and private homes and cottages. Incorporation, however, would add another layer of administration to the township as well as the costs of enforcing ordinances. A zoning board, requiring twelve or thirteen members, would add another expensive layer of government, and a concomitant increase in taxes.

As a transplant from a city, the township treasurer understands the issue of incorporation and zoning, and agreed that it would be beneficial if Chippewa Lake became incorporated or formed a zoning board. She stated this at the meeting, but tried to make it clear that the costs of such an endeavor would be prohibitive. It was very clear from the body language of the audience that the crowd was divided along clearly defined lines, the Lions Club members and old-timers nodding along with the treasurer, and the lake residents and newcomer candidates scowling and rolling their eyes.

As the lake residents were asking their questions and airing their concerns, there was little input from the longtime residents who were present in the room. Many of these were Lions Club members who were congregated along the back of the room where I sat, and I was able to hear their loud whispers and grumbling as the newcomers complained about the lack of services, the inability of the township board to manage the sewer, and the lack of eyesore ordinances. They did not add to the discussion, however, but instead allowed the candidates to address the concerns and provide their views on the subject. There was only one discussion topic that brought the longtime and back-of-the-room audience to life, and that was the fourth issue—community participation and volunteerism.

Volunteerism

While the first three issues illustrate divergent values and perceptions of local government and community, the topic of volunteerism elicited the most emotional response. The battle lines between newcomers and old-timers were clearly defined. After all, volunteerism and the concept of mutual assistance are one of the hallmark definitions of "community."

One of the candidates for office, a relative newcomer, diminished her chances of winning by criticizing someone who called on her to volunteer—saying the caller was rude to her on the phone. This comment, as well as others I have heard at the township board meetings, hints at an underlying tension between those who are longtime volunteers and who know the routine of events in the community, and newcomers who say they aren't asked, and when they come to help, they are ignored.

This unexpected topic of debate brought the Lions Club members away from the wall and into the fray. The moderator lost control of the group as people talked over each other, newcomers accused the old-timers of being unfriendly and exclusive, and old-timers accused the newcomers of the same traits and as being unfairly critical. Finally, one of the township board members, obviously frustrated by the discussion, responded: "Don't wait to be asked—just do something." At the end of the Candidates Night, a sheet of paper was passed around for anyone who was willing to volunteer to sign.

During the reception time after the meeting, the discussion continued in hushed tones in small circles, clearly defined by longevity and residence. In fact, the lake residents did not stay long. Clearly not feeling welcome, many left directly after the meeting, leaving mostly longtime residents and Lions Club members to complain about the unreasonableness of those who want to bring the city to the country and who don't understand how things work.

As a footnote to the above township meeting, the election was instructive. All but one of the elected officials has lived in the community for more than twenty-five years.

Discussion

As I observed this event and thought about it afterward, I tried to understand how this public event might serve as a mechanism for explaining the tensions and interactions between the various populations sharing Chippewa Township. Several points of contention were clear from my observations. Clearly defined axes of conflict highlight the intersection where longtime residents identify threats to their idea of rural community and rural identity, and where newcomers become disillusioned about that rural paradise that brought them to Chippewa Township.

First, the composition of the audience was worrisome to me. The members of the Lions Club represent primarily the nonfarming residents who have lived in the community for many years. However, there were few farming residents at the meeting from the rural township, and I was left to wonder if longtime residents had already decided for whom they would vote and didn't feel it necessary to attend a meeting. This attitude, however, defies one of the basic responsibilities of small-scale societies—the importance of participatory local government and lively debate on the issues.

Perhaps the absence of farmers foregrounds one of the complaints that we heard while conducting our interviews in the rural township areas—that the township today is concerned primarily with lake issues and not with the betterment of the community as a whole. Their concerns would seem to be substantiated by the issues discussed at the meeting. There was no overall discussion of the future of the community. There was no discussion of development in the rural township, or improvements such as roads or land use; nor was there a debate on development or growth.

Second, the dialogue and tone of the entire meeting served to reinforce the stereotypes that exist on either side: The longtime residents, standing quietly against the back wall, arms crossed, listened to the comments from the audience, but were somewhat judgmental in their demeanor and body language. Members of the audience, perched on metal chairs, expressed their concerns to a township board that shares none of their experiences as retired factory workers or white-collar professionals. The latter group, mainly men, tried to convince the longtime residents that there was another way to do things; yet, they were unable to understand why the old-timers weren't impressed by how things are done in Lansing.

Third, and most critical, the exchange of ideas exemplified how the newcomers embody the perceived threat to all that the longtime residents hold dear. To the longtime residents, the newcomers exemplify a group that is unwilling to participate in the daily life of the community—volunteerism and mutual assistance. Further, the ritual discourse of gossip and sanction do not affect them—they don't care what others think of them. To the newcomers, the longtime residents fulfill their stereotypes of rural people—resistant to change and narrow-minded. It is clear that their ideal of rural living differs markedly from the local ideal, and the breach will be difficult to bridge.

CONCLUSION

Interactions outlined in this chapter reinforce Janet Fitchen's findings on how longtime residents allow themselves to maintain their idea of a homogenous, idealized community.[3] In this scenario, old-timers categorize others as "newcomers," "transients," or "outsiders." By building social boundaries between "us" and "them," it becomes easier to discriminate, or in the present case, to justify maintaining the status quo. According to Fitchen, as a class, "newcomers" may be kept at bay for years or decades, usually to their consternation and dismay, even though as individuals they may be cordially received. Likewise, "outsiders" may receive rather unfriendly treatment, and "transients" may be ignored.[4] This process of categorizing is implicit in the conversations that we had with township residents, and was illustrated in the Candidates Night debate. In this case, however, the newcomers represented a visible and vocal faction. Though newcomers were not elected, their concerns were aired publicly, and it will no longer be possible to ignore their voices.

Nor can longtime residents claim homogeneity or "community values," as there is considerable variation in local feelings about potential growth and development. For example, many longtime residents supported the housing development and the campground. It was the summer residents who were most vociferous against these projects. Both longtime and recent residents are angered by the condition of the village, but they differ in how the problem should be solved. All residents would like to see development and new business ventures, but not with the expense of a formalized community-development organization or zoning control. It was a township board member who told me that if she won the lotto, she would buy all the land held by Barney, the absentee property owner, so that she could burn the buildings down and start the town over again.

While newcomers would like to see development in the form of additional services, better restaurants, gas stations, and other conveniences, longtime residents do not want Chippewa Lake to experience the process whereby the village is remodeled in the vision of Lansing, with a box store and franchise restaurants that would effectively kill the local businesses that are now barely clinging to life. Rather, they would like to see local businesses and churches thrive. They envision social events and activities in town, and a town pride where people care for their surroundings and take care of their property. They would like to hold onto the nostalgic past, the time when dances at the Grange and other social events tied families together.

Unfortunately, fewer and fewer families hold this nostalgic past in their memories as the years pass. From now on, the families that come to the community, attend events, and perhaps settle here will not share this history. While longtime residents watch their children move away to the cities to find jobs, they are simultaneously watching new people come into the town: retirees and commuters who bring with them their own vision of rural life. They see people building large homes on the lake that will ultimately impact the property taxes that they pay on their multi-acre farms; they see strangers placing trailers on smaller and smaller lots in the village and on the lake, demanding services that only higher taxes can provide; and they see the problems of the city coming to the country: methamphetamine labs in neighboring Osceola County, larcenies at cottages and homes, and general threats to their lifestyle.

So far, the worst fears of the local residents have not come to pass. The influx of newcomers has not yet resulted in the type of rapid economic change or development that some have feared and others have awaited. I personally can attest that the main street of the town has not grown in the past twenty years. In fact, the village has shrunk since I arrived, though the population has increased 23 percent. Since we moved into town, we lost the roller rink, a heavy-equipment/boat repair business, several bait shops, a restaurant, bank, car wash, beauty shop, stained-glass-window shop, a small campground, video arcade, and the village's only blinking traffic light. If we go back another ten years, we can add two grocery stores, a snack bar, gas station, and the dance hall to the loss column.

New residents, other than those who came to town specifically to take over existing businesses, have not brought businesses with them, nor are they often visible in the local restaurants or at events such as parades. Their participation in the political process is limited to issues that directly involve them, such as the milfoil weeds and the wake laws. They seem very frustrated when, as happened at the Candidates Night debate, people are not open to outside ideas, such as seeking outside contracts for the sewer. These encounters reinforce, rather than dissolve, the walls between these two groups, the lake residents accusing the elders of being intransigent and unwilling to change, and the longtime residents seeing the newcomers as arrogant city folks trying to bring their views to the community. The result is inertia.

CHAPTER 8

Social Networks

> *There's a lot of dissension among local groups [today].*
> *There's a lot of bickering. They don't work together like*
> *we used to . . . I think it's because no one is friends anymore.*
> *Back [then], they were all friends, even when they got mad*
> *at each other . . . It's not that they aren't around. It's that*
> *they have too much to do. They go to work to get that*
> *second paycheck, to raise and support their family.*
> *And when they get home, they are too tired.*
>
> —INTERVIEW WITH
> COMMUNITY RESIDENTS, 2005

WHEN LONGTIME RESIDENTS REMEMBER THE PAST, THEY DESCRIBE the community in terms of cooperation, struggle, and shared leisure activities. In many cases, memories are secondhand, based on stories they have heard from their parents and grandparents. Various types of events dominate these shared or revisionist memories: the local musicians who played their fiddles at dances throughout the community; the various dance halls, and dances at the Grange; and progressive card parties. Memories of cooperation revolve around stories of threshing parties and other forms of mutual assistance. Stories of struggle inevitably involve the challenges of winter survival, illness, and the lack of amenities.

In comparison, today's world seems mundane, and people today seem less involved in their neighbors' lives. Many residents we interviewed complained that people just don't have time for others any more—they are too busy. The number of newcomers is a source of concern for many—people just don't know each other anymore. Though most people lamented the loss of local commitment, a closer examination illustrates that under the surface of the sleepy community is a current of activity that becomes activated at certain times of the year (Chippewa Lake Days) and for certain occasions (funerals and tragedies). It is this undercurrent that still links members of the community together despite the outward appearance of apathy and neglect.

We will examine various types of community participation, the ways in which participation is embedded in local history and culture, and how these commitments are shifting as the composition of the community changes. We will also explore some of the social variables that affect individual and family participation in local organizations and events. Finally, we will look at local and regional institutions and how these simultaneously unite members of the community and extend family networks outward beyond the township.

FORMAL AND INFORMAL SOCIAL NETWORKS

Formal Organizations

As in the past, women provide the focus for many social and community-based organizations. Several women who live in northern Chippewa Township still belong to the Emerald Lake Birthday Club, which was founded in the early 1900s. In the early days, the club had two functions. One was to act as a monthly social group where birthdays were celebrated. The other was a "community service" function. They provided food and other necessities to families in need, and made quilts for families who had lost their homes or belongings to fire. Today, the descendants of the original members still participate, though the group is much smaller than in the past. They meet less frequently, though they still make quilts for fire victims and donate quilts for local fundraisers.

Closer to the village, several other groups have been very influential in providing women opportunities for both social activity and community. The Merry Circle was one such group that was dedicated to community service. They sponsored many projects in the community, and were an important part of the organization of the community building that serves as the social focus point for Chippewa and Martiny Townships. The Young Women's Club was formed in the 1970s, and I was one of the members of this group for almost ten years. In the early years of this organization, the YWC focused on children's activities, sponsoring the Easter Egg Hunt, Halloween Hayride, swimming lessons, children's games at the Chippewa Lake

Days, and co-sponsoring, with the Merry Circle, the Christmas party. They also sponsored the Hunters' Breakfast on November 15th and a Valentine's Day dance in February.

The community used to have a very active seniors group, but when the county organized the Commission on Aging and located their community center near Chippewa Hills High School, many of the local seniors became involved in the larger organization. Members of the original group were instrumental in the fundraising and organizing of the community building. The community building itself has an organizing structure, with a board that coordinates the rentals and use of the building and its grounds, which include a playground, baseball diamond, and tractor-pull area. The board takes care of the maintenance of the building and grounds.

The Lions Club is an international organization, and the local branch meets in Chippewa Lake and sponsors many local activities, particularly during Chippewa Lake Days in the summer. Recently the membership of the Lions Club has declined. According to one member, the membership tends to be cyclical and is in one of the downward trends. Members tend to be middle-aged community couples. Their mission is to raise money to assist the blind, and to make contributions to their local towns.

The volunteer Chippewa-Martiny Fire Department, in addition to their important firefighting service to the community, is also a service-oriented group that offers assistance in many ways. The fire department has sponsored many special events over the years. Their most visible contribution is the bonfire and hotdog supper they provide at the fire hall every Halloween night. Other local organizations make cash and food contributions for this annual event, which brings the neighborhood kids and their parents and friends together before and after trick-or-treating.

Spontaneous Networks for Mutual Assistance

The most generalized form of community involvement is reciprocity and mutual assistance. Many longtime residents noted the loss of local involvement as one of the major problems of living in the community today. Yet, upon reflection, they were all able to remember acts of kindness in their own experiences. They acknowledged that neighbors assisted them in some way when a family member was sick or experienced misfortune. Deb Carmichael Zielinski, a woman from a farming family who does not farm herself, joked about the time when her aunt and uncle, who ran a large beef farm operation, had to go to the hospital at the same time, and the entire extended family was called upon to take over the farm chores. She said that many relatives knew how to do one or two things, but no one could take over all the chores, so it took an entire extended family to hold the farm together while the aunt and uncle were in the hospital. Deb knew how to run the silo loader, so that was her job. She also knew how much grain and protein to give the steers because she had helped her uncle in the past. But there are so many things to know, that it is difficult for the nonfarmer to step in and assist a farm family who need help.

The willingness to help each other out is born from mutual need as much as from an inherent desire to help others. In all communities, urban and rural, networks form that enable people to help each other out—carpools, shared child care, or other services. These are not limited to small towns and rural communities. However, in small towns, these services are sometimes more critical than in the city, where daycare centers and kennels are available. How does a family take a vacation when it has horses, cows, and perhaps other animals to care for? I learned of this mutual assistance when we had three horses, chickens, a dog, and a cat. We exchanged services with our neighbor, who also had animals, feeding and watering their horses and dogs when they traveled in exchange for the same services when we were away.

Likewise, neighbors come to the rescue in times of health emergencies or accidents. I remember when my friend's husband had cancer, and many neighbors volunteered to take turns transporting him to the hospital seventy miles away for his tests and treatments. Others volunteered to take care of their children so that my friend could take her husband to the hospital or run errands. Without any fanfare, a schedule appeared at their house, and when people came to visit, they volunteered to drive, provide child care, or bring a meal to their house. Deb Carmichael tells another story of how, when her uncle's father died, the neighbors took care of his widow and children until they were on their feet again, got their crops off (harvested), and did whatever they needed.

Informal Networks for Mutual Assistance

While families and individuals help each other out in times of personal suffering, there are also informal networks that lie dormant, hibernating until tragedy strikes. These networks spring into action around an important community or family need. The most visible manifestations of these underground networks are the benefit potluck and memorial dinners. Traditionally, one of the services provided by the senior citizen's group was to organize funeral dinners. Until her death in 2008, Evelyn Nott of Martiny Township was the official calling committee for these events. Now others have taken her place. Whenever a death occurs in the village, the network springs into action, and community members get a call asking for "your special pistachio salad," baked beans, or sheet cake.

The various groups in the village have also sponsored many benefits over the years for individuals or families facing financial difficulties because of disease or accidents. These benefits are in the form of community dinners organized by a local group, usually one in which the family was involved. The community building often donates the use of the building, various organizations give money, and many individuals contribute food. Benefit dinners draw many local families, who come to support or help needy families in this way.

Since I have been a part of the community, there have been more benefit dinners than I can count—usually to help for hospital costs when a family lacks health insurance, or when costs exceed the family's ability to pay for special services not covered by insurance. Marty and Katie Miller are a young couple in the community. Marty is the son of Raymond and Judy, who are profiled in chapter 4. Katie is a former summer vacationer who came to the community when she was young. As an adult, she joined the army and served as a communications officer in many countries, including Belgium, the Netherlands, in the American Embassy in Paris, Saudi Arabia, and Kuwait during Desert Storm. Marty and Katie settled in Chippewa Township, living in a mobile home on a parcel of the Miller farm. Having no children of their own, they began to take in foster children and, over time, adopted some of them. As their adopted family grew, they built a home on the land. Marty got a job at a local potash plant, and Katie earned money working at several local stores, so she could be close to her growing family.

Their first foster child was a baby girl, Megan, who suffered multiple disabilities stemming from fetal alcohol syndrome. She was not expected to live long, but under Katie and Marty's care, she lived longer than anyone expected, and they eventually adopted her. During one medical emergency, Megan's hospital bills mounted, and the community put on a benefit to raise money for her hospital expenses and to help Katie and Marty have the necessary equipment on hand to care for her. At this event, the community raised $15,000. Megan finally succumbed to her illness in 2008 after seven years of triumphant life. To reciprocate, Katie is always one of the first people involved in planning benefits for others in the community who need assistance.

Another noteworthy example of community cooperation occurred in September 1987. Anyone who lived in Mecosta County during that fateful night will never forget it. Unexpected fall rains pummeled the county over a 24-hour period, resulting in horrendous flooding affecting small communities and Big Rapids. Many businesses in Big Rapids were demolished as small creeks grew into rivers and tore buildings apart, destroying "creekside" parks and a high school football field. In Chippewa and Martiny Townships, the flood raised the levels of Chippewa and Evans Lakes above their shores and threatened homes and trailers on the lakeshores. Roads were flooded, and the fire department was out directing traffic, keeping cars out of electrified water-flooded roads, and helping people out of their flooded homes. It was a terrifying night for everyone. Within hours of the news of the evacuations of families from Evans Lake in Martiny Township, the phone wires (those that were intact) were buzzing.

The community building was converted to a shelter, and individuals and organizations volunteered to provide food and time according to a schedule that materialized out of nowhere. All day and evening, volunteers were in the community building cooking food, making coffee, and entertaining children evacuated from the flooded areas. Others contributed drinking water, clothing, diapers, sleeping bags, blankets, and other necessities that evacuees needed. Members of the fire department worked around the clock, searching for families and monitoring the roads. As a relatively new member of the community at that time, I was truly amazed and emotionally moved as I watched this unfold. I have seldom felt the pride of community that I experienced as a participant in this extraordinary effort.

Spontaneous acts of kindness are part of all communities, and Chippewa Lake, despite complaints to the contrary, is certainly one of these communities. When our neighbor's barn caught fire, many neighbors were drawn to the blaze; some just watched, but others risked their lives, helping to save as many cows as possible from the stalls. Because the fire lasted so long, wives of the firefighters took thermoses of coffee and snacks to the farm to feed the firefighters and the family members who were all struggling to save their cows, even while simultaneously grieving the loss of some of their valuable animals.

Summer residents and retirees on the lake are often not aware of these events and do not experience the random acts of everyday kindness that rural people take for granted. Such unplanned tragedies bring out the best in rural communities.

COMMITMENT TO FORMAL ORGANIZATIONS AND INFORMAL NETWORKS

Economic and social changes in the community have had an impact on membership in social organizations. An anecdote from one of the organizations, the Young Women's Club, will serve to illustrate how economic shifts affected one organization. As a member of this group, I observed this transformation with some regret. When I moved into the community in 1982, I was a stranger. I was also wary of my uncertain future, living in the middle of nowhere with two small children and a seemingly useless Ph.D. in anthropology. Because my husband's family, the McCormicks, was one of the founding families in the township, and longtime residents knew my husband, people were probably curious about me and perhaps more forthcoming than they might have been otherwise. In any event, within months of our arrival, I received a phone call from one of the neighborhood women, who invited me to a meeting of the Young Women's Club. I did not consider myself a young woman, but I did have young children, so I attended a meeting in the house of one of the members, Terri. There were ten women of various ages congregated in the neat farmhouse, and Terri served home-baked dessert and coffee.

I very much enjoyed this group because I valued their child-centered goals and projects. The group was well organized, and it was not long before I started taking leadership roles. Each month we met in a member's house. I found that there was a certain competitiveness about the homemade desserts served. However, by the late 1980s, some of the members' husbands were being laid off in the factories, and women were seeking part-time or full-time jobs to fill the gaps. Other women, whose children were getting older, also began to look for jobs to supplement their husbands' salaries, and one member, Terri, lost her husband to cancer. Women began to complain that they didn't have time to clean their homes for meetings (an important consideration), and so we began to meet in the community building. The role of hostess continued to circulate among the members, but within a year, even the homemade desserts became a burden, and women began to bring store-bought desserts or cookies. As women got jobs and others were seriously dieting, it wasn't long before the desserts were dropped altogether, and women brought their own snacks and beverages. The transition was gradual, but reflected the changes that were happening in many women's lives at that time.

In 1991, I obtained a teaching position eighty miles from our home, and I left the group, though I have always been "on the list" for contributions and special events. As I obtained a sabbatical and started this project, I reconnected with the group and found that it had only one of the original members, and that it was dominated by a small core of dedicated women. Younger women in the group struggle with conflicts of jobs and child care, and meetings did not seem to be held regularly. Yet, they continue to offer many of the same community contributions that the original group did:

the Easter Egg Hunt (held in the snow that spring), Hunter's Breakfast, and Halloween and Christmas parties.

INTERGENERATIONAL AND INTERLOCKING MEMBERSHIPS

Urban social networks and rural social networks differ in several respects. One respect is the distinction between what Eric Wolf called "single-stranded networks" and "multi-stranded networks."[1] The former represents situations where individuals are members of families, churches, workplaces, and organizations; however, the social ties in these various networks do not overlap, and are thus weakly connected. One can quit a group and never see those people again. In contrast, networks in small communities are often "multi-stranded."

Individuals and families in small communities interact in various different contexts. First of all, most longtime residents are related in some way or another. While some of these ties may appear tenuous, people do connect themselves to others through kinship ties. Furthermore, membership in many organizations tends to run in families. Members in the Chippewa Lake Church, Lions Club, Emerald Lake Birthday Club, and even the Young Women's Club bring their children into the group when they are adults.

Away from the community, young parents, especially mothers, form multi-stranded relationships through parents' groups at school, sports and after-school activities, 4-H, and other events. As in all communities, certain families are associated with volunteerism, regardless of the ages of their children.

The transition from young adulthood to middle age is not an easy one in a small community, however. Our interviews with residents uncovered intergenerational tensions regarding community participation. Older residents, who remember when Chippewa Township was a bustling community with many active groups and lots of activities, said that the younger generation is not as interested in the community, and that they do not want to become involved in government or groups. In contrast, younger respondents complained that the older residents want to control the organizations and they don't want to consider new ideas or try new things. Many young people felt discouraged and quit various organizations because of these conflicts, and others said that they didn't get involved because of the elders in leadership roles.

The willingness of many people of all ages to become involved in local organizations or as volunteers demonstrates that people are connected through multiple memberships in local groups and organizations: church, various social organizations, school activities and organizations, 4-H, fire department, etc. It is very likely that any person is linked to any other by at least two networks and maybe more. While these interlocking networks reinforce social ties and allow for potentially strong personal ties, they can also result in long-term animosities as past errors, missteps, or insults are long remembered and often embellished over the years.

One of the ironies of small-town life is that its strength is also its weakness. Some people told me that "the best thing about Chippewa Lake is that everyone knows each other; the worst thing is that everyone knows each other." This paradox is apparent in understanding the participation of individuals and families in social organizations. Family feuds and other local animosities nurtured over the years affect social relationships and participation in local events. People will avoid social situations that bring them into contact with those whom they dislike or whose personalities clash with theirs. People know each other well enough to know who is well organized, bossy, know-it-all, or easy to get along with. Often, people gain reputations, sometimes based on limited contact with others or through stereotypes. Newcomers are seen as arrogant and critical of local norms; college-educated people or college students (known locally as pinheads) are suspected of being book-smart but lacking in common sense. It is often difficult to break down these stereotypes without reinforcing the images that people carry with them.

COMMUNITY CHURCH AND IDENTITY

The local church has long been a symbol of the unity of the community. When the Chippewa Lake Lumber Company built the church in 1885, it was established as a Congregational church. According to Virginia Ball, the local historian, the Methodists met in the town hall for several years, and in 1921 the Methodists took over the church. It continued as a United Methodist church until 2000. During the early days of the community, the church was the center of many local activities. As in many churches, the women were an integral part of church activities, such as the Ladies' Aid Society that served to raise money, organize dinners and other events, and in general contribute to the community.[2]

The Chippewa Lake Church was not the only church operating during the 1880s, however. Emerald Lake area had its own church, the Sparks Church, and there was a Lutheran church about three miles south of the village in Martiny Township. The Lutheran church served as a center for many of the German families who came to the area, some of whom settled in Chippewa and Martiny Townships.[3] The building where it stood has been inhabited by several small nondenominational congregations over the years.

In my memories, the Chippewa Lake Church was a focal point for many social activities, and our two oldest children participated in many of the events that mark the religious calendar. By the time our third child was old enough to participate, the church was plagued by a series of short-term pastors and discontent among the members. We became less active, as did many other families. It was always difficult to draw young families into the church, and complaints often mirrored those of the other local social organizations: that the elders of the church dominated the policies and the running of the church.

Nevertheless, during the 1980s, two pastors were successful in establishing a strong congregation of young and middle-aged people, as well as the elder core. The first of these was a very young minister who went through a divorce while serving the church. It is a testament to his popularity that he was able to survive this personal tragedy and also bring a new wife into the church, a very lively graduate student in biology who spent a lot of time in our barn stalking owls and collecting owl spoor. He served for five years, longer than most Methodist ministers.

Ironically, the next pastor, who served six years, was an elderly man who had also survived a divorce before coming to us, and whose second wife was ordained as a minister during their service. Both of these men had their followers and detractors, but they were able to provide a stable church to our community. That has not been the case since the second pastor left. Between 1990 and 2000, the church had six pastors.

There are several factors that mitigate problems in rural churches today, and several of these may be inherent in the Methodist procedure for placement of their pastors. Among many religions, the congregation hires their pastor, and there is an established system of vetting their qualifications and personal styles. In the Methodist Church, pastors are placed by the diocese. There is a perception that rural communities such as Chippewa Lake receive pastors who are being tested, or for some reason banished to the nether regions of the countryside as punishment for untold deeds. It is my perception that all of the pastors that I have known have a strong commitment to their faith, but become frustrated by the local customs. They are often not able to negotiate the minefield of small-town idiosyncrasies and personalities.

This problem is exacerbated by another feature of rural religion, and that is the consolidation of churches. The Chippewa Lake United Methodist Church was linked with the Barryton United Methodist Church, and the pastor's residence was in Barryton. Thus, the pastor tended two churches with often very different expectations and two church boards. Often the pastor was well liked at one church and merely tolerated at the other. This caused many conflicts and frustrations for the pastor and for the churches. Because Barryton is the larger congregation and the home congregation, it is seen as having more power, and Chippewa Lake residents have often argued, accurately or not, that they have lost good pastors because the pastors couldn't get along with the Barryton church board.

These issues came to a head in 2000. The details are sparse and contradictory. There seems to have been a general dissatisfaction with the Methodist Church. During this time, the national United Methodist Church made landmark decisions regarding acceptance of homosexuality in membership and leadership, and in support of gay marriage. While some members said that this was one of the factors in the church conflict, others denied it.

One of the complaints expressed most commonly was that much of the money contributed to the church went to the Methodist diocese, and there was not enough local control over the money they raised in the church. Others expressed dissatisfaction with the pastors who were sent to the community, and a desire to have more control over the church locally.

Whatever the reasons, participation in the church dropped between 1998 and 2000, and by spring of 2000, it had dropped to thirty or forty members. The remaining church members voted, and most decided to leave the United Methodist Church and form a nondenominational church, called the Chippewa Lake Community Church. Those who chose to remain with the organized church continued to meet in the church building, and the new church met in the community building. In 2001, the United Methodist district superintendent closed the church doors and gave the church building to the Barryton congregation, causing more bad feelings as the splinter church wanted to move into the original church building. There was a lot of discontent at this time, and members were trying to find local landowners who might donate or sell land for the building of a new church.

In 2002, the Barryton United Methodist Church donated the church back to the community and the Community Church moved in. One local woman served as the first pastor of the new church from 2000 to 2001, and they have had several pastors since that time. Many of the longtime Methodist members and others who were unhappy with the new group have started worshipping elsewhere.

One prominent local couple was very active in the Chippewa Lake Methodist Church but, with great regret, moved their membership to a Methodist church elsewhere. When I asked them why they left, they stated that the Methodist Church reaches out beyond the community. "For every tragedy, there is need . . . the church wants to reach out and help others, but this church [Community Church] doesn't want to send the money out of the community. They probably do good things, but it is in the community. I haven't heard of what they are doing." They added however, that they don't have hard feelings about the members of the new church. "They are all good Christians." One of their biggest regrets is that they had to leave the community to go to church, yet they felt strongly enough about the split that they decided to attend a Methodist church elsewhere rather than attend the nondenominational church in their own community.

The church has always had an important social function in the community, sponsoring dinners and participating in the Chippewa Lake Days in the summer. However, with increased religious diversity in the community, the church is less central to community events than it was in the past. Nevertheless, the new church has doubled its membership since becoming nondenominational and returning to the church building. The recent growth of the church has necessitated remodeling and adding onto the building. Many residents have indicated that the church is a very welcoming place, and friends encourage those of us who have left for other churches to return.[4]

IMPORTANCE OF COMMUNITY EVENTS
IN DEFINING COMMUNITY

We have already discussed the variety of lake events that draw audiences from the lake, township, and village. Other events also draw participants from the community, though they do not necessarily draw from all population groups. The major community event in Chippewa Lake is Chippewa Lake Days, which occurs the weekend before the Fourth of July every year. The parade draws the biggest audience, though it is not widely attended. The local organizations, including the local 4-H groups, have floats in the parade, and someone is asked to serve as judge for the best floats. In the past there was always an elderly couple designated as the king and queen. They rode in a car or a horse-drawn carriage. The fire department shows off its trucks, and others pull floats with their tractors. Several families ride their horses, and some families decorate their horse and carriage. During an election year, the size of the parade swells as local candidates walk the parade route handing out candy and brochures; otherwise, the parade has decreased in size and extravagance over the years. In non–election years, the parade takes ten minutes tops to move through town; during an election year, it might double.

The parade route ends at the community building, where the chicken barbecue and baked goods and craft sales draw people in. The Lions Club sponsors the chicken barbecue, with contributions from many in the community. Other groups sponsor a petting zoo, children's games, and handicrafts and bake sales. A softball tournament at the community building lasts all weekend, bringing teams from the Mecosta County area, but drawing only a small number of local observers. All profits earned by any organization go to the Community Building Association for its maintenance and expenses.

During Chippewa Lake Days, the horse and tractor pulls draw the local farm families and their friends together in a friendly competition. A track has been cleared for these pulls, which allow farmers to compete with their tractors in pulling cement blocks behind them. Horse pulls are also lively, though some may think them less than "humane" to the horses. Yet many farmers with Belgians work with them all year, increasing the weight that they can pull, just for these competitions.

The modern equivalent of horse pulls and tractor pulls involves the other paramount vehicle of rural America—the pickup truck. Peter Nellis organizes two mud runs a year, one on Memorial Day weekend, the other on Labor Day weekend. He floods a field, turning former grazing land into a mucky goo, through which participants drive their trucks. Mud covers the tires, and as the driver spins the wheels, mud spews outward over all the participants and observers. In recent years the event has drawn people from further away who have modified their trucks with huge, oversized tires. The mud run provides entertainment for the entire family, complete with food wagon and Porta-Johns.

The Fourth of July is a more relaxed weekend, with events primarily taking place on the lake. We have already learned of the fireworks, boat parade, and the poker run that bring the lake and village residents together for local festivities. When the Fourth of July falls on or near a weekend, there are more resort people on the lake, and local businesses such as the bar will draw customers in with live bands or karaoke. When it falls during the week, the primary celebrants are locals and those families who take their vacations over the holiday week.

FAMILY EVENTS AND RITES OF PASSAGE

Deer-Hunting Ritual

While families get together for many occasions, the event that draws the relatives to the community most is deer-hunting season. While many hunters come from the urban areas of the state to set up "deer camp" on state land, my interest is in the way that deer-hunting season brings families together, sometimes not in the friendliest way. First, there are actually three deer-hunting seasons. The first is bow season, which opens on October 1. Bow hunters are allowed to "bait"—that is, to leave piles of carrots or apples in a clearing to draw deer to a particular place where the hunter has raised a deer blind in a tree or on a platform. Bow hunters wear camouflage. On November 15, firearm season starts, and from that time, the bow hunter camouflage is replaced by bright orange vests, hats, and gloves. Until recently it was illegal in Michigan to bait deer during firearm season or to use raised platforms. The first was deemed as unfair to the hunt, and the second as dangerous when combined with a rifle. However, both are now legal, and every year hunters are killed by their own firearms as they climb up or down from their blinds. It is this season that I will write about. The third season starts when firearm season ends on November 30 and musket season begins. Fewer men are involved with this sport nowadays as men are more enamored of the semi-automatic weapons, but some purist hunters enjoy using the muskets, which are one-shot weapons requiring refilling of shot and powder each firing.

One of the tests of my courtship with my husband (at least that was how I saw it at the time) was to go to the farm for opening day of deer season. Before the expressway was built, the trip from Grand Rapids to the farm took over two hours on a two-lane secondary road that passed through countryside and numerous small farming communities. In the fall, it is a beautiful drive as the colors change, but by November, most of the color is gone, and the landscape is brown and stark. We arrived at the small farm-house early on November 14, the day prior to opening day, armed with a shotgun, sleeping bags, and a pile of orange clothing, as well as heavy socks, hats, and gloves. As a city girl who avoids cold weather at all costs, this all looked very ominous. The farmhouse, described in the preface, was very austere, with tar-paper shingles and an outdoor well. I had been to the house before, but it had been in the summer, and I had enjoyed the lake and hiking on their two 40-acre fields. It had seemed such a quaint town—existing in time somewhere between the Wild West and the Great Depression. Now, in winter, the kitchen was toasty warm from the wood stove that sat against the far wall. Grandpa Earl sat where he always sat—in an overstuffed chair near the fire. Grandma Cleva bustled in the kitchen as always, preparing food for the small army that was invading her home. Away from the kitchen, in the living room and upstairs bedrooms, the temperature dropped precipitously. Wind blew through ancient windows covered several years previously with plastic, now ripped and yellowed. We claimed our lower-status place on the floor of the upstairs attic, the parents and aunts and uncles having claim to the beds, and spread out our sleeping bags and collected any blankets we could find to make the night more comfortable.

By suppertime the family had all arrived: LaVail's parents and his younger sisters, two sets of aunts and uncles, and many cousins. On other occasions, there were others who would come, other shirttail relatives or friends of the family. Seeing so many guns in one place was unnerving as the ritual preparations began. Discussions about which gun one was to use—the pros and cons of the rifle versus the shotgun, the .45 or the aught-six. Once the weaponry had been decided upon, the next discussion focused on where everyone was going to sit. As patriarch, Grandpa Earl liked to designate who got the prime spots, and stories always ensued about where the best spots were, where deer had been spotted. It was soon decided who was going to get to sit on the west hill and who would be down by the stream. After a supper of fried pork and potatoes, everyone brought out the beer and the whisky offering to Grandpa Earl, and the stories began: about LaVail's first kill, encounters with deer and other wildlife, comparing the racks of the deer that had been killed by adults and cousins alike; stories of past trans-gressions, such as shining deer, illegal prior to opening day. At that time, I had a sense that these stories had been told before, and I was proved right in future years as I continued to participate in the opening-day eve's activities, but I ceased participating in the actual hunt. The same stories, duly embel-lished, have been passed down from year to year, generation to generation, and of course are amended each year as younger cousins reach the age when they can hunt for the first time.

Before dawn the next morning, I was awakened by the smell of bacon and the bustling of people as they took turns in the icy cold bathroom. Grandma Cleva prepared breakfast as everyone dressed. There was an elec-tric spark of excitement in the air as all the hunters anticipated their future success. Reluctantly, I donned the layers of thermal underwear, jeans, snow pants, and orange coveralls. Leaving the breakfast mess to Grandma, we filled thermoses and flasks with coffee and other warming liquids, and with the guns and ammunition, we all climbed into three pickup trucks and took off in the dark. Parking on the dirt road at the edge of the 40 acres where the family hunted, we trudged inland to the hunting land. Everyone grumbled because the orange plastic overalls I wore over my many layers of clothes rubbed together as I walked, making an annoying and deer-alerting crackle with each step. Finally, everyone settled into their assigned spots, separating at the top of hill, waiting for the dawn, and hoping. . . .

LaVail and I settled under a pine tree, where I immediately fell asleep—the story that has evolved about my first hunting experience was that I had drunk the warming liquid instead of the coffee and had been in a stupor for the entire time. I can neither deny nor confirm this accusation, because I don't really remember it. I do know that I did not see any deer on that first hunt, though I did on later excursions, and we see them every evening from our back porch.

Several hours after my limbs had become numb from the cold, with the sun high in the sky, the hunters returned to the house. I think that one of the uncles had killed a deer, and perhaps one of the cousins had killed one. Upon returning, Grandpa Earl was excited to hear the stories and examine the kill. Because of his age and disability, he had a special license from the state that allowed him to hunt on his tractor. Otherwise, this is against the law. So, his custom was to take his tractor to the edge of the 40 acres and hunt there. He was home long before the hunters regrouped for another hot meal and coffee. The deer were hung in the barn for all to admire, and after dinner (the afternoon meal is called dinner), some of the hunters went back out for another try. It is important to note here that it was not only the men who hunted. LaVail's mother and aunt also hunted. I was the only one who tagged along for the ride.

Over the years, after Grandma and Grandpa moved to Big Rapids, the farmhouse became dilapidated, and no one lived in it after them. LaVail's parents built a retirement house on the corner, and it is in this house that we lived when we returned from the Micronesian Islands. We now own both of the 40-acre parcels, the farm 40 and the hunting 40, and it is to our house that relatives still come to hunt; however, over the years, the group has become smaller.

At first, the aura of the earlier years continued in our house, as everyone came, found a sleeping spot, and used our house as their base of operations. For my husband and his cousins, their first deer hunt was a rite of passage. Now, the small group of hunters includes two of LaVail's nephews who are very successful bow and rifle hunters. Their great-grandfather would be very proud of them. They are continuing the family custom of hunting. Unfortunately, they are too young to have experienced that strong sense of belonging and the family bonding that accompanied the family deer-hunting ritual.

I never learned to hunt, and despite many efforts on my husband's part, I have not learned how to shoot a gun. Nor did any of our children inherit the interest in hunting, though our two oldest accompanied their grandfather, grandmother, and father on opening day from time to time. Stories now include the attempt of our daughter (a vegetarian at the time) to distract her grandmother when she saw a deer in the distance, and how our son fell asleep reading his book under the same pine tree where I had slept, and how his uncles, from their spot on the hill, saw a deer walk up to within two feet of him. The uncles had to decide whether or not they could get the deer and miss the kid.

In Mecosta County and elsewhere, there are deer sanctuaries where deer are raised for their antlers. Hunters pay thousands of dollars to hunt in the enclosed preserve for a guaranteed "rack." Despite this cynical form of hunting, it is important to remember that for many local families, venison and other wild game and fish are the basis for their annual meat supply. It is not a matter of getting a trophy deer, but a matter of having meat for the winter.

Other Rites and Events

One of the important things I learned when we moved to Chippewa Lake was the intensity of the intersecting networks. In many American suburban communities, there are few relationships that go beyond the household. Neighbors are not often invited to family rites of passage. In contrast, special events in rural communities are shared by a wide net of family and friends. Circles of neighbors or friends tied together by specific interests, such as horses in our case, will meet each other again and again at weddings, baby showers, and graduations.

High school graduations are important events, especially in the near past when few local students went on to college. Graduation receptions are usually held at home, if the yard is large, or in the community building for especially large families. Outdoor open houses will often have tents set up in case of rain, or sometimes the host family will clean the garage and set it up for the drinks. This prime location is where most of the men will sit, while the women and children will congregate in the yard, under the tent, or move to the inside of the house. Invitations to the open house are enclosed with graduation announcements and include not only family and close family friends, but the parents of the graduate's friends, neighbors, and even favorite teachers.

Members of the extended family assist in food preparation for huge crowds who come during the specified time, usually three hours. Families whose own child is graduating will get numerous open house invitations, and entire weekends can be spent going from open house to open house around the widely dispersed school district. Open houses are usually held on the weekends just before or after the actual graduation, spreading over Memorial Day weekend and into June. Graduation Day is reserved for families.

Most people give monetary gifts to the students, and this can amount to a considerable sum, considering the economic level of the community.

Likewise, weddings are usually local events, with receptions often taking place in the community building or under huge tents on family farms. Again, women take charge of the food production, distributing the responsibilities of the buffet choices. Like graduations, weddings bring people together from the entire community and beyond. Nevertheless, as young people move away and the practice of endogamy wanes, it is less likely that weddings are localized. Many young couples marry in the cities or in the hometowns of the bride. Fewer local families attend, because of inconvenience or unfamiliarity with the location, reluctance to travel to cities, and inability to rent hotel rooms overnight.

The continuation of family events is one of the most critical elements of shaping and reproducing a common identity. This is perhaps the greatest indicator of the shift in a shared community that I discovered. While these familial and kinship links draw the community together in multi-stranded relationships, they also serve as barriers to acceptance of newcomers and retirees. Surveys indicated that although 85 percent of township residents had family living in the immediate area, village and lake residents were least likely to have family living in the area (44 percent and 42 percent respectively). Thus, retirees and other newly arrived lake and village residents are not invited to those events that connect and crosscut already existing ties and might ultimately link them to local families. Until these residents cross that invisible barrier from "outsider" to "insider" through avenues of participation or friendship, they will remain on the margins of the community—living parallel lives, but disconnected from the activities that bind the members of the community together.

CONCLUSION

We have seen how Chippewa Lake, a village that seems "dead" from the outside, is enmeshed in webs of activity, both cyclical and spontaneous, that connect families in a complex network of relationships. Families participate in these activities based on a myriad of individual and familial factors: age, stage in life cycle, occupation, gender, and place and length of residence. At the same time, we can glimpse the barriers that segregate residents and serve to reinforce those stereotypes that form when rural and urban meet.

The lack of kinship ties that link newcomer families in everyday events is the most disturbing discovery of the research. Without a worldview that values joining in group goals and participating in the daily routine of life, a community splits along discernable lines, forming crevices between the newcomers and the longtime residents. This rift further prevents communication and cooperation necessary for the development of a re-created identity that takes the best from the old and the new and fosters a new community. In the next chapter, we will look at the impediments to such a re-created community as well as the possibilities for such a re-creation to occur.

CHAPTER 9

Social Networks beyond the Community

> *I started in 4-H when I was seven years old and I am still involved. I am the sewing leader and our kids have been involved in 4-H since they were little. Erica and Aaron would get up at 6:00 every morning to take care of their animals before school and then they did their sports after school. When they got home, they tended to the animals again. The animals always ate before the kids did. I am a strong supporter of 4-H because it keeps kids busy and teaches them responsibility.*

—SALLY JO EATON, CHIPPEWA LAKE, 2005

INCREASINGLY, RESIDENTS OF CHIPPEWA TOWNSHIP REACH BEYOND their immediate community. In many cases, the extension of local boundaries is forced upon them because of the consolidated schools and the need to seek jobs beyond the township and county. However, in some cases, residents seek social interactions that take them to surrounding towns and cities: shopping, volunteering, and searching for spiritual guidance beyond the local church. In this chapter we will look beyond Chippewa Township and trace the extended social networks that are shaping a more inclusive community identity. Then, we will examine those who are more likely to participate in volunteer organizations within and beyond the community.

ROLE OF CONSOLIDATED SCHOOLS
IN INTER-COMMUNITY NETWORKS

In the early days of the township, and indeed, in all communities, the school represented a source of local pride and community identity. In the 1800s, Chippewa Township had five one-room schoolhouses, each associated with a district of the township. To commemorate the early settlers, these schools were named after early residents in each district: Sparks, Johnson, Eaton, Tallman, and Brigham.[1] There are many stories about these schoolhouses, some of which were actually located in people's houses: the young mother/teacher moved the beds aside each morning to make room for the tables and chairs used by her students. One family told me how one of their ancestors, a young girl at the time, was paid to go to the school early and start the fire in the fireplace.

These one-room schoolhouses were used until the 1930s, though they served students until junior high school in later years. A high school was built in Barryton, eight miles away, and students from the small schools in Chippewa and Fork Townships met there to complete their high school education. At one point, this school burned down, and a new one was built. The Barryton school is currently one of the elementary schools that feeds into the large consolidated high school in Remus, another ten miles from Barryton, and twenty to twenty-five miles from the Chippewa Lake area.

The Chippewa Hills School District, formed in 1967, is the second largest in the state in area, encompassing 387 square miles, seventeen townships, seven villages and towns, and sections of three counties: Mecosta, Osceola, and Isabella.[2] The bus system covers 2,750 miles per day, transporting 2,300 of the 2,700 total students from their homes to the numerous elementary schools, the middle school, and the high school. With the exception of an affluent resort community in the southwestern region of the school district, most of the students live in working, lower- to middle-class families. Using the state criteria, 56 percent of the student population are considered socioeconomically disadvantaged, compared to 34.7 percent of students statewide. The student population is not ethnically diverse. In 2005, only 10 percent of the population identified with a racial or ethnic group; 7 percent of these students claimed Native American ethnicity, and 2 percent claimed African American ethnicity.[3]

While the consolidated school district allows students from rural areas to have access to affordable education, the location of the high school twenty miles away results in a loss of the school as a local focal point of activity. In a sense, the local elementary schools have allowed families to maintain proximity to school for their young children, and many parents are active in local elementary school activities, through volunteering and participating in school events. In fact, several recent suggestions that local elementary schools be closed or incorporated with other elementary schools at the central location of the high school have met with fierce resistance. Families desperately want their local schools, especially those families who live in communities where these schools reside: Barryton, Remus, Mecosta, and Weidman.

Despite the fact that the Chippewa Hills School District is not an affluent district, it has developed several valuable programs that have benefited its students. The first is a first-rate music program, both orchestra and band, that has opened many doors for students—either professionally, or to broaden their perspectives. The junior-high and high-school orchestras have received many firsts in state competitions. Like all schools, Chippewa Hills has a marching band that competes statewide. As parents of children who all participated in orchestra and/or band, I was always impressed by the extraordinary parental support of music in the school district. Concerts were always performed to full houses and had to be held in the discomfort of the gymnasium, instead of the inadequate auditorium.

Sports have always been important to rural schools, and in many communities, sports events provide an important social focus for the community. Chippewa Hills is no exception. Though Chippewa Hills does not produce championship teams, attendance at football and basketball games is an important way to socialize with neighbors and friends. Our children were more musically inclined than sports inclined, so we attended the home games to watch the half-time entertainment. It was always my contention that football was what they did before and after the marching band performed.

Though there is a strong commitment to education in the community generally, the lack of a local school has had an impact on participation of the general public at events. In many small towns, local sports events offer an opportunity for all residents to congregate, and the team spirit and town rivalries go beyond the athletes and their families. Teams represent towns. In large consolidated school districts, the link between the team and the town is weak, and with the possible exception of football, few people drive from their small towns to the sports events as a source of entertainment. Sports events and concerts, though well attended, are attended primarily by parents and grandparents, not the community at large. Attendance at any event requires driving long distances on country roads. No one lives within walking distance of the high school and new middle school, though a few families live on the same country road. This affects the desire and ability for the community at large to take advantage of the performances and athletic events that might otherwise serve to reinforce those multi-stranded relationships.

SOCIAL NETWORKS BEYOND THE COMMUNITY

Participation in intracommunity organizations builds networks that reinforce social ties, as we have seen. However, not all families are involved in these local organizations. Families are linked to others beyond the immediate community in a variety of organizations and institutions that are based on special interests and/or stages in the life cycle. The unique location of Chippewa Township, in the midst of larger villages and towns, and within the economic and political orbit of Big Rapids, influences this expanded sense of community. Chippewa Lake is not large enough to act as a centralized core for the region. Rather, local residents are drawn in all directions to larger and more active communities. Two regional organizations illustrate this centripetal force that draws people from the community outward, instead of inward.

4-H and the County Fair

One of these centripetal forces is 4-H. The 4-H organization is part of the Michigan State University Extension Service, and it is organized locally through various counties that sponsor individual clubs and the county fairs. Young people join 4-H groups according to their interests and residence. 4-H clubs form around different animals and crafts, so young people interested in horses, rabbits, or cattle will look for the group closest to them, or the group where they have friends or family already involved. Beyond this, many families choose to participate in the Osceola County Fair instead of in Mecosta County because they feel that their children have a greater likelihood of being competitive in the smaller county fair than in the larger, more competitive Mecosta County Fair. Within our community, there are various 4-H groups that crosscut school districts and counties.

As might be expected, township residents were more likely than lake or village residents to be involved in 4-H. Of twenty-seven township families, sixteen, or 59 percent, were involved in 4-H; in two cases the parents had also been involved in 4-H as children. The lake residents were second most likely to be involved in 4-H. Some of these were the children of families whose farms are located on the lake, or those who moved from farms to the lake after retirement. The village had the least participation, with only one child and one adult being involved.

Those who are involved in 4-H are committed to the values and skills that young people learn. One leader, whose third child was in her last year of eligibility for 4-H, is passionate about the values of the program. Young people, according to this mother-leader, have a commitment to their animals. Members must attend meetings and learn proper feeding and techniques for keeping their animals healthy. They learn record keeping, and also competitiveness when they take their animals to fair. This sense of responsibility follows with them in whatever they do as adults.

The Mecosta County Fair is held the week after the Fourth of July, and is a time of excitement for all the farming families in the area. As mentioned earlier, Mecosta County covers a large area, including five large population centers—Big Rapids, Barryton, Remus, Mecosta, and the Morley-Stanwood area—and three school districts: Big Rapids, Chippewa Hills and Morley-Stanwood. The Osceola County Fair is later in the summer.

The Mecosta County Fairgrounds, located north of Big Rapids, has an organizing board that plans the fair and maintains the buildings and equipment. Many 4-H groups participate in various livestock categories: pigs, sheep, rabbits, cattle, goats, chickens, and horses, as well as a variety of homemaking and craft categories: canning, baking, arts and crafts. My children were primarily involved with horses, though my sons were involved with rabbits for several years. The horse competitions are judged by professionals who evaluate the riders in many categories: fitting and showing, English and Western riding, trail, and speed. Individual riders are all members of a 4-H team, and riders are earning both individual ribbons and points for their teams.

All 4-H participants keep a record of their animals' upkeep, cost of food, inoculations, care of hooves, etc., and submit this to the 4-H committee on the first day of the fair. Every day there are scheduled competitions. The horse competitions are the most obvious as they take place in an outdoor arena. Horse trailers and stock trailers fill a large area of the parking grounds, and some participants, those who come from other communities, pitch tents or live in their horse trailers and spend the week at the fair. Others leave their horses but come in every day to participate and take care of the animals.

Each 4-H group has a schedule for individual participation: cleaning the stalls, feeding the animals, and staying in the barn (called barn duty) to watch the animals and protect them from the public, and vice versa. Keeping curious children's fingers out of the horses' mouths can be a full-time job. In addition, groups are assigned duties regarding the entire barn. Each day, one 4-H group is assigned to keep the barn walkway clean, picking up trash and raking the sawdust and keeping an eye on all the horses, not only those of their own group. Each night, a group is designated as night watchmen, spending the night in the barns to protect the animals from trespassers and to watch the horses in case they get ill or entangled in tack (harnesses, ropes, etc.). This is important, as there are activities going on all evening at the fair: the carnival and various concerts and performances on the racetrack. After these events and after closing, many young people think that it is fun to wander through the livestock barns, drinking, smoking cigarettes, and scaring the animals.

This same type of routine is set up for all of the livestock at the fair. Being in 4-H is an obligation, not only for the kids but also for their parents. When children are young, the parents are active participants in these chores, helping and teaching their kids how to feed and water the horses and keep their areas clean. It is also mothers who are the primary participants, both as leaders and as parental assistants. As the children reach their teens, and especially when they can drive, they take over many of the responsibilities and do not need (or really want) the parents to be around all the time—especially for night duty, which is a kind of rite of passage for teen participants, as it requires vigilance to protect thousands of dollars worth of horseflesh and tack.

For the other livestock, participants learn how to care for their animals, train them to perform certain skills, and then give demonstrations to the judges and audiences. The sheep, pigs, and cattle are sold at the auction, and the participant can earn good money by raising a well-developed animal. Local participants, individuals, restaurants, grocery stores, and business people will purchase the animals, getting their names in the paper for contributing to 4-H. Many of these individuals will donate the animal back to 4-H so it can be resold. Somehow, young people learn to accept the fact that the animal that they named, loved, and cared for will be sold at the local IGA or served as hamburger at a local restaurant.

Besides the livestock, there are many 4-H groups that also teach young people a wide variety of skills, such as gardening, quilting and other traditional arts, painting, photography, preserving produce, and baking. 4-H brings young people together in a spirit of competition, but also of cooperation. In the horse community, the young people involved in 4-H know each other from school, and some as members of high school equestrian teams. Big Rapids, Morley-Stanwood, and Chippewa Hills all have equestrian teams, and it is very possible that two people from the same 4-H group will compete against each other in equestrian. Because of these crosscutting networks, however, they all know each other well, and also know everyone's horses.

The participants know all of the horses' strengths and weaknesses, as well as the strengths and weaknesses of their competitors—who is proficient in English riding or fitting and showing. And this is the source of some of the more negative aspects of the competition. Not all horses are created equal, nor are all riders, but certain circumstances are certain to result in envy and critique. Some families who have established farms and long traditions of raising horses are able to purchase or obtain quality breeds for their children—Arabians, Morgans, and other purebred horses; others have standard breeds or "mutts," and these horses compete against each other.

It is unclear to what extent judges count or discount the breed of the horses, but there are always perceptions that a certain judge "loves Arabs" or "hates Appaloosas." Some young people also have, or are rumored to have, professionally trained horses, while most kids and/or their parents train their own horses by working them every day. Professional training is perceived as unfair, and some young people who are suspected or known to have these advantages are often accused, fairly or unfairly, of not having earned their blue ribbons by hard work, but because they had "push-button" horses. These riders may bask in the glory of many blue ribbons, but they are often the focus of backhanded gossip, as their competitors feel disadvantaged in the arena. These accusations reflect the differences between families who raise and breed horses—those families whose children were raised on horseback and in horse barns, and those whose horses are hobbies.

Criticisms and jealousies pertaining to horses are likely to be diluted if the horse family and the young people follow the customs of 4-H—that is, if they are friendly and willing to help out. Families that keep to themselves, and whose children don't feel that they need to do the "dirty work" of 4-H will get a bad reputation that will follow them to equestrian team and put them at the margins of the group. However, good riders with expensive horses are forgiven if they are generous with their time and share responsibilities and tack.

One of the features of the 4-H and equestrian programs is the sharing of time and tack. If someone's bridle breaks just before an event, everyone scurries to find another; this idea of sharing also crosscuts groups. Friends in another 4-H group will also help out—find a clean shirt, help clean a horse that decided to roll in the mud just before fitting and showing, and lend a shoulder when disappointment is overwhelming. The good rider who is charitable with her advice and tack is forgiven her advantages, as she displays generosity and acts as a team member, and not an individual out for her own fame.

Parents are also part of this sharing network. Mothers will grab a rider and horse out of line and rub a cleaning rag (always present in a back pocket) over a competitor's dusty boot, or straighten a saddle or a pant leg. Because the mothers (and often fathers) know most of the participants from 4-H and other school activities, there is a feeling of engagement in all of the competitions, even when one's own child is not participating in an event. There is disappointment if someone's horse "acts like an idiot" in fitting and showing, or "drops his lead" on a turn. After an event, winners console losers, and mothers complement all riders as they exit the arena. Again, those parents who don't display these generalized supportive behaviors are also marginalized by the group.

One more comment about horses, if I may. I have often referred to horse riders as "she." It is my experience in 4-H as well as equestrian team that the sport is dominated by young women. Even at the state finals, which I attended three times in the four years our daughter participated, it is clear that girls and horses "have a thing." It is also clear that certain events are gender-specific. Females participate in all areas of the sport: fitting and showing, English and Western riding, speed, and trail. Males are more likely to participate in Western riding and speed. Most clubs have rules that riders cannot participate in only one event; for example, a young man cannot only do speed events. Thus young men do participate in riding classes, jumping, and trail, but they dominate in speed events in the same way that females dominate in fitting and showing.

Speed is always the last event (called classes) and the most exciting, as these events earn group points that pit club against club. Events include barrels, cloverleaf, and flag. These are entertaining to watch, but they can be very dangerous if one's horse decides not to stop, or stops suddenly, throwing the rider over the gate. For speed events, unlike other classes, riders are allowed to decorate their horses, as long as safety is not compromised (for example, the horse's vision impaired).

At equestrian team events, especially the state finals, this is very exhilarating. Riders and horses are decorated in school colors—horses are spray-painted with school initials and other phrases that identify the qualities of the horse or rider. The competitors wear bright outfits, crisp jeans, colorful shirts, and cowboy hats that rarely stay on for more than one to two seconds. Horses' saddles are highly polished and adorned in bright silver trim that is not allowed in regular classes. As the riders swoop into the arena, the audience responds with whoops and hollers for the competitor.

The audience cheers with each successful run, and groans with each barrel knocked over or flag dropped.

State equestrian competitions are held yearly in Lansing or Detroit, and top teams from all over the state meet for a three-day competition. Teams are ranked according to the size of their schools. Because the Mecosta County schools have different rankings, it is possible that two teams will attend the state competition, and this heightens the excitement of the venture as students and their families pack up horses, tack, hay, and feed and trek across state with horse trailers attached to pickup trucks. This event pits local riders against riders from all over the state, encouraging both cooperation between previously competing local schools, and animosity, based on envy of the beautiful horses ridden by riders from affluent "down-state" school districts. Here, when a Mecosta County team wins a first, second, or third, all students rejoice—not unlike a tribal segmentary lineage cooperating to engage in warfare against a distant enemy. After three days of exhaustion, horses are piled back into horse trailers, and frazzled parents, children, and horses return home, hopefully with individual and team ribbons to display.

Mecosta County Commission on Aging

Another organization that pulls people from around the county is the new senior center. The Mecosta County Commission on Aging (MCCOA) is a very active organization that operates out of Big Rapids. Several years ago, they decided to build a new senior center, and instead of locating the center in Big Rapids, they built it on the east side of the county, where it would be accessible to the numerous rural communities where many of the county seniors live. This was an enlightened decision, one that surprised many who had assumed that Big Rapids would house the center, thus further reinforcing the urban-rural animosities that exist. The building is located conveniently to Mecosta and Remus, and within twenty minutes of Canadian Lakes, Barryton, and Chippewa Lake. It is approximately a thirty-minute drive from Big Rapids. The center sponsors many events, serves meals, and offers classes in various crafts. The organization also provides numerous volunteers who assist with driving people to appointments, delivering food, and helping out with housework and other activities.

The unintended consequence of this new building to Chippewa Lake is interesting, and did not occur to me until I talked to several seniors in the community. The Chippewa/Martiny Seniors' Group was very active for many years, sponsoring local activities and being an integral part of the fund-raising activities for the community building. When the senior center was built, many seniors began to be active there instead, participating in events or volunteering to help others. The focus of the local group shifted from Chippewa-Martiny Townships to the new center. Unfortunately, some of the seniors, who lacked transportation or motivation to become involved outside the community, felt marginalized, and the local, informal organization dissolved.

Some seniors have remained active in the community by joining other organizations or putting their efforts into the church; others, like Evelyn Nott, the official caller, remained active by volunteering for special events or activities. However, it remains important that the consolidation of the senior services has dispersed this potentially powerful group of citizens— those who volunteer and are often the backbone of local participation.

Informal Events that Link Families and the Larger Community

There are many rural events that draw people from various communities to one place. The first and most open of these is the farm auction. Auctions are advertised by means of flyers and ads in the community newspapers. They draw many people, farmers and nonfarmers, to look over the merchandise and bid on desired items. When one does the auction circuit, one sees the same group of people all the time, as well as others who are drawn by proximity or because of specific items being auctioned. There is a casual banter as attendees walk through the merchandise before the sale. Furniture, large and small appliances, antique furniture, and knick-knacks and linens are displayed outside the house and barn. Household and other items are displayed on wooden doors or pieces of plywood spread over sawhorses. Women tend to congregate in this area of the auction, fingering the household goods and examining the antique furniture and Depression glass. Men congregate around the barn or garage area where the tools and heavy equipment are displayed—old tractors, farming equipment, the accumulation of many years of farming and caring for machinery.

Before the auction starts, people have in mind what they want to bid on, and often have set a limit on what they are willing to spend. To be eligible to bid, each bidder or couple requests a number that is printed on a long, narrow piece of stiff paper. The auctioneer's assistant (often wife or grown child in training) will take the name and address down; this person is in charge of writing down all the items as they are sold, and assigning the number of the person who won the bid and the amount of the bid. After the auction, people settle their debts with the auctioneer's assistant and take their merchandise. The auctioneer has nothing to do with the signing up of the bidders or collecting the money.

There is a lot of trust involved in this process, as people will stack their purchases together in a chosen location until the end of the auction, since it is likely that their trucks are parked up the country road, perhaps a half mile away. People trust others not to take their purchases while they are bidding on other things. It would be very easy for someone to walk away with another's purchases in the confusion, but I have never heard of this happening. For his part, the auctioneer must trust that people don't leave without paying, and that their checks are good. The fact that the auctioneer and customer may know each other will lessen the temptation to steal from others or skip out on the bill.

There are a limited number of auctioneers in the region, most of whom are local to the Mecosta County area. Because the audience and the auctioneer often know each other, the mood at actions is often amiable. There is a lot of jostling and snickering when someone wins the bid: "Now what does Joe want with *that*?" In contrast, sighs of disappointment and awe go through the crowd as a much-coveted item, such as an antique secretary or collector's piece, is purchased for a large sum of money. When the auctioneer cannot get an opening bid on a junk box or dilapidated lamp, he will often improvise and point to someone he knows in the audience and say, "One dollar starting bid to Bob—thanks Bob." Bob looks up in confusion as he realizes what has happened, and those around him tease him for bidding on such a hopeless collection of stuff. Bob only hopes that someone is willing to outbid him, and someone almost always does.

One has to be very patient and persistent at an auction. It is not an event for the faint of heart, especially if one is interested in the large items, such as furniture and farm equipment, for those items are auctioned off last. To get to the valuable and highly valued items, one must wait through the knickknacks, linens, plastic dishes, broken lamps and toasters, and the mysterious junk boxes. By the time the furniture is auctioned off, many people have given up and gone home, especially if it is a bad day, rainy or cold. The psychology of auction sales is that people will stay for the furniture if they really want it, whereas if they auction off the junk boxes last, no one will be left to bid, and the family will not get a good price for their goods, or will be stuck with them.

The most common reason for auctions today is the death of the patriarch of the farming family, or when the husband and/or wife are moved to an adult child's home or nursing home. If the matriarch is still alive, she may sell off the farm and move in with a child, though sometimes women will stay on the farm and sell it on their own when they are ready, or when they know that their children are not interested in taking it over. Few retirees can afford to maintain a nonworking farm and pay the taxes and utilities.

Many farmers and those who raise horses also attend the various horse auctions. One must travel greater distances to these events, as they are conducted in several centralized locations at designated times. The closest horse auction to Chippewa Lake is in Marion, a small town at the northern edge of Osceola County. There are other auctions in Lake County, and some in southern counties where serious farmers and horse people buy and sell livestock. Unlike the farm auctions, these are much more formal, and without the banter. Buying animals is serious business. The livestock auctions are located in large barns at county fairgrounds. Animals are displayed in stalls, and people are free to walk around and look at the animals before the auction. This atmosphere is very lively. Farmers in bib overalls and John Deere caps; men and women in jeans, boots, and cowboy hats; young families seeking horses for their children; Amish fathers and sons—all seeking that perfect animal: the diamond in the haystack, to mix a metaphor.

The owners of the animals are there to answer questions and tell or disclose why the animal is for sale. There is a lot of spin (dissembling) involved here, as good animals are seldom brought to sale. People prefer to sell their animals, especially horses, on their own, where they can get better prices and be assured that the horse goes to a good family. The horses that are brought to sale are often old or lame, or unruly. Sellers are very crafty in describing their horses—"spirited" can designate "mean" or untrainable. Buyers need to be very careful and knowledgeable about horses, examining them carefully before bidding. Not all animals brought to auction are on their last feeble legs. Other animals, such as calves or sheep, are sold for a variety of reasons—to cull the herd, sell excess bulls, etc. But it is always important to know your breeds and have a working knowledge of livestock.

The auctions themselves are intriguing, and even one who attends with no intention of purchasing finds one or two animals that she would love to rescue and take home. People obtain bidding numbers as in the farm auctions, but there is little of the banter among the buyers or between auctioneer and buyers. Buyers sit in bleachers or stand along the rail to watch the animals as they are brought into the arena. The auctioneer describes the animal, its age, breed, history, weaknesses, and other pertinent information. Sellers will often have their children show the animals around the ring, as they evoke a sympathetic emotion in the buyers—poor little boy who has to sell his lamb. For horses, it is very common to have young women ride the horses, again to display the easygoing personality of the horse. What is not always known is that these young people who ride the horses are experienced riders, unlike the youngster who is looking for his or her first 4 H horse.

Some farmers, like the Amish, attend auctions regularly, bringing live-stock for sale and buying others. Some make a business of buying animals, feeding them or giving them some training and returning them for sale, but these are serious dealers—the faint of heart or the inexperienced buyer/trader is very vulnerable here.

PARTICIPATION

In the past, mutual assistance and a cooperative spirit were imperative in the success of families and the community as a whole. When I initiated this research, I believed that wage labor and a commuter population would result in a decrease in participation and the community ethic. Instead, I have discovered that the issue is more complex than I imagined. Several factors that I thought would be critical indicators of participation—such as commuting distance, occupation, and education—proved to be of questionable importance. I found that participation is related more to age, gender, and life stages than to economic factors. My survey of fifty-five families indicated that the participation rates were similar for farm and nonfarm families. Overall, 42 percent of our sample (farm, dual-income, and nonfarm) claimed membership or involvement in one or more social organizations. In general, farm families had a higher participation rate than nonfarm ; longtime residents (over sixteen years) had higher rates than more recent residents; older residents (over thirty-five years old) had higher participation than younger; and lake residents had lower participation rates than township or village residents. This last finding conforms to the concerns and tensions expressed at the "Meet the Candidates Night" episode.

Participation in social groups, instead of being related specifically to occupation, is more profitably seen as a function of work schedules, shared interests, stage in the life cycle, and gender, as our examples have shown. Let's look at some of these indicators and examine how they relate (or don't relate) to participation.

Occupation and Work Schedules

When I started attending the meetings of the Young Women's Club, I asked my neighbor Claudia, a hard-working dairy farmer, if she was a member of any of the local groups. She gave me a snort and a laugh. "I don't have time to go and drink coffee—I have too much to do here." And it was true.

She and her husband ran a dairy farm, and at that time their two children were too young to be much help. Twice a day, Claudia worked the milking machines for all of their cows. Her husband worked in the fields, planting and harvesting the food grains, storing them, cutting and storing hay, and caring for the herd in general.

From Claudia's statement, I assumed that most farm women did not participate in social activities, but I have learned differently. Most of the women in the Emerald Lake Birthday Club are farm women, or women whose husbands do part-time farming. The differences in these families and their participation in social activities are complex but related to various factors, including personality. In several of the families whose women participate in the Emerald Lake Birthday Club, the women were part of large extended families where the farm chores were spread among various brothers and others while the women's responsibilities were centered in the home. These women enjoyed baking and quilting, and joining a club allowed them to extend their interests and their domestic skills beyond the home and into the social arena. Quilting allowed women to share an activity and socialize at the same time. This pattern fits the category of wife as supportive homemaker, though I do not want to understate the contributions that these women make to the success of the farm.

In contrast, the two Miller families are independent units residing two miles apart but separated by a long-term feud. Instead of providing mutual assistance, they each maintain separate dairy farms, relying on their children and their hard-working wives to keep the farm going. Today, in both families, the adult sons help their parents on the farm, but none of them are interested in taking over, and all have jobs away from the farm. Neither Judy nor Claudia has time to attend meetings or quilting clubs. Judy and Claudia's spare time has always been spent running errands for the farm, hauling hay, caring for the cows, and maintaining the milking equipment. Judy and Claudia both clearly represent the farming-partner model described by Pearson.[4]

Yet, I have also learned that both Claudia and Judy, though they aren't members of the Young Women's Club or the Merry Circle, were involved in other activities with their children. Their children were active in 4-H and always had animals in the county fair. Judy's husband, Raymond, was a volunteer firefighter for many years, and both of his sons contribute their services to the fire department today. Until Judy's struggle with Alzheimer's Disease began, she was always very generous about providing food for funeral dinners or benefit suppers.

Once again, these conversations forced me to look beyond my urban conception of "participation" that is defined in terms of observable contributions, such as membership in local and regional organizations. Nonfarm families are more likely to join the service organizations, such as the Lions Club, Young Women's Group, and Merry Circle, that require attendance at meetings and regular participation in local events. In contrast, farm women make contributions that are also invisible to outsiders, especially those who do not participate in 4-H or see the hands that have prepared the food that fills potluck tables. Although they are not at the planning meetings, they are on that long list of people that Evelyn or someone else calls for funerals, dinners, and benefits.

I had also assumed that commuters would be less likely to participate than those who worked near the village, but the findings were surprising. While I found that those individuals who commuted more than twenty-five miles each way to work had the lowest participation rate (22 percent), I also discovered that those who commuted eleven to twenty-five miles each way (equivalent to the distance to Big Rapids or Evart) had the highest participation rate (50 percent). Of those who commuted fewer than eleven miles, 39 percent claimed participation in at least one organization. Clearly these findings indicate that commuting distance is not the primary variable in the decision to participate in local organizations. Instead, the strongest indicator in participation is residence. Once again confirming the local perceptions, fewer lake residents participate in local organizations (44 percent for township and village residents compared to 37 percent of lake residents). Nevertheless, this means that one-third of lake residents *do* participate in at least one organization.

Age

Data indicate that there is an informal age segregation in membership in particular groups. The Young Women's Group actually had few members in their twenties. When I was part of the group, it was comprised primarily of women between thirty and forty, with a few in their late twenties. Today, with several exceptions, the young women are actually young—predominantly in their mid to late twenties. In the past, the Merry Circle attracted middle-aged women who were likely to be grandmothers, as does the Emerald Lake Birthday Club. One of the younger members of the Birthday Club complained that the group was dominated by elderly women who had set ideas about what the club should do—after all, their mothers had been members, and the tradition of the group passed from mother to daughter. The younger member joked about how rigid the other members were regarding benefit potlucks. They had a certain idea of what foods were acceptable; "new" or "unusual" dishes were looked upon with suspicion. One young woman joked, "They always want the same thing—baked beans, scalloped potatoes or potato salad, rolls, and Jello salads . . . and you are expected to know the proper quantity, because if you bring too small of a bowl, you are criticized."

The Lions Club attracts middle-aged couples who are well established in the community, as does the Community Building Board—though, as we will see, these two organizations have a history of tension and don't usually have interlocking memberships. In fact, data on participation indicate that older residents have higher rates of participation. This supports the likelihood that membership is also affected by stage in the life cycle, as it is everywhere. Young women with children are more involved in school activities than with social activities. When the last child starts school, women have more freedom to participate in community activities and begin to involve themselves, if their labor is not required on the farm or they don't have other income-generating obligations. Likewise, men will join organizations according to the demands of their jobs and families. When women and men retire, they have more time to become involved and are more interested in activities beyond their families.

Conflicts do exist between the generations, however, as some young women have argued. Some women who would like to be more active find that they are not accepted into the gerontocracy. Membership is sometimes by invitation, especially to such organizations as the Community Building Board, and some women have expressed frustration when they try to participate in a group and find that they are ignored and overlooked.

Gender

The community organizations are overwhelmingly female-oriented. The Merry Circle, Young Women's Club, and Emerald Lake Birthday Club are all women's organizations. The Emerald Lake Birthday Club is a truly unique organization as its membership seems to transcend the generations and served as an important network for related and neighbor women for many years.

The Lions Club tends to be a couples' group, with the men and women taking complementary roles. Men are usually in leadership roles, but officers are assisted by their wives and the office is often seen as shared. Men are normally in charge of the grilling of chicken for the chicken barbecue at the Chippewa Lake Days, but women work in the kitchen, solicit the contributed food for the potlucks and dinners, and organize many of the other events. In fact, women are an integral part of many organizations. Women dominate in the female/children's organizations already mentioned, but they are also important in all groups, serving as officers and having strong voices as to the needs of the organization or the community. Women serve as officers on the Community Building Board and on the township board.

The Chippewa-Martiny Fire Department is an organization that has been both age- and gender-segregated. Traditionally the fire department served as a means for young men to initiate their involvement in the community. It provided them with status in the community and culminated in a complex network of male bonding and mutual assistance that went beyond the fire hall. Older men ultimately were promoted to fire chief and then retired, leaving this time-consuming and strenuous activity to the young. Until recently, the fire department was also a gender-segregated organization. An attempt by a woman to become a member about twenty years ago was unsuccessful, as the leadership claimed they couldn't get a uniform to fit her. As an army veteran who had worked as a firefighter in another community, she was highly qualified for the position. Today, however, there are two female firefighters. The gender barrier has been broken.

Women are very active in the 4-H organization. All of my children's 4-H leaders, for horses and rabbits, were women. It is often women who initiate community projects. When I worked on the Chippewa Lake Centennial Celebration in 1983, all of the formal committee members were women, though men were very helpful behind the scenes, collecting museum items and assisting with setup of the museum displays and activities. Women find time to participate if they possibly can. School, church, and community events would not occur if a cohort of women were not involved in the planning, cooking, organization, and cleaning up afterwards. Men are often in front, serving and involved in the public display of events—as auctioneers, chicken barbecuers, and major spokespersons—but behind the scenes, dozens of women have made critical contributions and made the event possible. These are women who also have children at home, have household responsibilities, and jobs (sometimes more than one). Their energy and commitment to community are truly remarkable.

CONCLUSION

In traditional cultures where social and economic classes do not exist, social distinctions are formed primarily on the basis of age and gender. Status, responsibility, and participation are defined by one's gender and age, with respect for men and women increasing with age. Likewise in Chippewa Township, there seems to be an invisible yet tangible age/gender ranking system. Some women have broken the glass ceiling of the fire department, but expectations about membership in clubs and activities are still understood implicitly. Men and women graduate from age grade to age grade based on their contributions as they get older, from school and 4-H to service organizations.

Men and women who are active in the community are proud of their contributions, regardless of age. While some are disappointed that more people don't contribute, as a group they are optimistic about the future of Chippewa Lake. They see the village as surviving, if not thriving as a community, and they all share the deeply engrained community effect that allows longtime residents to identify with their shared history and their hope for the future.

CHAPTER 10

Transformation and Contested Identities

Anytime a group of people get together to talk, it's a gain.
Nowadays, people are too busy making a living to be social.

—DUKE METCALF, 2004

AT LEAST TWO TRANSFORMATIONS ARE OCCURRING IN CHIPPEWA Township. The first is the transformation from farm community to commuter community, a process that has been occurring for many years, but which is culminating in the loss of family farms and the subsequent out-migration of many young families seeking jobs or other opportunities "off the farm." Those who remain are the descendants of longtime residents, tied economically and emotionally to the history of the community.

Second, and simultaneously, there is an influx of residents who are seeking both the rural ambiance and the lake environment as an ideal retirement community. Even though the recent arrivals and the descendants of the earliest settlers share the same dream—a small rural community surrounded by natural beauty—their definitions of community and natural beauty differ greatly. While the rural families who remain here do so because of their historic and kinship ties to the land and a "remembered" community, those who come here from the cities are seeking something that they feel they have missed: the idyllic peacefulness of the countryside.

Sonya Salamon describes this process in Illinois, where newcomers seek a "rural ambience, peace, safety, good schools, and nature rather than the unique identity and qualities of a particular small town so precious to old-timers."[1] Newcomers have not been a part of the history of the community, and they are not aware of the historical or social milieu in which the community has been shaped. Here we will look at the intersection of these divergent ideas of community.

IDEA OF COMMUNITY REVISITED

Since we are reevaluating the idea of community as it is perceived by newcomers and old-timers, it will benefit us to review some of the characteristics of community outlined by Sonya Salamon.[2] First, over the years, communities develop shared expectations of behavior that are reinforced by ritual discourse—rites of passage and social rewards, such as prestige and respect, as well as negative sanctions, such as gossip. Second, members of a community mobilize to achieve group goals or complete projects that will benefit the entire community—this includes mutual assistance in times of hardship. Third is a sense of identity that results from the shared values and norms whereby individuals characterize themselves as members of a community. Membership is linked with kinship ties in the community, but also with the multi-stranded social relationships that develop over years of interaction.

Fourth is a sense of egalitarianism. Egalitarianism does not mean equality, but rather a sense that everyone is more or less like everyone else, and shares similar economic conditions and values. There are sanctions against demonstrating wealth ostentatiously, and an implicit understanding that those who have more will contribute more to the community. Comparing the farming community, the village, and the lake communities allows us to examine in what ways these characteristics have persisted over time, and how they have evolved. We will look at the intersection of these three groups in order to understand how they interact and how they identify the important issues and values that define community.

Township

The ideal vision of a homogeneous community has always been exaggerated and probably never existed, even when the community was newly settled and the above values were taking shape. We have seen that early families came from a variety of backgrounds, from European homesteaders to loggers, mill owners, and doctors. Yet, it is very likely that all of these families, despite their differing situations, shared a worldview that defined them as members of a shared community. Today, the descendants of these early settlers are even less homogeneous than their ancestors. Yet, I found that most of these descendants also shared a vision of community that mirrored that of their predecessors.

Janet Fitchen, in her book *Endangered Spaces, Enduring Places*, captures the sentiment of many of the people I interviewed for this project. According to Fitchen, "The space as a whole, as well as each individual parcel of land, has a social history known and referenced by local people, and the very term 'locals' or 'local people' is a way of affixing people in the relationship to space."[3] This is very true in Chippewa Township, where rural residents identify themselves as rural, but their focus is on their relationship with the land. The farm and "the land" are where social relationships are grounded, held together by marriages and kinship bonds across generations. Longtime residents not only identify places as Sparks Corners, Stockwell Corners, Cowden Hill, the old Smith place, Pickerel Point, for example, but attach families to the land in meaningful ways. Consequently, the land is where events of social-cultural importance take place, such as deer and wild-game hunting, mud runs and tractor pulls. Even after death, local residents remain tied to the land. Each community within the township has a cemetery that corresponds to the earliest settlements: the Eaton, Chippewa, and Church cemeteries (named after a family, not a church).

In Chippewa Township, the lake has also been an integral part of this landscape, where summer and winter fishing and local festivals contribute to the social activities shared by residents. Thus, physical boundaries help to locate the community in a tangible way, according to landmarks, and in intangible ways, according to memories of past experiences and events.

As my students and I interviewed longtime residents for this project, and as I collected oral histories, we discovered that the shared values of mutual assistance, egalitarianism, volunteerism, and ritual discourse are still deeply engrained in the worldview of local families. When we interviewed the families who were currently farming or dual-income families, we found that they were generally happy about their life in the township. They noted the quiet, rural setting as what they liked most, or family and friendliness of the people.

Farm families were, and still are, committed to the obligation of participation in local events. Community participation was an integral component of the economic and social survival of early settlers. For many longtime residents, community participation is still the barometer for a successful community. Whether it is membership in a church or social organization, or merely one's willingness to help out one's neighbor in a time of need, the community continues to be defined in terms of these social relationships. Nevertheless, farm families today realize that the current economic system has forced a concomitant shifting of familial and social networks from the neighborhood to the city and beyond. Fortunately, modern communication has allowed families to maintain networks over longer distances than could have ever been imagined by their ancestors.

While nonfarming families complained about a lack of volunteerism in the community today, this was not an issue for full-time and dual-income farmers whom we interviewed. Instead, we found that more than half of them claimed participation in one or more organizations. Our discussions with families provide an excellent example of the benefits of open-ended questions as supplements to (or in place of) structured survey questions. Respondents often indicated in their answers to the survey questions that "people don't help each other any more" or "people don't get involved." When we asked respondents to give examples of the loss of community values, they often reiterated the old stories that have circulated about the "good old days," implementing the romanticized notion of past community, using the imagined past as the measuring stick for the present.

However, when I conducted follow-up interviews with these same families and recorded the oral histories, I often found that involvement in the community continues to be a measurement of the success of the community today. As they began to expound on their lives, their conversations always included current stories of mutual assistance among neighbors, and the continuation of networks reinforced over many years. As they related these stories, past and present, they often smiled as they realized that these networks are still a part of their lives—perhaps muted and diluted somewhat, since people are not as interdependent as they once were when few people had access to transportation, telephones, or pantries and freezers filled with food.

By 2008, only two families in the township were still dairy farming, and these were both struggling. Pat Nellis will likely be the last in the long line of Nellis farmers to raise dairy cattle. The ethanol initiative that promised a rebirth of corn farming has not benefited the farmers I know. The 2008 gas crisis has severely handicapped all farmers who depend on diesel fuel to run tractors, mowers, balers, and combines, and who are dependent upon chemical fertilizers for many of their crops. The costs of producing and transporting corn to market are prohibitive, and individual farmers cannot take advantage of this opportunity in the same way that corporate farms can. While corn prices are up, so are the costs of feeding their cattle. Increasing property taxes further hinder farm families with 200–300 acres of land. In this way, the global market, seemingly very distant, impinges on the daily livelihood of local farmers.

Farm families struggle to keep the land intact, while the sons and daughters drift off to find jobs elsewhere. As I revisited families in the summer of 2008 in preparation for finishing this study, I sometimes felt as if all the local families were reading from the same script. All of the farmers I talked with, husbands and wives, lamented the high costs and the inability to pay for the diesel fuel for their tractors, and had fears about how they would heat their old farmhouses in the coming winter with propane fuel costs so high. They spoke with a mix of relief and despair about how their children had found jobs off the farm—relief because jobs are difficult to come by, especially when many of these children have only high school diplomas, and despair because these jobs take them further away from the farming lifestyle.

Yet, as I drive through the countryside, I see new modular homes and doublewide trailers springing up on the edges of family farms, along gravel roads. In my interviews, I learned that the inhabitants of these residences are local adult children who, though working in Big Rapids, distant factories, or in local oil and gas fields, are choosing to live near their parents. Paul and Renee Miller have both built homes within two miles of their parents, as have Marty and Troy Miller. Jimmy Nellis lives one half mile from Peter, and Jon Nellis lives near his parents.

The hopes of the longtime nonfarming or part-time farming families to keep their children in the community are less likely to be fulfilled. The children of nonfarmers or part-time farmers are more likely to have college educations and become lost to the community. Leigha McCallum Compson, Wendy Ulrich, the Austin children, and even our three children are unlikely to return to Chippewa Township to live. My husband is feeling the same angst as many local families as he looks out over our 120 acres and wonders what will become of it in the future. Our "hunting 40" has been in the family for many years, and we hope that our children will always value this little piece of pristine real estate with forested hills and the Roundy Branch Creek flowing through it. LaVail's great grandparents settled on the "farming 40" acres where we are currently living, but none of our children are likely to return here to live unless a career opportunity presents itself. Our sons are living in cities, and our daughter and her husband are building their own farmstead at the outskirts of another city. The greatest fear of many people, including my husband, is that the land in the township will be divided up and sold in parcels, and that the history of the community will be lost forever.

Lake Retirees and Other Newcomers

The village and the lake residents are more diverse in their history and characteristics than are the longtime farm and village families. As such, it is difficult to generalize about their aspirations and values. Lake residents come from a variety of small towns and cities. Some have moved here permanently because of their childhood memories of past summers at the family cottage. Others found the lake by accident, seeking an affordable getaway from Lansing, a two-hour drive away. While some lake residents have lived here for many years, forming a community where their children grew up and where they forged those critical social and emotional networks that result in a strong sense of commitment to place and people, others have moved here somewhat recently, by local standards. Recent immigrants do not have the multigenerational experiences that characterize other local families. They raised their children in distant cities and towns, and these adult children have settled down elsewhere.

Retirees seldom form bonds beyond their closest neighbors, though some have formed strong friendships with village or lake residents with whom they share common interests or backgrounds. For the most part, they lack the characteristics that we already noted for community. They have not participated in the rites of passage that draw people together to celebrate the accomplishments of their friends and family, such as the high school graduation marathons. As probate judge, my husband officiated two weddings on the lake, and I was invited to attend these events. At both, the attendees were family members from elsewhere. In one case, the groom's parents hosted the marriage of their son. The announcements invited their friends and family to "their quaint cottage on the lake," and there was only one lakeside neighbor who attended.

Newcomers are not compelled by, nor are they often aware of, the ritual discourse that moderates rural behavior—for example, talking to the parents of a disrespectful child instead of calling the police, moderating their boating times to be considerate of early morning or early evening fishermen, volunteering for community events, or joining a service organization. It is not that newcomers are rude or unreasonable. In fact, for the most part, they are very friendly people who love living on the lake, and who if they had lived in Chippewa Lake for twenty-five years would probably fit in very well. They just don't know the rules. And the rules of behavior differ in rural areas from the cities where most of these newcomers originate. Thus, the newcomers bear the brunt of gossip and perhaps are the victims of exclusion, and being human, the newcomers retaliate with the same, and perhaps with an added dose of "redneck" humor. These misunderstandings fester and further segregate the newcomers and the old-timers, villagers and lake residents.

Newcomers, particularly the most recent homeowners on the lake, also violate the norm of egalitarianism. In American society generally, consumerism and ostentatious displays of wealth are the measures of success. Retirees and others who own cottages on the lake take pride in their remodeled or rebuilt summer homes, built in the style of urban suburbs; they flaunt their speed boats, multiple Jet Skis, or jet boats, pulled behind their monstrous SUVs. As in peasant society, such display of wealth, while intriguing, is more likely to result in ridicule than admiration. "What are they thinking bringing that huge boat to this lake? Before they idle up, they're on the other side." The powerful jet boats, more and more prevalent in the past few years, are even more disturbing to the local residents as they race from one side of the lake to the other, leaving huge waves in their wake, while pontoon boats are pulling small children on tubes and Jet Skis jump the wake. As I wrote the first draft of this manuscript in the early spring of 2005, there had already been one death on the lake as two nonlocal teenagers played chicken with their Jet Skis, crossing each other's wake—resulting in the death of a seventeen-year-old girl.

The perceived lack of community identification is also demonstrated in expressions of mutual assistance and participation in community events. While some lake residents, especially those who have lived in the area for a while, will contribute to or attend benefit suppers or other community events, most tend to limit their participation to those events that relate to the lake—the Fourth of July poker run, perhaps Chippewa Lake Days activities—but they are less likely to be involved in community organizations, or to use the community building for family and social functions.

Our survey indicates that there is a stronger incidence of participation among those who have lived in the community for more than twenty years. Because newcomers do not have the tight family networks and do not know many longtimers, they are less likely to attend benefits to raise money for special projects or families in need. These events further reinforce already existing ties between neighbors and family, and thus act as an impediment to newcomers in forming these ties and participating in the future. As potential agents of change, newcomers express a reluctance to attend and participate in meetings. They don't feel welcome at events, and also express a certain bitterness about the lack of acceptance they feel in the community.

Longtime residents tend to be unaware that their own actions are viewed as exclusionary. Further, they don't understand or remember the amount of social capital that they have invested over the years in order to achieve their position in the community. Descendants of early settlers do not recognize that their place in the community is partly inherited, and is constantly reinforced through continued contributions to the community and strengthened social and kin networks.

Other longtime residents feel that newcomers must "prove themselves," as they did themselves when they moved to the community. They must take the initiative to become involved, to forge friendships and invest in the community. They have little respect for those newcomers who do not contribute—or worse, who demand or complain to the township about services that others do for themselves.

Age and Generation

The issue of volunteerism provides a powerful point of contention in local discourse on community and the intersection of newcomers versus oldtimers, but it is not the only one. Many young families complained about the township elders in the same way. Several younger and even middle-aged respondents argued that the older residents want to control the organizations and don't want to consider new ideas or try new things, so young people feel discouraged and quit the clubs or don't get involved at all. For their part, the elders are aware that they dominate in community organizations, such as the Lions Club and the Community Building Board, and they often attribute this predominance to the disinterest of the young people, or, with more generosity, to the fact that jobs and child-care responsibilities place time constraints on them.

The elders place the same burden on the young as they do the newcomers, arguing that they need to earn their place in the community. According to their perspective, those who are descended from early families should step up and take their turn by joining the clubs that their parents joined, and maintaining the social networks already in existence. Young newcomers and retirees should take the initiative and participate in the community. People are limited only by their own reluctance to make the first move and become involved. If you aren't involved, you can't complain about how things are done, according to their worldview.

These fault lines are not limited to Chippewa Lake. They occur in all communities. One need only attend any public meeting in any small town to confirm that it is the older, established residents who dominate the leadership, and perhaps the audience as well. In small communities, the rule of gerontocracy is further embedded in complex webs of relationships, past and present. Established families are tightly linked to history and to place. Young people and newcomers both have a very difficult time bridging this historic chasm.

EXPANSION OF COMMUNITY BEYOND THE VILLAGE

In concluding the ideas presented in this book, I would like to return to Janice Fitchen's ideas on transformations in the rural area.[4] Her comments are pertinent to the dilemmas faced by residents of Chippewa Township and hundreds of other changing communities in the United States today. Fitchen explores the locus of conflict in rural communities between the nostalgic past and the reality of the modern world. First, she reminds us that "rural places . . . don't look the way they used to."[5] Farm equipment has modernized; huge tractors have replaced the horse-drawn plow; round bales have replaced square bales, which replaced hand-pitched hay; and cash crops supplement dairy or beef cattle operations. Successful farmers have been able to accept these changes and take advantage of the various opportunities that are available. According to Fitchen, rural residents need to make a distinction between form and function—"between outward physical appearances and underlying social meanings."[6] She further warns that rejecting new forms will not facilitate survival of either that idealized community or community identity. "Nostalgia . . . will not suffice. . . . If people believe that old-fashioned forms are the equivalent of rurality and rural identity, then adaptation to modern technological, economic, social and political realities will be more difficult."[7]

This revelation has relevance in Chippewa Township, where this struggle between form and function is played out in the daily relationships of all residents. While they understand that the world has changed, and they understand the economic realities of living in a community dependent upon transient populations, they have a difficult time rectifying the disjunction of the new permanent residents who will be the future of the community. The urban transplants and retirees are here to stay. The fact that newcomers were defined in this study as families here for fifteen or fewer years is indicative of the stability of the community over time. As they establish themselves in the community, form networks, and figure out the local patterns of participation, they will make their mark. The sooner the established families (those here for more than thirty years) embrace their differences and tap their financial and time resources, the smoother the transition will become.

For their part, the newcomers have the power to reshape the community in many ways. The most negative impact would be in promoting and demanding the type of homogenization of which Salamon warns us—demanding that Chippewa Lake be a little Lansing, with Starbucks and Walmart. A positive impact would be to step away from the lakeshore and establish themselves as "boosters" in the local community—volunteering their skills and their time to local projects, taking part in local and school activities, and shedding the stereotypes that they bring with them to the country. Even though the boundaries set up by some of the old-timers seem like impenetrable walls, they have chinks, and most people will accept ideas offered in good faith (as opposed to criticisms) and will invite newcomers into their organizations that are currently struggling to survive.

Fitchen further reminds us that a "strong and positive identity can be a crucial ingredient in community survival," and suggests that the survival of the rural community depends on reinventing those relationships that reinforced kinship ties in the historical community.[8] Indeed, this is an ongoing process for many families in the township as they continue to involve themselves and their children in 4-H, county fairs, school activities, and church. But the interests of those who retire here do not include those traditional shared experiences. Residents in Chippewa Township need to discover what those activities might be that will unite all residents and forge new networks of cooperation and mutual assistance. The township board needs to offer periodic forums so all residents can give input as to community goals, instead of either meeting in front of the same five residents at their monthly sessions, or in front of an angry mob at special sessions, where people accuse them of lack of transparency.

I was very encouraged when I interviewed several members of the township board in the spring of 2005, including the new supervisor, George, and one of the new trustees, Ron. It was clear that George and the board took very seriously the concerns expressed by the residents during the campaign. They had also reviewed the survey findings that I had submitted to them in a report, outlining the concerns of the township residents.

In response to the community concern about the condition of the village, George started taking photographs of the buildings owned by absent landowners, and talked to them about their responsibilities. He visited other families in the village to talk about cleaning up their properties. He agreed with many of the comments made by respondents to my survey, felt that the buildings and the areas around them could be dangerous, and was prepared to take action with the county if these properties were not upgraded. At the time of the final draft of this manuscript, the old roller rink and several old structures in the village had been demolished and several new modular homes built; the homes in the village are much improved, as is Millett Park, located next to the newly renovated diner that draws many local families and summer residents.

George and the board were also actively pursuing the creation of the new park and a new township complex with a larger community building, new fire hall, and township hall. While there is controversy about his vision, it is clear that a new sense of enthusiasm and optimism was brought to the community as a result of the last election. Today, George still does not consider himself totally successful, because there are still dilapidated properties in the village, and he has not yet fulfilled his dream of a new township complex. Nevertheless he ran for reelection in 2008, unopposed.

Because the transitions from an idealized past to an imagined community are occurring very slowly, it remains to be seen if the end result will be the suburbanization/homogenization that Salamon found in small-town Illinois, or an empty town, a skeleton of past community.[9] In her summary of *Prairie Patrimony*, Salamon gives us hope that rural inhabitants can build a community where members share a sense of belonging, and where people can mobilize and share group goals.[10] Such a community can produce social capital through forming new interpersonal relationships that generate strong social networks and reciprocity. Further, rural communities can provide cultural continuity amid the "flux of change" by reproducing cultural systems of land tenure and kinship relations characteristic of farming settlements. Diverse communities with "multiple cultures" can indeed share a worldview.[11] This worldview, however, must be carefully forged and maintained through mutual respect and conscious attempts to include and to listen to those whose views are new, young, or old-fashioned.

CONCLUSION

When we envision rural areas such as Chippewa Lake, the image of the pristine farming community persists. We carry within ourselves this vision of a simpler life in a better time and place, often associated with our own ancestors and ideals of "traditional values." We yearn for that time when everybody knows everybody and we can know about our neighbors simply by knowing their family tree. As in the Mexican community I studied for more than twenty years, longtime residents in Chippewa Township have all told me that "everyone is related here." I have often been told how my husband is related to the families that I have interviewed for this project. I have also found out how I am related to some of the local families, as my mother's family settled in a small community that exists astride Mecosta and Isabella Counties. At one interview, as I sat with a man and his wife and the man's nephew, deciphering a genealogy, we realized that everyone sitting at the table, including me, had ties to a tiny community optimistically named Sherman City, consisting of an intersection and a church, where my grandfather was raised and where my mother came to visit as a child—going to her grandparents' farm in the country.

We have already discussed whether or not these perfect communities ever existed, but the perception persists nonetheless, and it is probably embedded in some truth. Families did know each other and did work together to achieve common goals. Gossip and various leveling mechanisms very likely moderated behavior and provided an egalitarian ideal if not reality. Those qualities listed earlier are embedded in shared tenets of agrarian communities: shared values, density of connections, effective norms, and engagement and mobilization for the common good.

Ironically, it is this romanticized perception that draws many people to rural areas, and ultimately results in transformations in the social relationships existing in these small communities. While Chippewa Lake is unlikely to experience the same kind of suburbanization experienced by Big Rapids, it is experiencing similar processes of transformation as the population shifts from farming families who supplement their income with factory or other unskilled work, to nonlocal retirees and escapees from Big Rapids who seek that idyllic community while working elsewhere. It is the latter two groups that are likely to influence the future of the community. They are upgrading former cottages to full-time homes, affecting local property values; they are purchasing family farms for nonfarming living, or building expensive homes on farming land. They are beginning to take an interest in local politics, and their ideas about local government and development differ markedly from the native population's, as do their expectations about delivery of services and quality of life. In the village, refurbished modular or doublewide mobile homes are replacing dilapidated clapboard houses, rented by transient families and single mothers. Yet, businesses come and go, and those that stay suffer a frequent turnover of owners.

So, my question to those who complained about the community— who criticized the old-timers or the newcomers, who lamented the lack of activities or the presence of summer people—was "Why do you stay here?" Kristin, the young candidate for township trustee with whom I spoke about volunteerism and other community activities, put the issue into perspective for me. When I asked her why she and her husband didn't leave the community, she paused and admitted that it was worth it, living here. She told stories of how her brother, still attending school in Lansing, has to pass through metal detectors every day, about the problems of drugs and violence in the state capital. Here, she argues, "I always know where my kids are and who they are with; I know the teachers and the community."

Whenever I asked this question, it resulted first in a look of confusion, then a wry smile, then a shrug of the shoulders, and finally a sigh. What keeps them here is the lake, and the quiet, and the people, and the beautiful summers, and the lack of congestion and traffic, and the fact that their kids can go anywhere in the community and be safe. They are here because they either would not know how to live in a city, or have left one behind, or because their family is here and everything they know is here.

What is clear is that Chippewa Lake is a village like many others. As I was reminded by a close friend whose family has lived in Martiny Township for four generations, "The life of the village is not in the buildings." It lies under the surface and in the homes and dairy barns. Daily life is driven by small animosities and magnificent acts of kindness. Like other communities, it is currently located at the crossroads of the past, present, and future. Today Chippewa Lake seems trapped and strangled by inertia brought about by the convergence of at least two worldviews, one enmeshed in a rich farming history and the other imagined by newcomers seeking an ideal community. I feel encouraged by the willingness of people to assist each other.

One evening, as I stood in a neighboring farmer's front yard, watching their life burn up in their century-old farmhouse, I felt both bereaved and elated at the same time. In the shadows of the blaze and choking smoke, neighbors were planning a benefit dinner, because the owners could not afford house insurance. Peter Nellis was volunteering his services as auctioneer, and plans were being laid for shopping trips for clothes and household items. This is the community that I adopted and that accepted me—the city girl. And I am optimistic that, despite inevitable upsweeps and downturns, it will maintain the elemental characteristics that have allowed it to survive the booms and busts of rural America: persistence and hope.

Marijuana Mama

E DWIN AND M ARILYN T AYLOR'S ANCESTORS SETTLED IN C HIPPEWA
Township in the early 1900s.[1] The extended family owns several hundred
acres of land, including a farmhouse and several sections where they produce corn and hay for their dairy operation. Edwin and Marilyn raised four
children on the farm, two daughters and two sons. The Taylor brothers,
Jack and Bill, were hulking youths whose mannerisms intimidated other
children on the bus, and as adults they had a reputation as heavy drinkers
and fighters. According to local rumor, they had the dubious distinction
of being banned from every bar in three townships. When the Taylor boys
showed up, a fight was sure to break out—it was just a matter of time. They
were also suspected, though never prosecuted, for theft and other nefarious
acts of deviance.

The reputation of the Taylor "boys" continued into adulthood, even
after Jack and Bill established their own dairy farms within a few miles of
the Taylor homestead. Jack purchased a farmhouse and land to our east,
and Bill purchased land just to the north of us. Even after we moved to the
area, when Jack and Bill had children, there were sporadic rumors of thefts
and other deviant acts committed by them. For example, an expensive part
of a hay-mowing machine went missing in the area, and the victim of the
theft suspected that Jack had stolen it. As the story goes, one night the
victim went to Jack's barn and stole the part back. Jack's son, Carl, defends
his father, saying that it was his cousin, Jack's nephew Jimmy, who stole the
tractor and hid it in Jack's field. Jimmy, who has a history of theft, is a major
player in the drug incident discussed below.

There is also a story about a feud that Jack had with a local farmer that
resulted in a terrible example of rural retribution when the local farmer-
victim planted green metal stakes throughout Jack's hay field, so that when
Jack mowed, the stakes tore up his machine. Once discovered, Jack not only

179

had expensive repairs to his mower, but had lost precious time seeking out and removing the dangerous stakes.

In addition to Jack and Bill, Edwin and Marilyn Taylor had two daughters, Sally and Laura, who were tough women, known for their descriptive vocabulary and hot tempers. They married local men and lived in the area; Laura's house was adjacent to Jack and Gloria. Laura and her husband, Gary Gibson, had one son, Jimmy. After Laura and Gary divorced, Laura became involved with a nonlocal man, Harry, with whom she had a daughter. Harry owned a large parcel of land in the area that he rented to beef farmers for summer grazing. Laura worked as a rural mail carrier, holding one of the few prized federal jobs in the county. She also raised cattle and farmed with her son, Jimmy.

During these years, Laura and Jimmy got involved in buying and selling marijuana, using equipment leasing and gun purchasing as cover for their trips to South Carolina. Rumors began to circulate about Laura's trips south, and how she and Harry were managing a large herd of cattle. Most rumors centered around the possibility of cattle rustling in Texas, and when Laura returned home one year with a gunshot wound in the leg, the hint of drug smuggling and selling were added to the litany of alleged crimes. Local rumors were incorrect in several details. First, she was going to South Carolina, not Texas, and second, Harry was not involved in her operations.

Meanwhile, Jimmy was living far beyond the means of most farm children. In his early twenties, he was known for having huge parties and buying many pieces of electronic equipment, guns, and expensive trucks. Neighbors complained about the loud parties and the two menacing rottweilers that patrolled the property and chased after cars and pedestrians.

Mecosta County, like most rural counties, is part of a multicounty drug-enforcement team, comprised of state and local law-enforcement agencies. They work undercover, infiltrating drug rings and building drug cases until they have sufficient evidence to conduct raids and make arrests. Eventually, a case was built against Laura and Jimmy. The community rumors about drugs were proven correct, and for once, the truth far exceeded even the imagination of the most creative resident. The local newspaper screamed headlines, dubbing our local criminal "Marijuana Mama," and Chippewa Lake, whose positive qualities or events normally went unnoticed by the local press, got its six months of infamy as the newspaper followed the case.

The investigation uncovered a cache of guns and other weapons in the Gibson house, and a stash of marijuana hidden in Marilyn's basement. At this time, Marilyn was terminally ill with cancer. Because of her age, illness, and the uncertainty of her knowledge of and complicity in the crime,

Marilyn was not prosecuted, but her home and farm were seized by the state, per Michigan law. Marilyn died during this time, with many questions lingering over her part in the scandal, diminishing somewhat her reputation as a hard-working farm wife and mother.

The FBI investigation became the topic of intense gossip in the community, and the Taylor family, accustomed to small-town mechanisms for conflict resolution, underestimated or misunderstood the power of the federal government over their lives. The FBI, in their investigation of the guns and other stolen items found in Laura's home, began to interview local residents and others who had become part of the investigation. According to Jack's son Carl, Jimmy named his own mother as the major instigator and planner of the crimes, and pressured his friends to claim ownership of guns that were found cached in his house. Jack, who was not at all involved in these crimes, became embroiled as a family member and was trying to help his sister and nephew by talking to witnesses and holding back information from the FBI.

Although Jack was innocent of any crimes related to the drug smuggling and sales, he was prosecuted and found guilty of obstruction of justice. He spent eighteen months in prison, and then probation. Jack's younger son, Curtis, was also involved in the cover-up and went to prison for fifteen months for his role in the crime. Jack's probation was particularly harsh for a farmer as he was not allowed to use a gun. His family, like most farm families, was dependent upon venison as a primary source of meat, and not being able to hunt was a major hardship. Thus, when he was caught on his own land with a friend on opening day with a rifle, he was sent back to jail, although he and his friend claimed he was showing the rifle to the friend, who wanted to buy it. Even though it was suspicious that the DNR officer would be conveniently working in that area on opening day, Jack's story was weak.

Carl, the older son, removed himself from the family scandal. He moved to a piece of land that adjoined the family land to the south, purchased a trailer, and found a nonfarming job. Carl and Curtis were estranged as a result of this conflict, and it was nearly ten years before they would renew their sibling relationship.

During the time that Jack and Curtis were in prison, Gloria ran the farm by herself. Carl took over many of the chores of the farm in addition to his off-farm job. Neighbors assisted Gloria with her seasonal chores, such as cutting and baling hay and cultivating corn. Because Gloria had always been in charge of the milking operation, this was second nature to her.

Jack's sister Laura and nephew Jimmy went to prison, even though only a small amount of marijuana was actually found with them. Jimmy was convicted of felony possession of firearms since he had violated his previous felony restrictions, and received a seven-year sentence, of which he served three-and-a-half years. Based on Jimmy's testimony against his own mother, Laura was convicted of drug charges and received a thirty-year sentence. She is still in prison to this day. Harry took custody of their young daughter. Jimmy and Curtis are now free, as is Jack. Because of the animosity surrounding Jimmy's involvement in the crime, and the anger aroused when he implicated his mother and friends to cut his sentence, Jimmy has not returned to Chippewa Lake. The home he lived in with Laura was also confiscated by the government, as were all the farm implements and guns. If this crime had occurred in an urban area, and the family had been a different one, it is unlikely that the sentence would have been as harsh as it was. That a woman would spend thirty years in prison for possessing and selling marijuana is an interesting testimony to the local ideas of justice, crime, and punishment. Since this rural drama played out in the urban court system of Big Rapids also sheds some light on the stereotyped images of farmers that town residents have.

Once home, Jack and Gloria continued to farm, but life was not easy for them. When Curtis was released, he moved into a trailer behind the milking barn. He married and started a family, but as a convicted felon, he had difficulty finding a job. He helped his parents on the farm and did odd jobs for neighbors. Recently, his brother, Carl, helped him get a job, and Curtis and his family have built their own home nearby.

Despite the terrible events that strained their family and their relationship with their neighbors, Jack and Gloria have reestablished themselves in the community. More serious and responsible as they age, those who know them recognize their commitment to the community and their struggles to keep their farm intact. They finally succumbed and sold their dairy cattle in 2005, and are currently crop and hay farming.

During the early spring of 2005, Jack and Gloria's home caught fire. One evening, after dark, we saw and heard fire engines rushing up and down our road. This is not unusual in the spring, as grass fires often break out in the dry fields. Later, when my husband walked outside, he saw the flames flashing above the trees that separate our farms. It was Jack and Gloria's house that was on fire. Arriving at their house minutes later, we found that three fire departments had been called, and a fourth arrived later with additional air for the Scott packs that the firefighters wore. The air was filled with smoke as the firefighters fought back the flames leaping from the lower- and upper-story windows.

Gloria and Jack had been in the milking barn when the fire broke out in their house. They and Curtis managed to enter the house and rescue the television, Jack's mother's dishes, and the breadbox where they stashed their cash. They lost everything else, and because of cost, they had no insurance coverage. It is believed that the fire started as a result of a power surge.

Other family members and neighbors, such as ourselves, were drawn to the fire. While we stood choking from the smoke, the plans for a benefit were already being laid. Peter Nellis offered his services as auctioneer for a benefit auction. Others were asking what size shoes Gloria wore, as all she now owned were the barn boots she was wearing when the fire broke out.

Two days after the fire, we walked up to their farm, where the remnants of their house, broken windows, and lumber lay smoldering around the brick chimney, still standing as a reminder of what was lost. We were surprised to see a used mobile home in their yard. Inside we found Gloria and a friend sorting through a box of food. We discovered that the owners of the mobile-home sales business in Martiny Township had given them the trailer on loan until the auction, which was already being planned. Friends and neighbors hooked them up to electricity, propane gas, phone, and their well. Others brought clothes, food, and furniture. Not to be outdone, we walked home, hooked our trailer onto our car, and then returned to their new abode with our outdoor swing. We placed it in their front yard, and Jack immediately sat down, a wide smile exposing his toothless grin. His huge body, clad in his trademark bib overalls, swung back and forth, back and forth.

Within a month, the benefit auction took place in the community building. There were two volunteer auctioneers, Peter Nellis and Andy Lattimore, the son of the owner of the mobile-home business who donated the trailer to the Taylors. Many local residents and businesses, including some from Big Rapids, donated items and gift certificates for the auction. The Young Women's Club sponsored the kitchen, with all of the food donated by local businesses or club members. There were two 50/50 raffles, and both of the winners (including me) donated their winnings back. Over the course of the evening, nearly one hundred people came to the auction, and the event brought in nearly $4,000.

The link between the Taylors and my husband's family go back several generations. When he was young, LaVail lived with his grandparents, Earl and Cleva McCormick, for several years and had visited the Taylors with his grandfather. After LaVail moved to Grand Rapids, he returned to his grandparents' farm in the summer months and worked for Edwin Taylor, baling hay and stacking it in the barn.

He remembers dinners in the cluttered farmhouse, and the deep friendship between Edwin and his own grandfather. When we moved to the township to live in 1981, with two young children in tow, Jack and Gloria became good neighbors, plowing us out during the hard winters and bringing us sweet corn in the fall. We have allowed them to use our land for hay or corn production, and our barn (before it collapsed in a strong wind) to store it in. We watched their sons grow up, and they watched our three children mature. We contributed to benefits when Curt was in an ATV accident, and I worked in the kitchen for the fire benefit. We were not as close to Bill and Barbara's family, but their daughter, Marcie, brought her horse over to our house for our daughter Sarah to ride, and was one of the young women who kindled our daughter's love of horses.

For as long as I can remember, as I became introduced to, and later entrenched in, the local community, the Taylor families had a reputation as ne'er-do-wells—heavy drinkers and fighters, suspected whenever anything disappeared from a barn or garage. Yet we encountered each other over the seemingly insurmountable chasm of different educations, professions, and world travel. We connect over the shared experience of parenthood and rural living.

When the rumors of Laura and Jim's illegal activities were proven true, and when Curtis and Jack became involved after the fact, the community responded in many ways, depending on their preconceptions of the family. Those who knew the Taylors by reputation or by misadventure looked on their misfortune with a sense of weakly disguised glee and a "what do you expect" attitude. As the scandal unfolded and the family disgrace deepened with each daily grapevine update and newspaper headline about "Marijuana Mama" and her band of wayward kinfolk, the family became more and more marginalized. Jack's complicity in the crime can be examined in the context of those values that we have outlined in this book. His attempts to protect his sister and nephew were viewed very differently by the legal system, which considers such behavior in terms of "obstruction of justice" and perjury.

That some of these same neighbors who had been implicated in some way or other during the investigation by the FBI were at the benefit is a testament to the strength of friendship and shared history. Not all residents shared this goodwill toward their wayward neighbors. As one of the members of the Young Women's Club was collecting food contributions for the benefit, one person, a recent resident, grumbled that the Taylors had received more than their share of largesse: "Why should we help them with another benefit?" When several members of the club discussed this later, we could not understand that feeling. Another member said, "Do we keep a tab on misfortune . . . only one misfortune per family?"

Several people, who do not know them well, complained afterward because Jack and Gloria did not address those who attended the benefit. Rather, they sat near the door, embarrassed at the generosity of their neighbors and friends. It was difficult for Jack to even enter the building—he hovered outside for quite a while. Those who know them understand their reticence. There are many ways to say "thank you." Friends know that Jack and Gloria are grateful to everyone for their assistance, and friends know that Jack and Gloria will do the same for anyone else who suffers misfortune—because that is what people do here.

Notes

INTRODUCTION

1. A. Gunder Frank, "Development of Underdevelopment in Latin America: Underdevelopment or Revolution" in *Latin America: Underdevelopment or Revolution* (New York: Monthly Review Press, 1969).

2. Immanuel Wallerstein, *The Modern World System: Capitalist Agriculture and the Origins of the European World Economy in the Sixteenth Century* (New York: Academic Press, 1974).

3. Alice O'Connor, "Modernization and the Rural Poor: Some Lessons from History," in *Rural Poverty in America,* ed. Cynthia Duncan (New York: Auburn House, 1992), 215–16.

4. Diane K. McLaughlin, "Changing Income Inequality in Nonmetropolitan Counties, 1980–1990," *Rural Sociology* 67, no. 4 (December 2002): 514–15.

5. Sherry Ortner, "Theory in Anthropology since the Sixties," *Comparative Studies in Society and History* 26 (1984): 126–66; Rural Sociological Society Task Force on Persistent Rural Poverty, *Persistent Poverty in Rural America (PPRA)* (Boulder, CO: Westview Press, 1993); Enzo Mingione, *Fragmented Societies: A Sociology of Economic Life beyond the Market Paradigm*, translated by Paul Goodrich (Cambridge, MA: Basil Blackwell Ltd., 1991).

6. Rural Sociological Society, *Persistent Poverty in Rural America*, 95–96.

7. Sonya Salamon, *Prairie Patrimony: Family, Farming, and Community in the Midwest* (Chapel Hill: University of North Carolina Press, 1992); Sonya Salamon, "From Hometown to Nontown: Rural Community Effects of Suburbanization," *Rural Sociology* 68, no. 1 (2003): 1–24.

8. Salamon, *Prairie Patrimony*, 226–28.

9. Salamon, "From Hometown to Nontown," 8.

10. Ibid.; Janet M. Fitchen, *Endangered Spaces, Enduring Places: Culture, Identity, and Survival in Rural America* (Boulder, CO: Westview Press, 1991), 254.

11. Salamon, *Prairie Patrimony*, 226–28.

12. Salamon, "From Hometown to Nontown," 4–5.

13. Fitchen, *Endangered Spaces, Enduring Places*, 253.

14. Ibid., 254–56.

15. Fitchen, *Endangered Spaces, Enduring Places*; Janet M. Fitchen, *Poverty in Rural America: A Case Study* (Prospect Heights, IL: Waveland Press, 1995); Laura B. DeLind, "Close Encounters with a CSA: The Reflections of a Bruised and Somewhat Wiser Anthropologist," *Agriculture and Human Values* 16 (1999): 3–9.

CHAPTER 1. THE GEOGRAPHY AND INDIGENOUS PEOPLE OF MECOSTA COUNTY

1. Mecosta Conservation District, *Mecosta Conservation District Resource Assessment and Implementation Plan, 2001* (East Lansing, MI: Michigan Conservation Districts, 2001) [hereafter MCDRA], 3.
2. Ibid., 2.
3. *Chippewa Lake Community and Environment Assessment* (Big Rapids, MI: Environmental Management Studies Center, Ferris State University) [hereafter CLCEA], 16.
4. MCDRA, 3.
5. Ibid., 1.
6. CLCEA, 13.
7. MCDRA, 1.
8. *Chippewa Lake Community and Environmental Assessment*, 14, 16.
9. MCDRA, 3.
10. I use the term "Ottawa" instead of the alternative term "Odawa" for this group as it is the term employed in the historical documents and the term used in the major ethnographic source used in this chapter: James Clifton, George Cornell, and James McClurken, *People of the Three Fires: The Ottawa, Potawatomi, and Ojibway of Michigan* (Grand Rapids, MI: Grand Rapids Inter-Tribal Council, 1986).
11. Wilbert B. Hinsdale, *Archaeological Atlas of Michigan* (Ann Arbor: University of Michigan Press, 1931), maps 7 and 8.
12. George Cornell, "Introduction," in Clifton et al., *People of the Three Fires*, iii, iv.
13. Ibid., iv.
14. Ibid., v.
15. James McClurken, "Ottawa," in Clifton et al., *People of the Three Fires*, 3.
16. Ibid., 8–11.
17. Ibid., 11–12; James Clifton, "Potawatomi," in Clifton et al., *People of the Three Fires*, 70. For Ottawa history, see www.tolatsga.org/otta.html.

18. McClurken, "Ottawa," in Clifton et al., *People of the Three Fires*, 13–17.
19. Ibid., 16.
20. Ibid., 18–19.
21. Ibid., 19.
22. Ibid., 20–21.
23. Ibid., 22–26.
24. Information for this section obtained from the document "Treaty with the Ottawa, etc., March 28, 1836" at www.1836cora.org/documents/1836march 28treaty.pdf.
25. James M. McClurken, "Ottawa," in Clifton et al., *People of the Three Fires*, 29.
26. Ibid., 30–31.
27. Ibid., 31–32.
28. Information for this section obtained from the document "Treaty with the Ottawa and Chippewa, July 31, 1855" at digital.library.okstate.edu/kappler/vol2/treaties/ott0725.htm.
29. National Archives and Records Administration [hereafter NARA], Letter to Commissioner, dated Ionia, Michigan, August 29, 1855, and signed by eleven members of the Ottawa delegation, NARA-DC, RG49, Indian Reserve Files, Entry 29, box 7, August 29, 1855.
30. National Archives Microform [hereafter NAM], Letter and amendments sent to George Manypenny, dated November 24, 1855, and signed by Henry C. Gilbert, Indian Agent, NAM M234 R.404, 815–21.
31. National Archives Microfilm, Letters Received by the Office of Indian Affairs, 1856–1857, NAM M234 R.405, 533–36.
32. Ibid.
33. Ibid.
34. National Archives Microform, Letter from Henry Gilbert to George Manypenny, October 22, 1856, NAM M234 R.405, 168–71.
35. McClurken, "Ottawa," in Clifton et al., *People of the Three Fires*, 34.
36. Ibid., 34–35.
37. James M. McClurken, "Grand River Band of Ottawa Indians Ethnohistorical Response to Office of Federal Acknowledgment Technical Assistance Letter," dated January 26, 2005 (Lansing, MI: McClurken Associates, 2005), 33–35.
38. Ibid., 31–32.
39. McClurken, "Ottawa," in Clifton et al., *People of the Three Fires*, 36–37.
40. U.S. Department of the Interior, Census Office, *Report on Indians Taxed and Indians Not Taxed in the United States (except Alaska) at the Eleventh Census: 1890* (Washington, DC: Government Printing Office, 1894). The census

data state that there were 5,625 Indians in Michigan, but the county-by-county totals only add up to 3,633. There is no explanation of the discrepancy in the document.

41. *Records of the Bureau of Indian Affairs: 1870 Annuity Rolls of the Chippewas and Ottawas* (Durant Rolls, 1908), Washington, DC: National Archives, General Service Administration, 1983. My thanks to Joe Quick at McClurken and Associates for introducing me to the Durant Rolls of 1908, and for researching the Mecosta County registrants on my behalf.

42. Personal communication with Dr. Richard Santer, local historian, November 13, 2011.

43. McClurken, "Grand River Band of Ottawa Indians Ethnohistorical Response," iv.

44. Ibid., viii–x.

45. Ibid., 37.

46. The article cited here, "The Indian Trail," was written by Nettie Smith for the *Chippewa Hills Courier* in the mid-1970s; the specific date is unknown.

47. Today, Native Americans constitute a small yet visible percentage of the local population, though the origins of these families are diverse and they are probably not descendants of those outlined in this chapter.

CHAPTER 2. LOCATING CHIPPEWA TOWNSHIP IN TIME AND PLACE

1. Virginia Taber Ball, "Memories of an Old Timer," *Good Old Days Magazine* (January 1970): 5–6; Ball, "A Story of the History of Chippewa Lake," unpublished manuscript (1968); and Ball, "Chippewa Lake Methodist Church Has Served Community for Years," *The [Big Rapids] Pioneer*, n.d.

2. "Chippewa Lake Woman Recalls Brother's Accomplishments," *The [Big Rapids] Pioneer*, July 14, 1980, 1.

3. *Chippewa Lake Community and Environmental Assessment* (Big Rapids, MI: Environmental Management Studies Center, Ferris State University, 1994), 1.

4. Willis Fredrick Dunbar, *Michigan: A History of the Wolverine State* (Grand Rapids, MI: Wm. B. Eerdmans Publishing, 1965), 623; Ball, "A Story of the History of Chippewa Lake," 2.

5. E. L. Hays, comp., *Atlas of Mecosta County* (Philadelphia: C. O. Titus, 1879).

6. Elden L. Brigham and Laura Brigham Jagger, *Emerald: History of a Pioneer Community* (Evart, MI: The Evart Review, 1972), 5.
7. Ibid., 91; Chapman Brothers, *Portrait and Biographical Album of Mecosta County* (Chicago: Chapman Brothers, 1883), 484–85.
8. Brigham and Jagger, *Emerald: History of a Pioneer Community*, 6.
9. Ibid., 16.
10. Ibid., 77–78.
11. Ibid., 2.
12. Hays, *Atlas of Mecosta County*.
13. Brigham and Jagger, *Emerald: History of a Pioneer Community*, 68–69.
14. Information on the Schroeder family is extracted from their family oral history, *From Prussia with Love*, original author unknown, updated by Michael Schroeder, n.d.
15. Brigham and Jagger, *Emerald: History of a Pioneer Community*, 16.
16. Ibid.
17. Ball, "A Story of the History of Chippewa Lake," 3.
18. Brigham and Jagger, *Emerald: History of a Pioneer Community*, 19.
19. Ibid., 5; Hays, *Atlas of Mecosta County*.
20. Dunbar, *A History of the Wolverine State*, 623.
21. Hays, *Atlas of Mecosta County*.
22. P. A. Meyers, J. W. Meyers, and C. H. Cameron, surveyors and draftsmen, *The Plat Book of Mecosta County, Michigan* (Minneapolis: Consolidated Publishing Co., 1900).
23. Dunbar, *A History of the Wolverine State*, 471.
24. *Chippewa Lake Community and Environmental Assessment*, 1.
25. Ball, "A Story of the History of Chippewa Lake," 1.
26. Brigham and Jagger, *Emerald: History of a Pioneer Community*, 8.
27. *Chippewa Lake Community and Environmental Assessment*, 1; Dunbar, *A History of the Wolverine State*, 562–63.
28. Brigham and Jagger, *Emerald: History of a Pioneer Community*, 9.
29. *Chippewa Lake Community and Environmental Assessment*, 1; Dunbar, *A History of the Wolverine State*, 562–63.
30. *Chippewa Lake Community and Environmental Assessment*, 1; Ball, "A Story of the History of Chippewa Lake," 1.
31. *Chippewa Lake Community and Environmental Assessment*, 1; Dunbar, *A History of the Wolverine State*, 562–63.
32. Chapman Brothers, *Portrait and Biographical Album of Mecosta County*; Meyers et al., *The Plat Book of Mecosta County, Michigan*; Dunbar, *A History of the Wolverine State*, 475n572.

33. Chapman Brothers, *Portrait and Biographical Album of Mecosta County*; Meyers et al., *The Plat Book of Mecosta County, Michigan*.
34. Ball, "A Story of the History of Chippewa Lake," 3.
35. Ball, "A Story of the History of Chippewa Lake," 3; Ernest Nott, personal communication, 1983.
36. *Chippewa Lake Community and Environmental Assessment*, 1.
37. Dunbar, *A History of the Wolverine State*, 623.
38. *Chippewa Lake Community and Environmental Assessment*, 1.
39. U.S. Census Bureau, *1990 Census*, available at www.census.gov/main/www/cen1990.html.
40. *Chippewa Lake Community and Environmental Assessment*, 2.
41. Interview with Mabelle Preston, Ilene Preston Stein, and Valorie Stein Kullman, 2004, Chippewa Township.
42. Interview with Irvin and Edna Austin, 1983, Martiny Township.
43. Interview with Debra Carmichael Zielinski and Robert Zielinski, 2004, Chippewa Township.
44. Curtis Stadtfeld, *From the Land and Back* (New York: Charles Scribner's Sons, 1972).
45. Ball, "Memories of an Old Timer."
46. Personal communication with Jack Langell, one of the owners of the Sweet Note during this time period, 2004.
47. There is extensive literature on the impact of the farm crisis on rural communities. For more reading on this subject, see Jane Adams, ed., *Fighting for the Farm: Rural America Transformed* (Philadelphia: University of Pennsylvania Press, 2003); Barry J. Barnett, "The U.S. Farm Financial Crisis of the 1980's," in *Fighting for the Farm: Rural America Transformed*, ed. Jane Adams, 160–71; Kathryn Marie Dudley, *Debt and Dispossession: Farm Loss in America's Heartland* (Chicago: University of Chicago Press, 2000); and Steve H. Murdock and F. Larry Leistritz, eds., *The Farm Financial Crisis: Socioeconomic Dimensions and Implications for Producers and Rural Areas* (Boulder, CO: Westview Press, 1988).
48. Rural Sociological Society Task Force on Persistent Rural Poverty, *Persistent Poverty in Rural America* (*PPRA*) (Boulder, CO: Westview Press, 1993), 1.
49. National Agricultural Statistics Service of the USDA, *Census of Agriculture, Mecosta County Profile, 2002* (Washington, DC: NASS County Profiles, U.S. Department of Agriculture, 2002), available at www.nass.usda.gov.
50. Ibid.
51. Mecosta Conservation District, *Mecosta Conservation District Resource Assessment and Implementation Plan, 2006* (East Lansing, MI: Michigan Conservation Districts, 2006), 4.

52. Interview with Jerry Lindquist, Michigan State University extension agent, published as part of "The Future of Agriculture," by Candy Allen and Brandon Fountain, in *The [Big Rapids] Pioneer*, August 16, 2008, 1, 6–9.
53. Mecosta Conservation District, *Mecosta Conservation District Resource Assessment and Implementation Plan, 2001* (East Lansing, MI: Michigan Conservation Districts, 2001).
54. Wilbert B. Hinsdale, *Archaeological Atlas of Michigan* (Ann Arbor: University of Michigan Press, 1931); Richard Santer, "Historical Overview of the City of Big Rapids" (2007), available at http.ci.big-rapids.mi.us.
55. Santer, "Historical Overview of the City of Big Rapids"; Richard Santer, "Big Rapids Historical Timeline" (2007), available at http.ci.big-rapids.mi.us.
56. Anna Howard Shaw, *The Story of a Pioneer* (Cleveland: Pilgrim Press, 1994).
57. Santer, "Big Rapids Historical Timeline."
58. U.S. Census Bureau, *2000 Census*, available at www.michigan.gov/cgi.

CHAPTER 3. FARM FAMILIES IN TRANSITION

1. Curtis Stadtfeld, *From the Land and Back* (New York: Charles Scribner's Sons, 1972).
2. Sonya Salamon, *Prairie Patrimony: Family, Farming, and Community in the Midwest* (Chapel Hill: University of North Carolina Press, 1992), 226–27; Sonya Salamon, "From Hometown to Nontown: Rural Community Effects of Suburbanization," *Rural Sociology* 68, no. 1 (2003): 1–24.
3. Janet M. Fitchen, *Endangered Spaces, Enduring Places: Culture, Identity, and Survival in Rural America* (Boulder, CO: Westview Press, 1991); Janet M. Fitchen, *Poverty in Rural America: A Case Study* (Prospect Heights, IL: Waveland Press, 1995).
4. Salamon, *Prairie Patrimony*, 227.
5. Ibid.
6. Ibid.
7. Fitchen, *Endangered Spaces, Enduring Places*, 255–56.
8. Kathryn Marie Dudley, "The Entrepreneurial Self: Identity and Morality in a Midwestern Farming Community," in *Fighting for the Farm: Rural America Transformed*, ed. Jane Adams, 182–83 (Philadelphia: University of Pennsylvania Press, 2003).
9. Ibid., 183–84.
10. Fitchen, *Endangered Spaces, Enduring Places*, 253–54.

11. Dudley, "The Entrepreneurial Self," 183–84.

12. Salamon, "From Hometown to Nontown," 8.

13. Salamon, *Prairie Patrimony*, 226–28.

14. Jessica Pearson, "Note on Female Farmers," *Rural Sociology* 44, no. 1 (1979): 189–200.

15. Stadtfeld, *From the Land and Back*.

16. Fitchen, *Poverty in Rural America*, 161–62.

17. Ibid., 163.

CHAPTER 4. CHIPPEWA TOWNSHIP AS RURAL COMMUNITY IN TRANSITION

1. 2000 U.S. Census, available at www.census.gov/main/www/cen2000.html.

2. Jessica Pearson, "Note on Female Farmers," *Rural Sociology* 44, no. 1 (1979): 193–94.

3. Peter Nellis, personal communications, Summer 2008.

4. Allen and Lois Schroeder, interviews, Summer 2005. Also Michael Schroeder, comp., *From Prussia with Love: Our Family History*, unpublished manuscript, n.d.

5. Janet M. Fitchen, *Endangered Spaces, Enduring Places: Culture, Identity, and Survival in Rural America* (Boulder, CO: Westview Press, 1991), 253.

CHAPTER 5. TOWNSHIP IN TRANSITION

1. Janet M. Fitchen, *Endangered Spaces, Enduring Places: Culture, Identity, and Survival in Rural America* (Boulder, CO: Westview Press, 1991), 253.

2. Ibid., 254.

3. Since the final draft of this manuscript was completed, the new township supervisor has overseen the demolition of the roller rink and the military bunker home, the latter being replaced by a modular home. The diner is in business again with new owners, but the restaurant near the marina has closed. The only grocery store is abandoned and for sale.

4. In recording this data, I used the years of residence of the spouse who had lived in the township for the longest period of time. This was usually the male, but not always.

5. Three of the households of fourth-generation residents were not counted here, as they represent relatives, and counting their families twice would skew the data.
6. See table 2 in chapter 4 for data on education and occupation.
7. Katherine S. Newman, "Deindustrialization, Poverty, and Downward Mobility: Toward an Anthropology of Economic Disorder," in *Diagnosing America: Anthropology and Public Engagement*, ed. Shephard Forman, 121–48 (Ann Arbor: University of Michigan Press, 1997).

CHAPTER 7. CONTESTED IDENTITIES

1. Janet M. Fitchen, *Endangered Spaces, Enduring Places: Culture, Identity, and Survival in Rural America* (Boulder, CO: Westview Press, 1991), 254.
2. Sonya Salamon, "From Hometown to Nontown: Rural Community Effects of Suburbanization," *Rural Sociology* 68, no. 1 (2003): 9.
3. Fitchen, *Endangered Spaces, Enduring Places*, 256.
4. Ibid.

CHAPTER 8. SOCIAL NETWORKS

1. Eric Wolf, *Peasants* (Englewood Cliffs, NJ: Prentice-Hall, 1966).
2. Virginia Taber Ball, "A Story of the History of Chippewa Lake," unpublished manuscript, 1968.
3. Michael Schroeder, comp. "From Prussia with Love," unpublished manuscript, n.d., 4–5; Elden Brigham and Laura Brigham Jagger, *Emerald: History of a Pioneer Community* (Evart, MI: The Evart Review, 1972), 83.
4. Chippewa Lake Community Church website: www.clcc.homestead.com.

CHAPTER 9. SOCIAL NETWORKS BEYOND THE COMMUNITY

1. Elden L. Brigham and Laura Brigham Jagger, *Emerald: History of a Pioneer Community* (Evart, MI: The Evart Review, 1972), 19.
2. The largest school district is in the Upper Peninsula of Michigan.

3. *Chippewa Hills School District School Improvement Plan for 2006–2011*, June 2006, 13, available at www.chsd.us/admin. (Follow link for District Reports, then District Improvement Plan.)

4. Jessica Pearson, "Note on Female Farmers," *Rural Sociology* 44, no. 1 (1979): 191–93.

CHAPTER 10. TRANSFORMATION AND CONTESTED IDENTITIES

1. Sonya Salamon, "From Hometown to Nontown: Rural Community Effects of Suburbanization," *Rural Sociology* 68, no. 1 (2003): 8–9.

2. Sonya Salamon, *Prairie Patrimony: Family, Farming, and Community in the Midwest* (Chapel Hill: University of North Carolina Press, 1992), 226–28; Salamon, "From Hometown to Nontown," 7–8.

3. Janet M. Fitchen, *Endangered Spaces, Enduring Places: Culture, Identity, and Survival in Rural America* (Boulder, CO: Westview Press, 1991), 251.

4. Ibid., 260–63.

5. Ibid., 260.

6. Ibid.

7. Ibid., 263.

8. Ibid.

9. Salamon, *Prairie Patrimony*; Salamon, "From Hometown to Nontown."

10. Salamon, *Prairie Patrimony*.

11. Ibid., 227–28.

EPILOGUE. MARIJUANA MAMA

1. Pseudonyms have been used for the Taylor family to protect their identity.

Works Cited

Adams, Jane, ed. *Fighting for the Farm: Rural America Transformed*. Philadelphia: University of Pennsylvania Press, 2003.

Allen, Candy, and Brandon Fountain. "The Future of Agriculture." *The [Big Rapids] Pioneer*, August 16, 2008, 1, 6–9.

Ball, Virginia Taber. "Chippewa Lake Methodist Church Has Served Community for Years." *The [Big Rapids] Pioneer*, n.d.

———. "A Story of the History of Chippewa Lake." Unpublished manuscript. 1968.

———. "Memories of an Old Timer." *Good Old Days Magazine* (January 1970): 5–6.

Barnett, Barry J. "The U.S. Farm Financial Crisis of the 1980's." In *Fighting for the Farm: Rural America Transformed*, ed. Jane Adams, 160–71. Philadelphia: University of Pennsylvania Press, 2003.

Brigham, Elden L., and Laura Brigham Jagger. *Emerald: History of a Pioneer Community*. Evart, MI: The Evart Review, 1972.

Chapman Brothers. *Portrait and Biographical Album of Mecosta County*. Chicago: Chapman Brothers, 1883

Chippewa Hills School District School Improvement Plan for 2006–2011. June 2006. http://www.chsd.us/admin/.

Chippewa Lake Community and Environmental Assessment. Big Rapids, MI: Environmental Management Studies Center, Ferris State University, 1994.

Chippewa Lake Community Church website: www.CLCC.homestead.com.

"Chippewa Lake Woman Recalls Brother's Accomplishments." *The [Big Rapids] Pioneer*, July 14, 1980, 1.

Clifton, James A. "Potawatomi." In *People of the Three Fires: The Ottawa, Potawatomi, and Ojibway of Michigan*, ed. James Clifton et al., 39–74. Grand Rapids, MI: Grand Rapids Inter-Tribal Council, 1986.

Clifton, James, George Cornell, and James McClurken. *People of the Three Fires: The Ottawa, Potawatomi, and Ojibway of Michigan*. Grand Rapids, MI: Grand Rapids Inter-Tribal Council, 1986.

Cornell, George L. "Introduction." In *People of the Three Fires: The Ottawa, Potawatomi, and Ojibway of Michigan*, ed. James Clifton et al., iii–v. Grand Rapids, MI: Grand Rapids Inter-Tribal Council, 1986.

DeLind, Laura B. "Close Encounters with a CSA: The Reflections of a Bruised and Somewhat Wiser Anthropologist." *Agriculture and Human Values* 16 (1999): 3–9.

Dudley, Kathryn Marie. *Debt and Dispossession: Farm Loss in America's Heartland.* Chicago: University of Chicago Press, 2000.

———. "The Entrepreneurial Self: Identity and Morality in a Midwestern Farming Community." In *Fighting for the Farm: Rural America Transformed*, ed. Jane Adams, 175–91. Philadelphia: University of Pennsylvania Press, 2003.

Dunbar, Willis Fredrick. *Michigan: A History of the Wolverine State.* Grand Rapids, MI: Wm. B. Eerdmans Publishing, 1965.

Fitchen, Janet M. *Endangered Spaces, Enduring Places: Culture, Identity, and Survival in Rural America.* Boulder, CO: Westview Press, 1991.

———. *Poverty in Rural America: A Case Study.* Prospect Heights, IL: Waveland Press, 1995.

Frank, A. Gunder. "Development of Underdevelopment in Latin America." In *Latin America: Underdevelopment or Revolution?* 3–94. New York: Monthly Review Press, 1969.

Hays, E. L., comp. *Atlas of Mecosta County.* Philadelphia: C. O. Titus, 1879.

Hinsdale, Wilbert B. *Archaeological Atlas of Michigan.* Ann Arbor: University of Michigan Press, 1931.

McClurken, James M. "Grand River Band of Ottawa Indians Ethnohistorical Response to Office of Federal Acknowledgment Technical Assistance Letter." Dated January 26, 2005, McClurken Associates, Lansing, Michigan.

———. "Ottawa." In *People of the Three Fires: The Ottawa, Potawatomi, and Ojibway of Michigan*, ed. James Clifton et al., 2–38. Grand Rapids, MI: Grand Rapids Inter-Tribal Council, 1986.

McLaughlin, Diane K. "Changing Income Inequality in Nonmetropolitan Counties, 1980–1990." *Rural Sociology* 67, no. 4 (December 2002): 512–33.

Mecosta Conservation District. *Mecosta Conservation District Resource Assessment and Implementation Plan, 2001.* East Lansing, MI: Michigan Conservation Districts, 2001.

———. *Mecosta Conservation District Resource Assessment and Implementation Plan, 2006.* East Lansing, MI: Michigan Conservation Districts, 2006.

Meyers, P. A., J. W. Meyers, and C. H. Cameron, surveyors and draftsmen. *The Plat Book of Mecosta County, Michigan.* Minneapolis: Consolidated Publishing Co., 1900.

Mingione, Enzo. *Fragmented Societies: A Sociology of Economic Life beyond the Market Paradigm.* Translated by Paul Goodrich. Cambridge, MA: Basil Blackwell Ltd., 1991.

Murdock, Steve H., and F. Larry Leistritz, eds. *The Farm Financial Crisis: Socioeconomic Dimensions and Implications for Producers and Rural Areas.* Boulder, CO: Westview Press, 1988.

National Agricultural Statistics Service of the USDA. *Census of Agriculture, Mecosta County Profile, 2002.* Washington, DC: NASS County Profiles, U.S. Department of Agriculture, 2002. Available at www.nass.usda.gov.

National Archives and Records Administration. Indian Reserve Files, Entry 29, box 7, August 29, 1855.

National Archives Microform. Letters Received by the Office of Indian Affairs, 1853–1855. NAM M234 R.404 (1853–1855): 815–21.

———. Letters Received by the Office of Indian Affairs, 1856–1857. NAM M234 R.405 (1856–1857): 168–71, 533–36.

Newman, Katherine S. "Deindustrialization, Poverty, and Downward Mobility: Toward an Anthropology of Economic Disorder." In *Diagnosing America: Anthropology and Public Engagement*, ed. Shephard Forman, 121–48. Ann Arbor: University of Michigan Press, 1997.

O'Connor, Alice. "Modernization and the Rural Poor: Some Lessons from History." In *Rural Poverty in America*, ed. Cynthia Duncan, 215–33. New York: Auburn House, 1992.

Ortner, Sherry. "Theory in Anthropology since the Sixties." *Comparative Studies in Society and History* 26 (1984): 126–66.

Ottawa History: www.tolatsga.org/otta.html.

Pearson, Jessica. "Note on Female Farmers." *Rural Sociology* 44, no. 1 (1979): 189–200.

Records of the Bureau of Indian Affairs: 1870 Annuity Rolls of the Chippewas and Ottawas (Durant Rolls, 1908). Washington, DC: National Archives, General Service Administration, 1983.

Rural Sociological Society Task Force on Persistent Rural Poverty. *Persistent Poverty in Rural America* (*PPRA*). Boulder, CO: Westview Press, 1993.

Salamon, Sonya. "From Hometown to Nontown: Rural Community Effects of Suburbanization." *Rural Sociology* 68, no. 1 (2003): 1–24.

———. *Prairie Patrimony: Family, Farming, and Community in the Midwest.* Chapel Hill: University of North Carolina Press, 1992.

Santer, Richard. "Big Rapids Historical Timeline." 2007. Available at http.ci.big -rapids.mi.us.

———. "Historical Overview of the City of Big Rapids." 2007. Available at http .ci.big-rapids.mi.us.

Schroeder, Michael, comp. *From Prussia with Love: Our Family History.* Unpublished manuscript, n.d.

Shaw, Anna Howard. *The Story of a Pioneer.* 1915; Cleveland: Pilgrim Press, 1994.

Smith, Nettie. "The Indian Trail." *[Barryton, MI] Chippewa Hills Courier*, n.d.

Stadtfeld, Curtis. *From the Land and Back*. New York: Charles Scribner's Sons, 1972.

Treaty with the Ottawa, Etc., March 28, 1836. Available at www.1836cora.org/documents/1836march28treaty.pdf.

Treaty with the Ottawa and Chippewa, July 31, 1855. Available at digital.library.okstate.edu/kappler/vol2/treaties/ott0725.htm.

University of Maine Cooperative Extension. "How to Tap Maple Trees and Make Maple Syrup." Bulletin #7036, 2007. Available at http://www.umext.maine.edu/onlinepubs/pdfpubs/7036.pdf.

U.S. Census, 1990. Available at www.census.gov/main/www/cen1990.html.

U.S. Census, 2000. Available at www.census.gov/main/www/cen2000.html.

U.S. Department of the Interior, Census Office. *Report of Indians Taxed and Indians Not Taxed in the United States (Except Alaska) at the Eleventh Census: 1890*. Washington, DC: Government Printing Office, 1894, 330–35.

Wallerstein, Immanuel. *The Modern World System: Capitalist Agriculture and the Origins of the European World Economy in the Sixteenth Century*. New York: Academic Press, 1974.

Wolf, Eric. *Peasants*. Englewood Cliffs, NJ: Prentice-Hall, 1966.

Index

auctions, 80, 152, 156–58, 183; horse, 158–59

Austin family, 39, 90–91, 100, 118, 169, 192 (n. 42)

Ball, Virginia Taber, 27, 29, 34, 40, 135

Barryton, 3, 17, 46, 67, 136–37, 148, 149, 151, 155

Big Rapids, 1–2, 4, 15, 68, 131–32; economic and political influence of, 44, 115, 150–52, 155, 161, 182, 183; history of, 17, 25, 31, 32, 36, 43–44

Bovay family, 30

Brigham family, 32, 34, 148

Carmichael family, xi, 31, 32, 40, 47, 61, 93, 129–30, 192 (n. 43)

Chippewa Lake Church, 3, 34, 37, 73, 134, 135–38

Chippewa Lake Days, 103–4, 128–29, 138–39, 162, 171

Chippewa Lake resort, 1, 3–4, 16, 17, 27–28, 83; changes to, 98, 100–103; characteristics of residents of, 97–101, 116–17, 118–20, 159, 170–72; community effect in, 106–7, 170–71; contested community in, 109–14; Eurasian milfoil in, 112–14; history of, 30, 37; sewer system in, 118–20. *See also* Chippewa Lake Days; Chippewa Lake village; Chippewa Township; community effect/personality; contested community

Chippewa Lake village, 3–4, 86–87, 100, 115–16, 194 (ch. 5, n. 3); changes to, 84–86; contested community in, 13,

84–86, 110–11, 120–21; development of, 101–3; history of, 3, 35–37, 40–41; in regional context, 1–3. *See also* Chippewa Lake resort; Chippewa Township; contested community

Chippewa Township, xi–xii, 4, 15–16, 51–52, 63–64, 87–89, 128–29, 143–44; changes to, xiv–xv, 3–4, 101–3, 165–66; characteristics of residents of, 57–61, 64–65, 71–81, 88–92, 100, 129–35, 159–63, 167–69; community church in, 135–39; community effect in, 12–13, 52–57, 84, 143–44, 166–69, 175–77, 185; contested community in, 12–14, 106–7, 109–10, 115–18, 121–25, 144–45, 165, 166–69; development of, 101–3, 104–7, 124–25; early settlers in, 29–35; economic conditions in, 65–67, 70, 92–94; education in, 67–70; history of, 27, 29–31, 35–41; indigenous population in, 17; location, 27–28; organization and structure of, 2, 115–16, 120–21; in regional context, 1, 2, 43–46, 65–67, 93–94, 147–59; township board in, 110–21, 163, 175. *See also* Chippewa Lake resort; Chippewa Lake village; contested community

Christiansen family, 90, 93–94

Commission on Aging, 155–56. *See also* senior citizens organizations

Community Building Board, 129, 131, 139, 162, 163, 172

community effect/personality, 11–12, 52–57, 106–7, 127–28, 166. *See* Chippewa Lake resort; Chippewa Township

commuting, 90, 93–94, 161

201

Native Americans, 16–24, 49, 188 (n. 10); access to land, 15, 20–24; in Chippewa and Martiny townships, 17, 25, 26, 64, 148, 190 (n. 47); Grand River Band, 25; in Mecosta County, 16–17, 21–22, 23, 24, 25–26; missions and schools, 20–22, 23–24; Saginaw-Chippewa Reservation, 22, 23; Three Fires Confederation, 18, 19; treaties with, 20–23, 29–30

Nellis family (Peter), x, 78–80, 109, 139, 169, 177, 183

Nellis family (Wynne), x, 49–50, 72–75, 76, 168, 169

nonfarm families, characteristics of, 88–92, 159, 161, 168, 169. *See also* nonfarm occupations

nonfarm occupations, 44–45, 65–67, 70, 72–81, 92–93; commuting and, 90, 93–94, 161; education and, 67–70, 76, 80, 92; women and, 66–67, 76, 92–93, 94

Nott family, x, 1, 32–33, 130, 156, 161

participation. *See* social life, participation in; volunteerism

Patterson, Dr. , 37, 85

Pollock family, 30

practice theory, 11–12

Preston family. *See* Stein (and Preston) family

residence patterns, 65, 91–92, 100, 144, 169

rites of passage, 68, 138–44, 152

schools, xiii, 67–70, 134, 143–44, 148–50; activities in, 143–44, 149–50, 152–53, 154–55; and early settlers, 34–35, 67–68. *See also* farming, education and; nonfarm occupations, education and; Native Americans, missions and schools

Schmidt family, 99

Schroeder family, 33, 63, 80–81

Scotland and Ireland, xi, xiii, xiv, 12, 30, 31, 32, 61

senior citizens organizations, 129, 130; and Commission on Aging, 155–56

Shaw, Anna Howard, 43

Smith, Nettie, 26, 29, 30

Social embeddedness. *See* practice theory

social life, participation in, 40–41, 159–63; community church and, 135–36, 138; formal organizations and, 128–29, 132–35; 150–53, 155–56; lake, township, and village compared, 150–51, 159, 161, 171–72; mutual assistance and, 34, 129–32; special events and, 138–39, 143–44. See also *individual organizations*; volunteerism

Stein (and Preston) family, x, 38–39, 66–67, 75–76, 118

Sparks family, 30, 31, 35, 135, 148, 167

sugar bush, 49–50

Taylor family, 179–85

township board. *See* Chippewa Township

Ulrich family, 89, 90, 169

volunteerism, 104–5, 111, 121–22, 130–32, 134–35, 171–73, 177, 183. *See also* social life, participation in

Wheatland Festival, 74

World Systems Theory, 9–10

Worth, Lawrence, 52

Wylie family, 30, 35

Young Women's Club, xiii, 117, 128–29, 133–34, 159, 160, 161, 162, 183, 184

Zielinski, Debra, 32, 129